ZOO RENEWAL

White Flight and the Animal Ghetto

LISA UDDIN

A Quadrant Book

UNIVERSITY OF MINNESOTA PRESS
Minneapolis · London

Quadrant, a joint initiative of the University of Minnesota Press and the Institute for Advanced Study at the University of Minnesota, provides support for interdisciplinary scholarship within a new, more collaborative model of research and publication.

http://quadrant.umn.edu.

Sponsored by the Quadrant Environment, Culture, and Sustainability group (advisory board: Bruce Braun, Daniel Philippon, Christine Marran, Stuart McLean) and by the Institute on the Environment at the University of Minnesota.

Quadrant is generously funded by the Andrew W. Mellon Foundation.

The University of Minnesota Press gratefully acknowledges financial assistance for the publication of this book from Whitman College.

Published by the University of Minnesota Press
111 Third Avenue South, Suite 290
Minneapolis, MN 55401–2520
http://www.upress.umn.edu

ISBN 978-0-8166-7911-9 (hc)
ISBN 978-0-8166-7912-6 (pb)
A Cataloging-in-Publication record for this book is available from the Library of Congress.

Printed in the United States of America on acid-free paper

The University of Minnesota is an equal-opportunity educator and employer.

21 20 19 18 17 16 15   10 9 8 7 6 5 4 3 2 1

To my father and mother, who arrived in the United States in 1959 and 1965, respectively, met in St. Louis, and left for Canada.

CONTENTS

Acknowledgments   ix

Introduction: On Feeling Bad at the Zoo   1

1. Shame and the Naked Cage   27

2. Zoo Slum Clearance in Washington, D.C.   71

3. Mohini's Bodies   125

4. White Open Spaces in San Diego County   157

5. Looking Endangered   191

Afterword: Good Feelings in Seattle   223

Notes   231

Index   269

ACKNOWLEDGMENTS

This book began a decade ago when I was troubled at the San Diego Zoo. Coming to understand that trouble has involved a polyphony of research and writing across different scholarly communities, zoos, cities, and life events. My gratitude and respect run deep.

My brilliant advisers at the University of Rochester deserve first acknowledgment. A. Joan Saab has been a strong, reassuring presence over the years, teaching me how to pursue questions with energy and substance, how to think about public culture, and how to engage its vernacular without apology. I am forever thankful for her belief in my scholarship and dazzled by her chutzpah. John Michael gave me hope from the outset that humanistic inquiry still matters, as do familiar questions about the American experiment. Robert J. Foster encouraged me to ask about global world making and championed my initial forays into animal studies. Reviewers of the book manuscript contributed their excitement, skepticism, and valuable recommendations. Their astute feedback gave me a new set of interlocutors and a second wind for this project. Pieter Martin at the University of Minnesota Press has been an attentive, patient, and enthusiastic shepherd throughout this publishing endeavor. Kristian Tvedten has been a skilled wrangler of images. Douglas Armato has always understood the thrust.

Many wonderful people brought me into their worlds and helped me develop the major currents of this book. In Washington, D.C., Pamela Henson's openness to visual approaches to institutional history and expert guidance through the vastness of the Smithsonian Institution made research joyful. My fellow researchers at the Smithsonian Institution Archives—Courtney Fullilove, Brian Daniels, Taika Dahlbom, Erika Figueiredo, Marie Plassart, Martin Thomas, and Heather Ewing—did as well. In Providence, participants in the 2008–9 Pembroke Research Seminar at Brown University moved me from dissertation to book with their staggering intelligence and curiosity about nonhuman otherness: Nancy J. Jacobs, Leslie Bostrom, Pooja Rangan, Sandy Alexandre, Jason Lindquist, Peter Heywood, Wendy Chun, and Elizabeth Weed. I give special thanks to Astrid Schrader for countless meals and intense exchange. In Minneapolis I benefited from impressive intellectual resources and kindness in and around the Institute for Advanced Study at the University of Minnesota. John Archer, Bruce Braun, Dan Philippon, Katherine Solomonson, Rembert Hueser, Christine Marran, Teresa Gowan, Nancy Luxon, Stacey Alaimo, Ann Waltner, Susannah Smith, Karen Kinoshita, and Anne Carter nourished my emerging claims and introduced me to the virtues of large public research universities. Matthew Huber was a particular pleasure to think with. Other amazing scholars responded to my work with warmth and productive critique, especially Nigel Rothfels, Susan McHugh, Donna Haraway, Tom Tyler, Jonathan Burt, Kari Weil, Kathy Rudy, Christina Chia, Eva Hayward, Jane Desmond, Matthew Brower, Cate Sandilands, Dawn Biehler, Emily Pawley, Harlan Weaver, Scout Calvert, Tora Holmberg, Ann-Sofie Lönnegren, Robin Veder, Leora Maltz-Leca, Daniel Harkett, Jeremy Kargon, Kelly Quinn, Victoria Wolcott, and Joseph Heathcott. I have learned much from each of them.

Several librarians and archivists made this book possible, answering my often-scattered requests and pointing me in the right directions. My sincere thank-you to Ellen Allers, Tammy Peters, and Tad Bennicoff at the Smithsonian Institution Archives; Mehgan Murphy and Jessie Cohen at the National Zoological Park; Michèle Gates Moresi and Esther Washington at the National Museum of African American History and Culture; Faye Haskins, Mark Greek, and Michele Casto of the D.C. Public Library's Special Collections; and the kind staff of the San Diego Public Library's California Room, the Escondido Public Library's Pioneer Room, the San Diego History Center, the San Diego State University Library's Special Collections, the Art, Design, and Architecture Museum at the University of California Santa Barbara, the San Diego Museum of Art, and Mel Hall. My research put me in helpful contact with Catherine Christen at the Smithsonian Conservation Biology Institute, Steve Johnson of the Wildlife Conservation Society, Mary Kazmierczak at the Zoological Society of Milwaukee, and the Licensing Team and Ted Molter of the Zoological Society of San Diego. Early research was routinely aided by Stephanie Frontz at the University of Rochester's Art and Music Library, and later research by Jen Pope at Whitman College's Penrose Library.

I reserve specific thanks to the organizations that enabled me to pay for my doctoral education, travel for research and lectures, and cover illustration costs. These include the Social Science and Humanities Research Foundation of Canada, Québec's Fonds de recherche sur la société et la culture, the Program in Visual and Cultural

Studies at the University of Rochester, the Susan B. Anthony Institute for Gender and Women's Studies, the Landscape Architecture Foundation and Garden Club of America, the Smithsonian Institution Fellowship Program, the Pembroke Center Postdoctoral Fellowship Program, the Quadrant initiative at the University of Minnesota and the University of Minnesota Press, the Corcoran College of Art and Design, the Rhode Island School of Design's Department of History of Art and Visual Culture, Duke University's Program in Women's Studies, Morgan State University's School of Architecture and Planning, Whitman College's Office of the Provost and Dean of the Faculty, and the Department of Art History and Visual Culture Studies at Whitman College.

Friends made important marks on this research. I am a better scholar after spending time with fellow interdisciplinarians Catherine Zuromskis, Peter Hobbs, Daniela Sandler, Norman Vorano, Michael Williams, Leanne Gilbertson, Lisa Soccio, Aubrey Anable, Derya Ozkan, Hossein Khosrowjah, Mara Gladstone, Aviva Dove-Viehban, Victoria Pass, Daniel Worden, and Margot Bouman. New colleagues and friends in Walla Walla, Washington, assisted this work in its final stages and inspired me to embark on new projects. Pronounced thanks to Matthew Reynolds, Matthew DeTar, and Adam Gordon for thoughtful reads; to Jen Cohen, Melisa Casumbal-Salazar, Nicole Pietrantoni, Michelle Acuff, and Sarah Hurlburt for fresh conversation; to Dennis Crockett for sound counsel; to Pat Sorenson and Richele Loney for administrative know-how; and to Helen Kim, Noah Leavitt, Lucy Schwallie, Anne Helen Peterson, Melissa Salrin, James Warren, Devon Wooten, Jessica Cerullo, David Schulz, and Leesa Phaneuf-Reynolds for necessary gatherings. Thanks as well to Ralph Ghoche, Sarah Litebody, and Elleni Centime Zeleke for decades of connection and to Doc for five delightful days.

It is difficult to convey my appreciation for the enduring love of Anna, Ricardo, Palma, and Emerson Camargo; Monica Uddin; Derek, Otis, and Annika Wildman; and my parents, Eva and Jamal Uddin. They sustained me at all stages of authorship with ideas, material, fact checks, room and board, R&R, and a sense of place. Tack så mycket. My greatest and ongoing thanks go to Joshua Slepin, who romanced me as a dissertator, married me as a postdoc, and became a parent with me as a book writer. His exquisite care, threshold for adversity, and general magnificence reenchant me daily and keep me alive. And to Marie Slepin, my before, during, and after all of it. Family hug.

INTRODUCTION

On Feeling Bad at the Zoo

During a recent trip to the Oregon Zoo in Portland, my family and I wandered into a minor event familiar to many zoo goers. Fresh off our pleasant look at the otters, we made our way to the underground viewing area for the sea lions—all facets of the Oregon coastal habitat exhibit, Steller Cove. The contrast between a cavelike theater space and the luminous 230,000-gallon saltwater pool was effective. We approached the plate-glass window between them with the anticipation of seeing something enchanting, especially (for) our toddler. But a split second later our path was suspended in confusion. The pool was a haze of blue-green liquid, still and empty. We stood in front of and within the cloudiness. Then a sea lion gradually emerged from the interior, brushing the full length of its sleek and massive body against the glass and retreating back into the opacity. Our uneasiness assumed its own presence, jockeying for position alongside the wonder. None of us spoke. Curators did not skip a beat, having posted "keeper notes" beside the window that briefed us on the daily rigors of maintaining the exhibit and the current job of replacing filtration equipment. We stayed for a while, watching the sea lion repeat its slow and murky swim cycle and disregard our furrowed brows, before we moved on to things that could more reliably lift our spirits.

This book probes similar episodes at and about zoos and the conditions of their probability. Amid the many delights and virtues of public animal display, what is it about zoos that provokes our bad feelings? Does it hinge on the exchange of looks between expectant humans and sad-looking animals or perhaps, as the British art critic John Berger suggests, the impossibility of the exchange altogether? Initially published as an essay titled "Why Zoos Disappoint" in 1977, and again with other

writing under the title "Why Look at Animals?" in 1980, Berger's compelling interpretation of bad zoo feelings has become a staple of contemporary zoo criticism and
reads as follows: reduced to a consumer spectacle like any other, and of which their
millions of spectators are all on some level aware, the animals housed and displayed
in modern zoos have been stripped of their wildness and are no longer interested in
or able to return the human gaze. Berger famously writes that "nowhere in a zoo can
a stranger encounter the look of an animal. At the most, the animal's gaze flickers
and passes on. They look sideways. They look blindly beyond. They scan mechani-
cally. They have been immunized to encounter."[1] Zoos here render "real" animality
fugitive, the remaining animal a mute object, and humanity at an embarrassing loss.
Meaningful relationships are impossible in this dynamic, despite some good intentions. Our bad feelings are symptomatic of this failure.

"Why Look at Animals?" scratches an itch for anyone who has paused to absorb the persistent fact of a zoo animal's captivity coupled with its compulsory-
yet-elusive visibility. The sprawling description of human–animal alienation under
capitalism, an alienation of which zoos are the culmination, seems to conform to
and confirm many visitor experiences at the beginning of the twenty-first century.
Exhibiting animals in public space still registers as more than a little exploitative
toward its charges and, for zoo goers, a guarantee of at least some ambivalence. But
there is good cause to take issue with Berger's melancholic mass culture critique
that treats looking itself as morally suspect and underplays the psychological and
physical complexity of modern human–animal relating, however uncomfortable.[2]
Further, the discomforts of zoos have undercurrents that are shorter, sharper, and
livelier than Berger allows, but which tend to be reserved for antizoo scholarship,
art, and activism.[3]

Berger's own thoughts were formulated during a concentrated moment of bad
zoo feelings that propelled major shifts in zoological thinking and practice throughout capitalist societies. During the 1960s and 1970s a professionalizing class of zoo
experts and advocates embarked on the large-scale revitalization of public animal
displays. Concrete and tile were often and variously minimized, while exhibit square
footage (or acreage) grew. Eliminating visible barriers like wire fencing and iron bars
became a paramount concern, as was refining materials and arrangements that could
simulate habitats called natural and stimulate behaviors called natural. In conjunction with the revitalization of the built environment, reformers sought to revitalize
their animal collection through intensive programs of biopolitical control. The decades after World War II witnessed the development of vitamins, antibiotics, vac-
cines, disinfectants, nutrition regimens, enrichment activities, and the coordinated

breeding of select rare and endangered species.[4] By the late 1970s scores of metropolitan regions in industrializing and postindustrializing countries could point to variations on a "new zoo" whose central paradox was the reconstruction of a more natural nature through increasingly sophisticated architectures and forms of animal science.[5] While indexing the global span of zoo modernization is beyond the scope of this book, attendance at the First International Symposium on Zoo Design and Construction in 1975 flags the breadth of interest in the "new zoo." Held in Paignton, England, the event attracted delegates representing sixty-three zoos from twenty-two different countries, including "Japan, New Zealand, West Africa, Brazil and California, and even a delegation from Moscow across the Iron Curtain."[6]

Stories of a new kind of zoo with a new kind of nature display circulated widely in the zoological community and popular media, while a handful of institutionally affiliated historians and design critics also wrote about revitalization until as late as 1997.[7] Running accounts emphasized a commitment to worldwide nature stewardship. Changes to the zoo, the story went, were breathing new life, figuratively and literally, into sagging public institutions by prompting citizens to rethink their privileged places on the planet and restoring animal populations at home and abroad. Reporting on a symposium on zoos and conservation funded by the United Nations Organization for Education, Science and Culture in 1964, for example, the editor of the five-year-old *International Zoo Yearbook* informed her colleagues that "the problem of the destruction of the natural environment and the consequent disappearance of wildlife is so serious, so extensive, that the only hope of halting the process will be through world-wide pooling of knowledge and resources," which a transnational federation of zoos could provide. R. Michael Schneider, a landscape architect and former secretary of the Minnesota Zoological Society, offered a biblical version of the outlook when he wrote in 1969: "It behooves mankind to take a lesson from a book as old as the ages and build Noah's arks around the world before the tidal wave of human population swallows up the remaining space on this planet."[8] Generally missing from these accounts was a discussion of how the new zoo's concerns for the conservation of wildlife overlapped with concerns about the conservation and reproduction of normative civic life that they concomitantly espoused. Many accounts perpetuated the overlap. In the same 1969 prompt, for example, Schneider speculated: "The riots and struggles within our cities may be due . . . to a lack of understanding of the overall meaning of life. Truly, the only place that communion with life can occur is within a natural setting, such as the modern zoo."[9] David Hancocks, a zoo architect and former director of Seattle's Woodland Park Zoo, came close to exploring the overlap but fell short of the mark, writing in 1970:

> It is no coincidence that at the same time that we are obliterating the forest habitat
> of the aye-aye in Madagascar or of the orang-utan in Borneo, our concrete city
> jungles are becoming intolerable places for people. . . . we can learn how to build
> a better environment not only for animals but also perhaps for ourselves.[10]

The omission in Hancock's reflection, as in others, was any analysis of the aesthetic or symbolic aspects of intolerability, and the valences of a better postconcrete jungle.

Zoo Renewal attends to this substrate of institutional reinvention by examining expressions of burgeoning zoo environmentalism for bad feelings about American cities in the long postwar period. While new zoo making was an international phenomenon in aspiration and enunciation, its resonances were also curiously native. Here, I focus on the revitalization of U.S. zoos and place it within the highly mediated climate of urban decline that, by the 1960s, had made the central city into an object of fear and concern for many Americans. My use of the term *zoo renewal* denotes this imbrication of American zoos and their cities by knitting together the history of renovating animal exhibits with the postwar culture and politics of "urban renewal" more broadly. Marked by specific federal initiatives, such as the Housing Act of 1949 and 1954, and the Federal Highway Act of 1956, urban renewal unfolded as liberal-minded, state-sanctioned interventions into the built environment to reverse perceptions of decline and its demographic fallout. An influential urban planner in the 1960s, Robert C. Weaver, understood the phrase as referring to "many activities—slum clearance and redevelopment, highways and public works, demolition and construction privately financed—all of which change the structure of a city."[11] The present study inhabits an archive that speaks to urban change of this kind and consequence. Oral histories, institutional correspondence, and the landscaped and architectural boundaries of animal exhibits are my primary texts. So too are the channels through which those exhibits were figured and "visited" from a physical distance: zoo photography, membership and marketing ephemera, and popular media. My readings of this often vibrant and bizarre material detail how zoo makers across the United States proposed renewed forms of public life to Americans of diverse backgrounds who were repelled by the constant buzz of racial conflict in the cities and searching for relief. Crucial for me is how the movement toward naturalistic exhibits of rare and endangered animals was entangled with experiences of white middle-class endangerment and those who aspired to whiteness in and around U.S. urban regions. These entanglements spanned the metaphorical—where denizens, caretakers, and visitors came to precariously stand in for each other, and the material—where zoo animals were treated as city dwellers in their own right, entitled to their piece of postwar prosperity. Dwelling on these dense and surprising connections, this book narrates specific stories of zoo rebirth and elaborates on the racial dynamics of American urbanism that helped define their terms and texture. What I am after is an account of improvement that gives sustained attention to the itineraries of race and species, and grounds for reconsidering how it is that Americans have felt bad—and good—at the zoo.

WRITING ZOO HISTORY

As a counternarrative of American zoos and their revitalization, the pages that follow work against what historians have identified as the evolutionary character of official zoo history—that is, histories written within or close to the institution that are prone to amnesia, hyperbole, and progressivist models of time.[12] Such histories tend to chronologize each period of animal exhibition as a decisive improvement from the last, particularly with respect to the treatment of zoo animals and the quality of the zoo-going experience for visitors. This style of writing zoo history has made it possible to declare a series of watershed moments in the life of the institution, moments that reject their predecessors and take the zoo form itself to higher levels of enlightenment, making it truly "modern."

The well-recognized status of America's first zoo is a case in point. Histories that classify the Philadelphia Zoo, planned in 1856 and opened after the Civil War in 1874, as the nation's founding public zoo point to a number of its definitive features: the institution's formation via a private zoological society, a mandate that emphasized scientific research, education, and nature recreation for all citizens, a collection of several hundred animals from all over the world, and an architectural plan that exhibited the collection in permanent buildings located within a large, landscaped public park.[13] Many of these histories, however, also elide the fact that other zoos were exhibiting a range of animals for free in park space well before the Philadelphia Zoo's opening and so might also qualify as some of the nation's first public zoos. As one of these overlooked zoos, New York's Central Park Zoo, established but also opened in 1856, quickly emerged as a popular site that attracted working-class city dwellers from different racial and ethnic backgrounds. Crowds could see exhibits of grazing Cape buffalo, a modest deer park, temporarily housed animals from P. T. Barnum's collection and other circus operators, and a selection of "poor man's monkeys," as dubbed by the urban elites who were disgruntled by the zoo's widespread appeal.[14] But for the historian Vernon Kisling, Philadelphia's lively antecedent in New York, together with Chicago's Lincoln Park Zoo of 1868, are best understood as "small urban menageries" lacking in the grand architectural vision, civic purpose, and scientific program of a "modern" zoological garden.[15] The

Central Park Zoo was "used as a dumping ground for unwanted pets and unwanted touring carnival animals." Despite earning official zoo status in 1873 and maintaining a decent-sized collection of animals that included a black bear, Virginia deer, raccoons, foxes, eagles, and parrots, Central Park's facility, for Kisling, "remained a menagerie until well past 1900," leaving the exalted title of the first American zoo open to Philadelphia and giving a new public tradition a virtuous point of origin.[16]

Nigel Rothfels traces this kind of historical writing to the second half of the nineteenth century. In these decades, public zoos like Philadelphia's began to flourish within a bourgeois civic culture that included museums, libraries, theaters, and concert halls. As zoos became socially respectable staples in the urban landscape, historically inclined members of their zoological societies set out to systematically document previous and current animal holdings, and insert those holdings and their display into particularly optimistic narratives that continue to this day.[17] These narratives begin somewhere around the barbarity of the Roman animal spectacles and conclude with the naturalistic utopias of, for example, the San Diego Zoo's Wild Animal Park. In between are the princely and commercial menageries that predate the French Revolution and the public zoological gardens that materialized thereafter as part of a wider phenomenon of public culture formation.[18] Homing in on this latter shift, Rothfels stresses that the lavish menageries built by and for royal families and their cohorts entailed more than evidence of aristocratic decadence, and likewise, the nineteenth-century public zoo cannot be taken unilaterally as a more enlightened form of animal exhibition.[19] Claims of this sort overly periodize the story of zoos in ways that miss meaningful ties between these two eras, and others besides. They whisk by physical, social, experiential, and conceptual continuities in favor of defining "revolutionary" turns in the zoo world that are consistently beneficial for humans and animals alike.

Zoo reformers after World War II were no exception. Their refrain of a "new zoo" often overlooked how an emergent strand of zoo naturalism owed something, aesthetically and ideologically, to American zoo makers a hundred years prior, who also sought to replicate an animal's native habitat for breeding purposes and offer visitors lessons in wildlife conservation. New zoo makers also minimized the extent to which zoos had already incorporated key naturalistic design elements before the purported revolution, taking their most notable cues from the barless mixed-species panoramas of the German animal exhibitor Carl Hagenbeck in the early twentieth century.[20] Built in the 1920s, the San Diego Zoo's iron-free, open-air exhibits that sheltered animals in shallow outward-facing grottos are one example of early zoo naturalism in the United States. The 1941 African Plains exhibit at the Bronx Zoo is another, modeled after the African savanna, with antelope, birds, and lions sepa-

Figure I.1. *Postcard of African Plains exhibit at the Bronx Zoo, circa 1940s. Courtesy of the Wildlife Conservation Society Archives.*

rated by moats (Figure I.1). The changes to zoos were also hardly transformative. Many U.S. zoos built their conservation-oriented exhibits in a piecemeal and snail-paced fashion among existing enclosures. The Bronx Zoo's World of Darkness from 1969, for example, was designed with the retinal needs of nocturnal small mammals in mind and hailed as being on "the frontiers of environmental conservation." But it would be almost another decade before large carnivores were given new housing, and forty years until the Beaux-Arts Monkey House from 1901 was emptied of its residents.[21] Conversely, a given zoo's course of renovation could be swift and time sensitive. What was considered a revolutionary exhibit in 1965 could be an embarrassment by 1971, as was the case with the National Zoo's modernist Great Flight Cage, discussed in chapter 2.

These temporal complexities position the revitalization of zoos in the 1960s and 1970s less as a definitive overhaul in the physical display of animals than as a spatialized and multispecies discourse *about* animal display coproduced by directors, designers, members, publicists, critics, and critters, and consumed by a national zoo-going public numbering annually in the tens of millions. Zoo renewal, so defined, was a prescriptive discussion that set the parameters for what was materially possible in American zooscapes, not a description of developments that actually transformed them. Problems with periodization also raise questions about the impulses that sparked and sustained renewal as a necessary path. From where and when did they come? This book posits that the "new zoo" was not especially new in conception or execution, and that aspects of its expression echoed and made newly relevant long-standing investments in the civilizing promise of the nonhuman world amid the double weight of species depletion and urban crisis. American zoo renewal was, in this sense, a revitalization of the mutual intelligibility of wildlife and city life.

The question of intelligibility in zoos is as fraught as their history. Critical studies of animal representation, including mine, favor a productive analytic tension over how, and if, zoos are meaningful. On the one hand, public zoos have been conceptualized as a kind of master symbol, crafted by elites, performed by animals, and taken up by a mass public with varying degrees of literacy. Here, the zoo is frequently interpreted as a raced/sexed/classed instrument for the elaboration and legitimation of imperialism, nationalism, and other normative constructions of being and belonging. Zoos function as microcosms or fragments of empire; they solicit versions of the ethnographic gaze, model captive wildlife in the image of human colonized subjects, and situate all zoo participants within panoptic visual structures.[22] The insights of this twenty-year body of scholarship cannot be overstated, having positioned the work and pleasure of public animal display as coextensive with other ideological and disciplinary modes of social control. On the other hand, and often in the same studies, zoos have been recognized as notoriously slippery mediums of communication. Instead of wholly structured and discrete texts and sites, zoos can be understood as triggers for a spectrum of simultaneous ideas, attitudes, associations, and experiences, none of which can be decisively managed by their producers. Seldom if ever has a visitor seamlessly digested a zoo maker's communicative intent, if indeed it is ever so digestible. Zoos, in this frame, are contests of indeterminate meaning, well-equipped to corroborate Fredric Jameson's thesis that mass culture articulates both the repressive dimensions of social power and its utopic content, however faint, disorganized, or ineffectual.[23]

The indeterminacy of zoo meanings extends most vividly to animals themselves, both within and beyond the zoo. A wellspring of critical studies within the humanities and humanistic social sciences have made clear that nonhuman organisms are not necessarily "good to think with," to paraphrase Claude Lévi-Strauss.[24] When an animal appears on the page, screen, stage, or within everyday range, its presence cannot always be sufficiently engaged through forms of human difference, racial or otherwise. An irreducible alterity disrupts any easy consumption of them as markers of something or someone else.[25] Cary Wolfe's reading of the gray gorilla mob in Michael Crichton's novel *Congo* endures as a useful illustration. Wolfe recognizes (before he problematizes) that Crichton's portrayal of a violent subspecies of gray gorillas, armed with complex language and tool use, might recode colonial representations that collapse distinctions between nonhuman primates and black people. More specifically, Wolfe argues that *Congo* is "nearly impossible not to read" as an allegory of American race politics in the 1980s by offering "a cautionary tale to white technocratic upwardly mobile America in the early Reagan years about the dangers of believing that 'blackness' can be domesticated and made productive for the social project."[26] But for Wolfe, the particular figure of the gorilla mob forms something more indistinct, and menacing, than a black racial metaphor. The hillside assembly of hundreds of murderous gorillas suggests "the demonic multiplicity of Deleuze and Guattari's 'pack' animality"—a deindividuated, desubjectified mass of otherness whose terrors defy comparison, even description.[27] The mob's semantic unreceptiveness, its inability to signify anything at all about human subjectivity, exemplifies the posthumanist gambit that nonhuman creatures pose serious threats to our learned and deeply problematic sense of what is human.[28] The gorilla mob is, in Steve Baker's related terms, the "postmodern animal" par excellence, further troubling the already troubled matter of human identity through an ineluctable animality that cannot be made to stand in for anything but itself.[29] Animals like these, in other words, draw attention to the fragility of a human way of being that has always been defined, usually unjustly, against an other of some sort. Moreover, they invite us to consider retiring the categories of animality and humanity *tout court,* or at least radically reformulating their content and form, an invitation that also extends from the life sciences, biomedicine, agribusiness, and other arenas of the biopolitical.

Without deflating these possibilities, it seems crucial to appreciate that the "old" possibilities—historical problems, really—laid out by social constructionist frameworks invite continued exploration.[30] The scholarly work of interrogating what and how animals mean, however badly, persists along with the configuration of racialized animals and animalized people, neither of which can be assumed to be the most immediate reading of a given representation. Dating from the period of colonial conquest, animality has served as a powerful reference point for constructing hierarchized social difference in Western cultures.[31] In particular, racial ideology in the United States has found much traction in representations of nonwhite people as animals, and vice versa. Conventions of ethnographic media and live displays, freak shows and wildlife documentaries, to name a few, evidence the signifying relay between race and species.[32]

Zoos have played their part as well, despite their initial passion for constructing distinctly Anglo-American wildernesses in the city. While native species and land-scapes held a certain appeal, visitors to the nation's first public zoos sustained cravings for the exotic that were cultivated by dime-store museums, circuses, and menageries, and to which managers responded.[33] The 1906 exhibition of a Congolese Pygmy named Ota Benga at the Bronx Zoo is a prominent example in the historical record. Benga arrived at the zoo having appeared in the anthropological exhibits at the Louisiana Purchase Exposition in St. Louis, and eventually joined non-human primates in the monkey house. He was ostensibly employed as a keeper, but also as a specimen on display, complete with a sign listing his physical and geographic specifics.[34] Benga's career is an uncharacteristically vivid part of a more informal practice of racial representation in early public zoos that included press reports of phenotypic and behavioral similarities between captive primates and African Americans, ethnological shows of American Indians, and giving animals Irish names.[35] American zoo makers have also evoked the presence of African and Asian people through architectural association. Detroit Zoo's giraffe exhibit from the 1930s, for example, featured striking Egyptian-like temple reliefs and seated figures as a backdrop.[36] Zoo Atlanta's current giant panda complex includes an elaborate open-aired Chinese Plaza and Panda Veranda in imperial red and gold. These techniques of conflation and analogy help explain the enduring pull of *not* being recognized as animal for Americans whose origins lie beyond northern and western Europe. They also underscore the stakes of conceptual moves to decenter the idea and status of the human through another kind of engagement with animality.

As one of the early and eloquent voices in this latter project, Donna Haraway offers infectious hope and a reminder that posthumanist thinking at its best attends to the vicissitudes of gender as well as race while holding out the power to undo all categories of human(ist) identity. Framing the issue as a feminist one that is still very much concerned with the condition of humanity, Haraway writes:

> Humanity is a modernist figure; and this humanity has a generic face, a universal shape. Humanity's face has been the face of man. Feminist humanity must have another shape, other gestures. . . . They cannot be man or woman; they cannot be the human as historical narrative has staged that generic universal. Feminist figures cannot, finally, have a name; they cannot be native. Feminist humanity must, some-how, both resist representation, resist literal figuration, and still erupt in powerful new tropes, new figures of speech, new turns of historical possibility.[37]

Exhibiting animals that were variously poised to write some new figures of speech, American zoos after 1960 failed to realize their own historical possibility. Their potential to serve as sites for a humanity conjugated through fallibility, flux, and the animality always already therein was continuously thwarted as zoo reformers variously reinscribed, and strove to keep reinscribed, the terms of a generic, universal human being onto a wider set of living beings who had yet to profit from that status.

Zoos could have taken another direction by partnering with other contemporary representations of U.S. public life gone awry and seeking alternative terms for—or alternatives to—being recognized as human. The movements for black and brown power, second-wave feminism, and gay liberation, to name the period's cornerstones of minoritized identity formation, each attempted a complication of generic universal human being with which the new zoo makers might have interacted in more generative ways. Instead, they used their animal displays to tacitly fortify familiar standards of civic worth—especially, though not exclusively, the standard of whiteness. American zoos under renewal were rife with inventive examples less of how species sought to undo race than of how species reinforced race. These examples signaled and enacted endorsement of an idealized Enlightenment human subject racialized white through immersion in its own fantasy of autonomy, reason, benevolence, morality, mobility, and invisibility.

The process was multifaceted and mutable, reliant on two-dimensional images and text, and validated through the substance of three-dimensional spaces and species embodiments. At certain points during renewal, reformers linked their animals to nonwhite people who fell well below the ideal, imbuing nonhuman creatures with objectionable traits, forms of behavior, and living conditions associated with racial and ethnic minorities. By depicting existing pathways blighted by iron railings and excessive concrete, for example, the National Zoo's master plan report of the early 1970s, like other zoo reports of its time, drew visual comparisons to the dehumanizing neighborhoods occupied by poor African Americans; surely, as these photographs implied, the zoo could do better for its charges (Figure I.2). The tuberculosis and toxoplasmosis afflicting certain animals in the collection provided more reason to link the problems of the Federal City's zoo to those of other communities in crisis.[38] At other points—points of institutional pride and regeneration—the new zoo makers suffused animal imagery with the codes of whiteness, figuring animals as protohumanist subjects in full kinship with a zoo-going public whose postwar whiteness was also under construction. So, for example, when the Zoological Society of San Diego debuted a new sprawling gorilla enclosure as a matter of "Keeping Up with Our Gorillas," they inverted the historical blackness of the primates by constructing the troupe as a normative, upwardly mobile family worth watching and emulating in the vein of "keeping up with the Jones'" (Figure I.3). At 210 feet long and 80 feet deep, the moated enclosure was a "rustic retreat" surfaced with Kikuyu

Figure I.2. *"Existing Conditions," in* Master Plan Report, National Zoological Park, *circa 1974. Smithsonian Institution Archives, Image SIA2014–01229.*

grass and semidecomposed granite found in the neighboring hillside. The addition of oak trees, cut back to sturdy branches, and a two-foot-deep swimming pool were additional "refinements" that curators "feared . . . the gorillas might not respect," but whose adaptation "surprised everyone." Zoo photographs displayed the residents engaging in vigorous, wholesome outdoor play, while a final image reconstructed "a gorilla's view of the Park," and a white subjectivity rooted in the power to observe others, risk-free (Figure I.4).[39] These racial representations were neither secure nor particularly self-conscious, confirming the riotousness of racial meaning that John Hartigan identifies as the stuff of American public culture more broadly.[40] Iterable and operational through inference, accident, and the uncanny, they were nonetheless pivotal to the reworking of a bourgeois urbanism that passed for generic, that counted for what was most human in American life, and that had always been highly racialized. As I discuss in chapter 1, this was the same urbanism that, since the mid-nineteenth century, privileged the presence of the white bourgeoisie in park space, a group that fashioned themselves as a universal type, sometimes to the physical exclusion of other people, and other times in ways that set the terms of what inclusion could be (maintaining decorum, dressing well, looking intently at nature, etc.). And it was the same urbanism that proved desirable to those who, while not comfortably located in that racial profile, sought out such distinction all the same or were drafted into it. In collaboration with participant animals, the new zoo makers renewed this type and in doing so demonstrated a preoccupation with the question of whiteness in the United States of the 1960s and 1970s.

READING ZOO URBANISM

The preoccupation with whiteness is a point I take from research that frames the larger story of U.S. postwar cities through the lens of identity formation. Urban historians have done invaluable work by asking how differences of race, class, gender, and sexuality come to bear on metropolitan culture and its extensions.[41] Historians of race in particular have helped rethink urban renewal and suburbanization since World War II as a class-specific process of constructing racial identities.[42] Collectively their research describes a pattern of racial self-discovery in which a rising middle class of Italians, Jews, Germans, Greeks, Asians, Latinos, and African Americans came to disidentify with the nation's urban cores as sites of physical and moral collapse and, with it, the struggles of a socially disenfranchised black poor. These communities embarked on a historical event that is now widely discussed as a period of "white flight" and which Eric Avila frames as the pursuit of "a classless but deeply racialized fantasy of suburban whiteness."[43] For Avila, white flight was defined as much by the reconfiguration of identities as the physical relocation of a specific demographic group. It entailed "a renegotiation of racial and spatial identities, implying a cultural process in which an expanding middle class of myriad ethnic backgrounds *came to discover itself as white*" (my emphasis).[44] From this perspective, a range of racial and ethnic communities, none of them uniform in themselves, escaped to and reaffirmed the suburban ideal. Abandoning inner cities, middle-income Americans variously embraced a particular spatiality that became synonymous with white culture, a geography that was sanitized, routinized, secluded, and beautified by natural-looking flora and fauna.[45]

Patterns of white flight manifested across the United States. While urban critics vilified cities like New York, Detroit, Philadelphia, St. Louis, and Washington, D.C., a parallel practice of Sun Belt boosterism constructed cities like Houston, Phoenix, and San Diego as a respite from the disorder, partly because their postwar identities were staunchly antiurban and organized around the clarity and consistency of automobile travel.[46] In these sun-filled, arid locations lay the possibility of easier, more prosperous living, comparatively free of crime and decrepitude. Urbanists have argued that this rejection of a fading industrial city life was influenced more by public

Figure I.3. *"Keeping Up with Our Gorillas,"* Zoonooz, *March 1973. Courtesy of the Zoological Society of San Diego.*

rhetoric that paired urban decline with menacing blackness than by sociological data or lived experience. The rhetoric was multilayered, incorporating social critics, the news media, advertising, and popular film. Its power, as Steve Macek asserts, was in structuring and informing a "panic over inner-city pathology" in ways that "consistently blamed the victims of urban crisis for their plight and constructed the central city as an object of middle-class fear."[47] As Anglos and passable racial and ethnic minorities moved away from the nation's purported trouble spots, any empirical or firsthand knowledge that might have dissipated the fear became more unlikely. Their physical disengagement from city life paired with a steady diet of urban decline discourse fueled more bad feelings over what downtowns could barely contain and suburban enclaves promised in their place. This book argues that the renovation of American zoos followed similar compulsions toward "democratized" whiteness, unfolding as both a thorny symbol and a vital slice of an antiurbanism that was negatively charged with racial difference.

My interpretive emphasis on race recognizes that renewal discourse was keyed

Figure I.4. *"A Gorilla's View of the Park,"* Zoonooz, *March 1973. Courtesy of the Zoological Society of San Diego.*

not only toward white racial identities but also toward those discernible as hetero-sexual, masculine, or feminine, and middle class. The reproductive sagas of "charis-matic megafauna," for example, underscore how these new zoos were saturated with gender and sexual normativity.[48] My account of white tiger breeding in chapter 3 is particularly mindful of the production of whiteness vis-à-vis sexualized discourses of male–female colonial contact and desexualized discourses of maternal fitness. At the same time, it would be quite conceivable to offer a reading of zoo renewal as a reinscription of economic affluence in the setting of public zoos, which is de facto white in its racial composition. Such a reading might posit that if renewal pitted whiteness against other racial identities, it also pitted wealth against poverty, perhaps more so. David Roediger's remarks about the subordination of race by class in traditional Marxist analyses begin to address why race was pivotal in zoo renewal and ought not to be absorbed into class.

> The privileging of class over race is not always productive or meaningful. To set race within social formations is absolutely necessary, but to reduce race to class is damaging. If, to use tempting older Marxist images, racism is a large, low-hanging branch of a tree that is rooted in class relations, we must constantly remind ourselves that the branch is not the same as the roots, that people may more often bump into the branch than the roots, and that the best way to shake the roots may at times be by grabbing the branch.[49]

Roediger's arboreal metaphor is handy for its cautions about reduction and how identity and power are experienced on the day-to-day level of the "branch." But the metaphor also inadvertently flags a potential problem with Marxist-inflected readings of zoos by suggesting that class and race share the stability of trees. An interpretation of race in American zoo renewal as an offshoot of class would seem to require that middle-class whites be as empirically white as they are empirically middle class, making the condition of race as fixed as that of class. Critical studies of race in the United States, however, have complicated such fixity.

Contra entrenched nineteenth-century ideologies of racial realism, these studies take as their foundation that categories of race are not biologically or otherwise intrinsic to human subjects. While race is usually assigned to, or claimed by, a human subject, it does not emerge from that subject, existing instead as, in the oft-cited words of Michael Omi and Howard Winant, an "unstable and 'decentered' complex of social meanings constantly being transformed by political struggle." The instability of meanings is far from a free play of signification. Omi and Winant also posit the social organization of racial meanings and the ways in which U.S. society is organized by said meanings, arguing for race as "an element of the social structure rather than as an irregularity within it." This insistence on both the representational and structural dimensions of race form the basis of what the authors have influentially theorized as "racial formation," defined as "the sociohistorical process by which racial categories are created, inhabited, transformed, and destroyed."[50] Race, here, functions as a dynamic and contested sign system, whose sense of realness can be attributed to, on the one hand, its power to verify and perpetuate unequal shares of wealth and opportunity, and on the other, its materially rooted—and most often corporeal—signifiers, such as skin and eye color, hair texture, nose and eye shape.[51]

Scholars of American whiteness have narrowed in on the sign system that has enjoyed and inflicted its privilege by appearing both ubiquitous and off the social radar. The task of studying whiteness—the sense of and authority in being white—has been to expose it as such, to make it visible and vulnerable to the same inspection given to other racialized groups; to bring whiteness out from behind de facto assumptions. In bell hooks's phrasing, this approach "allows for the recognition that progressive white people who are anti-racist might be able to understand the way in which their cultural practice reinscribes white supremacy without promoting paralyzing guilt or denial."[52] To this end, research on the cultures of whiteness has examined the extent to which being white is an effect of representational practices, whether textual, visual, or spatial.[53] Social histories and sociological studies of whiteness have emphasized how particular communities over time are able to profit from the social privileges of the sign system, thereby fashioning themselves as white.[54] In George Lipsitz's formulation, "Whiteness is invested in, like property, but it is also a means of accumulating property and keeping it from others."[55] Matthew Frye Jacobson demonstrates that the pursuit, and denial, of whiteness in American culture has been "a fairly untidy affair," characterized by debates over what being white means. The nineteenth-century confusions and conflicts over racial designations like *white, Caucasian,* and *Celt,* for example, illustrate the nature of white consciousness as an intricate competition over meaning as much as an effect of distributive inequalities.[56] Together, this research helps clarify how whiteness is the product (not the cause) of various forces that jointly constitute who and what hold power in American society. In this regard, to be white is to claim and/or identify with one or many axes of power. Moreover, it is to demonstrate that many axes of power exist *as* racialized positions, defined against an imagined or abandoned otherness, and from which a range of people speak at different historical moments.

While my study extends the work of historicizing distinctly urban processes of white racial formation, it also seeks to redress urban history's disinclination to tackle the question of the animal. A deeper analysis of American urbanism does well to scrutinize not only the ways that racial identities manifested in specific forms of modern urban life but also how feathered, furry, scaly, slimy, and microscopic creatures shaped its very possibility, lest historians risk repeating the anthropocentric miscalculations of midcentury urban reformers. These architects, developers, politicians, writers, and activists were often well meaning, but variously habituated to notions of modernity that reinforced the sanctity of the Enlightenment human subject to the detriment of those who had other-than-human experiences of the city. Wrote the urban reformer Charles Abrams in 1965:

> A city, even an American city, is the pulsating product of the human hand and mind, reflecting man's history, his struggle for freedom, his creativity, his genius— and his selfishness and errors. It is the palimpsest on which man's story is written, the record of those who built a skyscraper or a picture window, fought a pitched battle for a play street, created a bookshop or a bakeshop that mattered.[57]

What would it mean instead to appreciate how cities pulse not only with the product of the human hand and mind but with a multiplicity of organisms, of unfamiliar, agential corporealities that have supported, and challenged, the category of human at every turn and its record of civic decline and progress? What would it mean to feel for that pulse, taking it, not as a cue to forge an expanded liberal democratic pluralism—a case of "critters are people too"—but as the feeling of the always already interspecies character of the city and the starting point for social and environmental justice? Geographers have responded to these blind spots by mapping the interconnectedness between all species in urban environments, such that omissions of nonhuman life from physical and cultural geographies of the metropolis now seem anachronistic in the discipline.[58] The corrective offered by academic feminists (eco and otherwise) has been a robust investigation of the constructive powers of material bodies of various kinds within the social world—less as Foucauldian objects of discourse than as agents of its very production.[59] These responses are allied with my own, which is more directly bolstered by (1) Jonathan Burt's insight that zoo animals are active, techno-implicated subjects within and of modernity, and (2) the probability that renewal at the zoo was a multispecies "contact zone," in Haraway's reworked sense of the term, where resident animals and their caretakers were copresent with each other in the unstable work of communicating America's civic decline and rebirth.[60]

Zoo Renewal helps initiate the "animal turn" in urban history by examining a site that urban historians often neglect or undervalue, thanks partly to the zoo's identity as a metropolitan "elsewhere" with concerns that run counter to the city and/or are explicable through parallel institutions such as the prison or the asylum. Michel Foucault's speculative framing of zoos as heterotopias is particularly seductive in that it positions the spaces of public animal display as utopias-in-action: places where extraordinary things are possible on account of them being "outside of all places, even though they may be possible to indicate their location in reality." More specifically, Foucault sees zoos (via the garden) as "the smallest parcel of the world and then it is the totality of the world."[61] Such elastic thinking diminishes how zoos and zoo going are always somehow calibrated to the cities that finance, locate, promote, and attend them. Similarly, aligning zoos with other spaces of incarceration, spaces that Foucault identified as heterotopias too, also takes the zoo out of the city. The zoo-as-prison or zoo-as-asylum sets up the institution for ethical judgments often made at the expense of understanding its urban life as, what Jennifer Wolch calls the "zoöpolis," a place of routine human–animal interaction that forms the epistemological and ontological precondition for eco-socialist, feminist, and antiracist urban futures.[62] Patrick Wirtz's description of cities in the industrial age makes the concept audible, noting "a cacophony of sounds emitting from the industrializing landscape; the crash of metal upon metal within factories, the chugging growl of the combustion engine, the scream and whirl of street cars," but also "the roar of lions, the bark of seals and the chattering of monkeys."[63] For Wirtz, the story of early public zoological parks and gardens is the story of urbanism itself. Here, too, I foreground the urbanism of zoos in order to recognize other species as everyday figures and agents whom we imagine or meet in our vicinities—something akin to neighbors.[64] Where did these neighbors belong in struggles over urban decay and rebirth, and suburban growth? How did captive wildlife resonate with blackness and brownness in the city, but also whiteness, and for whom? What aspects of zoo renewal made those associations alternately probable and improbable, and always tenuous? In what ways were the rubrics of wildness and exoticism revived, and rebuffed? What racial assumptions were designed into enclosures that emphasized unrestricted views, more territory, animal privacy, and room to reproduce? How did zoo animals collaborate with or confound their eventual portrayal as happier, healthier creatures living in rejuvenated cityscapes and their suburban edges? Which animals were given these privileges, and why? These are some of the questions that animate this book, which insists that humans are not the only urbanites warranting study, and that reading the visual, print, and material culture of zoos is one way to access the presence and contributions of other breathing, breeding city dwellers.

The question of access is tricky. I am both frustrated and inspired by Nicole Shukin's assertion that "signs of animal protest awaiting counterhegemonic production are strewn all over the social texts of modernity, as yet unactivated links to repressed histories of animal capital."[65] It is hard enough to reconfigure a history of urban redevelopment beyond the exclusivity of the human, but how does one write an account of zoo change that activates repressed animal histories, histories that upset market forces with their own chronologies, spaces, and actors? How to read for a pulse that is anything other than instrumental to the normative project of building a whiter zoo? Erica Fudge has identified the problem of studying historical animals on their own terms (whatever those might be), given history's humanist orientation toward abstraction and periodization: animals do not keep records of their own, nor do they keep historical time.[66] Shukin has complicated matters in her utterly convincing argument that animals do not easily escape the logics of capitalism that fix them as fetishized figures and usable flesh. What research strategies remain available to us in the face of these disciplinary and structural conditions?

A deeper commitment to the zoo archive offers a way in. I agree with Fudge that any venture into the history of animals is one that begins with the centrality of animal representation—that is, the centrality of texts created and read by humans about animals. But, as Fudge also notes, this form of history does not have to end with the centrality of the human at either end of the production–consumption circuit. Bracketing off the issue of how animal representations are, from a materialist standpoint, interspecies productions, the issue of how they can be read nonanthropocentrically is what concerns me here, largely because my experience with archives is routinely punctuated by unexpected gasps, thumps, and tears, by the embodiments and embeddedness that make knowledge possible, whether it is about animals or not.[67] For this, I turn to Roland Barthes's 1970 analysis "The Third Meaning" and ask what a semiotic approach pushed to its limit can do for a historical research practice that aspires to take animals seriously. My interest in Barthes is a cautious one, heeding Haraway's astute point that poststructuralist concepts such as the "death of the subject" (and, in Barthes's case, "the death of the Author") emerged at the same moment when raced/sexed/colonized subjects were beginning to constitute themselves *as* subjects of representation, in all their necessary fragmentation and specificity.[68] What is more, Barthes's criticism and theory fits nicely into the annals of anthropocentrism with its relative disinterest in anything other than human-to-human experience.

But what kind of human? Looking at a set of film stills by the Russian filmmaker Sergei Eisenstein, Barthes undoes the sense of epistemic mastery customarily afforded to its viewer; that scenario in which a given text generates a definitive meaning and positions me as its definitive meaning maker, hovering above a given text in full command of its content and form. Amid definitive meanings, Barthes tells us, lies the third or "obtuse" meaning, the most ambiguous layer of Eisenstein's images, extraneous to and more supple than the denotative or the connotative, the informational or the symbolic. It is the one "too many . . . at once persistent and fleeting, smooth and elusive."[69] In its capacity to outplay meaning as such, the third meaning appears as a blunted, highly singular, and capricious luxury. It bends back beyond the ninety-degree angle that Barthes associates with the "legal perpendicular of the narrative" and "seems to open the field of meaning totally," setting itself to its own temporality and ethics. He writes: "Imagine 'following' not Euphrosyne's schemings, nor even the character (as diegetic entity or symbolic figure), nor even, again, the face of the Wicked Mother, but merely in this face, this attitude, this black veil, the heavy, ugly flatness—you will then have *a different time-scale* . . . a different film" (my emphasis).[70] Bumping up against the details of a cinematic figure, details that have migrated from their narrative utility and manifest as enigmatic form, is the moment of third-meaning production. For Barthes, the encounter with this different timescale is also the discovery of what is possible to love. While the third meaning does not represent anything per se, its transient, accidental dimension has the power to instill love toward the nonnarrativized (read: other-than-humanized) object of knowledge, creating space for a mutual "understanding" that is signaled by Barthes's response to the Eisensteinian people as "essentially loveable."[71]

The degree of intimacy, humility, and vulnerability needed to register third meanings seems appropriate for historians who seek to excavate the animals of the past. These modes enable us to ponder and attach ourselves emotionally to those elements of an animal's representation that defy human explanation and narrativization, and more, that confront us with the porousness of the "human" as a decontaminated, autonomous agent of her or his own rational–critical capacities.[72] Barthes, for one, could be quite noncognitive in his orientations. His tenure as a theater critic, for example, bespeaks a fascination with the body's role in the production of meaning, not only as sign but also as a strange participant in the process of writing, one that forms a "second horizon of possibilities" framed by the biological rather than the historical.[73] His humanism, in other words, was not entirely that. Whether third meanings are the location of "real" animals in the archive is less important to me than identifying these meanings as the raw and lively material for a different kind of zoo history, and historian. This is a zoo history in which animals came to embody America's civic endangerment and rebirth—often through forms of racial representation—but also slipped out of the labor of instrumental signification, not unlike the face of the Wicked Mother, and left some loveable residue of the uncooperativeness. Put differently, staying open to third meanings is one way to understand the tenuousness of zoo renewal, given its reliance on the semiotic transparency of zoo animals, and entering into some of renewal's other-urban-worldliness. This is to say, at minimum, that the humanist drives that directed midcentury zoos and the urban development of which they are a part were also always opened up by the contingencies of reading representations. As in the zoo, so too in the zoo archives.

FEELING BAD IN FIVE CHAPTERS, TWO ZOOS, AND TWO SPECIES

The history of feeling bad in and about American zoos in the long postwar period coheres around the visual trope and material conditions of the "naked cage." The naked cage was identified by the British zoologist Desmond Morris in 1968 but predates its label as a form of animal display at once highly singular and diffuse. In chapter 1, I focus on the seminal role of this widely condemned design staple by tracking its iterations across radically different sites of American zoo renewal, and the specific ways in which it incited a shame historically felt and marshaled by white middle-class liberals. My interest in this shame lies less in its possibilities for transforming social relations in zoos and their cities than how it affirmed and advanced racialized discourses of urban crisis that positioned cities as derelict spaces in need of wholesale intervention. The naked cage, I argue, found its affective heritage in nineteenth-century urban reform campaigns. Synthesizing studies of urban, environmental, and critical zoo history, I discuss early American zoos as part of a larger movement for urban improvement that understood the city as a site of civilization's collapse. Early zoo makers responded with the construction of recuperative spaces defined by the example of western European zoological gardens and a racially specific American nature ideal. These elements would resurface a hundred years later when zoo makers of the 1960s and 1970s constructed and confronted the problem of modernist animal displays whose artificiality reproduced the racial registers of postwar urban deviance.

The particularity of the case studies that follow combines with their illustrative function. While few if any urban and zoo histories can claim national comprehensiveness, the choice of examining the National Zoo in Washington, D.C., and the Zoological Society of San Diego's two campuses in San Diego County as somewhat exemplary of U.S. zoo renewal is a move in that direction. Recognizing that renewal was a discursive formation, rendered through the reconfiguration of space and species, the "Smithsonian National Zoological Park" and the "World Famous San Diego Zoo" (as dubbed by its midcentury director) were prominent sites through which to imagine the revitalization of zoos and their cities around the country. Both made early and strong commitments to physically improving their grounds and establishing *ex situ* (off-site) breeding programs for select species, effectively securing their place as leaders among a generation of "new zoos." The National Zoo built on its esteemed history of free admission, bison breeding, and the landscape aesthetics of Frederick Law Olmsted, to name a few touchstones, while the San Diego Zoo threw its resources behind the public breeding and display of African and Asian species on the open veldt. For zoo reformers, these institutions, along with a roster of other key institutions, were testaments to the changing face of zoos in the United States.[74] Placing both in the foreground of my study is an effort to mine these powerhouses of wildlife conservation activity and what they suggest about zoo renewal as a na-tionalized project to "green" these institutions.

At the same time, each zoo undertook renewal in ways that spoke volumes about the regional experiences of urban and suburban development. The National Zoo's improvement involved reclaiming its role as a truly national zoo amid the eyesores of District decline, and acquiring, displaying, and reproducing high-profile animals, such as Mohini, the Bengal white tiger, and later, Hsing-Hsing and Ling-Ling, the Chinese giant pandas. The Zoological Society of San Diego took a different shape, capitalizing on its entrepreneurial energies, military culture, and Southern California climate to renovate the original downtown zoo and build its San Pasqual Valley outpost in the spirit of suburban growth. The society's program of renewal culminated in the suburbanization of twenty southern white rhinoceroses imported from South Africa. The respective stories of these similar but divergent sites serve as bookends for the over two hundred commercial and nonprofit institutions that make up the category of "American zoos" in my period of study and the metropolitan centers and peripheries to which they were correlatively and constitutively bound.

Chapter 2 traces the renewal of the National Zoo through twenty years of master planning. Rooted in a critical racial analysis of Washington, D.C., and its renewal program, the chapter situates changes in the zoo's physical geography within a civic culture gripped by the shame of its decline and the promise of uplift. The National Zoo experienced its own strand of urban crisis through racially charged rhetoric, antiurban activism, and architectural efforts to bring visitors back into the city with-out realizing they were there. At each stage of renewal, complex junctures of racial and species difference racialized the zoo's grounds and its occupants, mirroring larger shifts in the Federal City's revitalization and giving it a zoological shape. My account follows these stages and begins to rethink zoo space as expressive of and responsive to an American way of life geared to escaping the perceived menace of its inner cities and getting back to nature.

Chapter 3 gives more attention to nonhuman life in National Zoo renewal, gen-erated by my archival infatuation with a single animal named Mohini. Mohini was a magnetic female Bengal tiger acquired from India, displayed on zoo grounds, and bred for her white coat, pink lips, and blue eyes until the early 1970s. Tracking her acquisition and early exhibition, I begin by demonstrating how the tiger enticed the District's zoophiles with her dazzling whiteness, restaging a colonial dynamic between the United States and India that inscribed Mohini as a postwar exotic. Next, I analyze a domestic and maternal tiger body image that zoo reformers placed into kinship with, and as model for, white middle-class women. With a focus on Mohini's breeding program and the postpartum care for her cubs, the chapter locates Mohini's reproductive body within a civic culture of American eugenics and pronatalism. What emerges from this short feline biography is the sense that animals confirmed, but also threatened, the National Zoo's reconstruction as a breeding ground for white racial identities.

Chapter 4 moves the story of U.S. zoo renewal to Southern California and the modernization program of the San Diego Zoo. The chapter investigates the suburban attitudes and borrowed views embedded in San Diego's zoo designs by reading the planning and promotion of their open-air, mixed-species exhibits against a regional history of race and real estate. Of primary concern is how zoo designers and advocates adapted the postwar planning concept of open space to animal exhibits on the zoo's downtown site and a new eighteen-hundred-acre wildlife outpost. Locating each campus within the spatial politics of "becoming white" in Southern California, I detail how these two overlapping phases of zoo renewal sustained preferred residential styles and settings for the city's suburbanizing population as much as the biological well-being of vulnerable and endangered species. At the San Diego Zoo, open space took form as wild animal suburbs that were sensitive to species-specific spatial needs, but also the comfort-zones of human spectators. The new San Diego Zoo alternated between nonhuman versions of midcentury modern home design and family life, as well as regional investments in the pastoral aesthetic and frontier mythologies that historically define white middle-class membership. Echoing chapter 2's treatment of the National Zoo, this case study offers more evidence of how zoos in the 1960s and 1970s spatialized white fear and longing.

Chapter 5 narrows in on the signature species of the San Diego Zoo's second campus and offers another animalcentric analysis of zoo renewal. I take up the regionally specific ways that Wild Animal Park planners figured the southern white rhinoceros as endangered, asking how San Diego's herd came to embody the quality and status of endangerment in the midst of a Southern Californian public uncertain of its own survival. I survey a longer tradition of visualizing race through rhinos before turning to a process of relocation and display that made recurrent use of the wilderness safari genre. Fresh off a popular craze for African wildlife tourism and Hollywood safari films, the park's version of safari refined the genre by reconnecting zoo goers to an esteemed colonial pastime pursued by white elites and adapting it to a 1970s audience yearning for up-close-and-personal encounters with a nonthreatening, natural-looking nature. The chapter foregrounds how white rhinos were instrumental in this line of white racialization by appearing as peaceful, authentic subjects themselves, but also figures whose racial whiteness, so conceived, was at risk of being lost.

By concentrating on not only two institutions but also the examples of white tigers and white rhinos therein, this book aims to understand the role of nonhuman actors in constructing postwar whiteness. At an obvious level, each species was implicated in historical claims to whiteness through their common names. At another level, whiteness was the negotiated outcome between different mammalian bodies, behaviors, and agendas. The variety and intricacy of these negotiations demonstrates just how dexterous racial discourse can be when animals are in the picture, and its peculiar energy in this period of zoo and urban history. Moreover, the prevalence of two quite distinct forms of whiteness—with differences *within* those forms—suggests that the whiff of race in American zoo renewal was integral to its reasoning and experience, and likely discernible in relation to other creatures.

An afterword gives a sense of the legacies of zoo renewal by reflecting on the peculiar state of feeling good in zoos today. Amid the perennial uneasiness of captive animal display, a recent public controversy at Seattle's Woodland Park Zoo points to local hope, gratitude, and pride around current wildlife conservation tableaux. Situating the controversy in the proliferation of zoo exhibits that now feature humans as an integrated part of vulnerable habitats, I take the happy zoo goers at their word and consider how their pleasure spurns nonwhite racial identities. My condensed visitor study reveals the mood of contemporary zooscapes to be continuous with the story of white racial formation in midcentury American cities.

Zoo Renewal is not an attempt to explain away or fix that sinking feeling we might experience when looking at a living animal in its zoo enclosure; its tonalities may well exceed interpretation or remedy. But given the extreme presentism of zoos today combined with an environmental futurity that leans heavily on children, inquiring into the not-so-distant past and the urban specificity of bad zoo feelings is a necessary critical procedure. The question worth answering is not, as Berger might have posed it, why do people feel bad at the zoo, but what are the idioms and interactions through which feeling bad has been cultivated, amplified, relieved, and disavowed? The stories that follow reorient us in this direction and toward the analytic practices required for their telling.

1

Shame and the Naked Cage

In a 1971 issue of *Curator,* a publication of the American Museum of Natural History, Dale Osborn, curator at large of Chicago's Brookfield Zoo, offered some recommendations for renovating animal exhibits. Under the title "Dressing the Naked Cage," and with four references to barren cages in the first five sentences, the problem was clearly defined. Osborn was critical of the classic animal house with its "display of rows of brightly lighted, 'naked' cages," a setting in which "sterility is the keynote" and furnishings consisted of "a shelf on the back wall, a piece of tree wedged into a corner, and perhaps a wooden nest box on the hard bare floor." These conditions were considered too similar to "a rat cage of wire mesh" and positioned zoo denizens as "just another animal in another cage." For Osborn, the cage remained a basic conceptual and material unit for zoo display; what one did with that cage was the pertinent issue. Cages could be illuminated with red fluorescent light and painted with non-reflective colors for nocturnal animals to feel concealed at daytime. The units could be refit to create "places to rest, hide, exercise, sleep, bear young, etc." Screening techniques such as stencils, artificial stones, and photomurals were useful to "hide undesirable cage features, add depth to a cage scene, and eliminate the feeling that one is looking into a cell." Such elements suggested that even on small budgets, "innovations can be made in barren cages to improve the plight of animals and relieve the public of monotony." Not only were these animal spaces aesthetically, biologically, and pedagogically better than "naked cages," they also offered "an experimental proving ground for future building plans," the scope of which was left unnamed.[1]

Osborn's fixation on cages, naked and dressed, would have been familiar to even the most casual zoo visitor, and certainly to other curators. Coined by the British zoologist Desmond Morris in a 1968 *Life* magazine article, "The Shame of the Naked Cage," the term described the poor state of animal space in midcentury zoos. In the United States, the naked cage was not always identified as such, but it was always identifiable. Typically marked by cramped and dilapidated enclosures, "unnatural" building materials like iron and tile, and a tendency to produce aberrant animal behavior such as pacing, the naked cage became shorthand for advocates of U.S. zoo renewal, a widely condemned staple of wildlife captivity and display. Crucially, the cage was less an actual design convention than a complex representation of bad design. More often than not, an American zoo's built environment in the postwar years was an eclectic mix of exhibition spaces including moated, outdoor grottoes and islands with heaps of artificial rockwork, New Deal structures in neoclassical forms, and recently built children's zoos designed in miniature.[2] From the late 1960s onward, however, the figure of the naked cage came to dominate the rhetorical environment of American zoos and trump other ways to understand contemporary zoo exhibits, exemplified by the sheer range of forms that the cage took as signs of the atrocity of unrenovated space. Indeed, the absence of a prototypical naked cage was part of the discourse's strength. Invoked by curators, designers, muckrakers, and artists in and around select institutions, the naked cage's multivalent contours and connotations offered a necessary "before shot" picture that could point to a number of infractions in American zoos and fuel their large-scale redevelopment throughout the latter half of the twentieth century.

No account of zoo change in these years was complete without some allusion to the naked cage. Reports of Brookfield Zoo's own changes one year after Osborn's essay testified to the cage's discursive grip. According to *Inland Architect,* for example, 1972 saw the Brookfield Zoo's new Design and Exhibition Department engaged in the formidable task of "transforming the traditional tiled-and-barred zoo cages into living environments," including the creation of three-dimensional domed modules for the existing lion house and a new fifty-thousand-square-foot primate house with a walk-through rain forest and savannah. Similarly, a profile of the Bronx Zoo in a 1970 issue of *Design and Environment* noted how a certain model of exhibit was being phased out: "Here, the captive animal sits in a cage utterly alone, cramped in discomfort, bored and frustrated in his concrete or white-tile, easy-maintenance, sanitary enclosure. Such a repressive environment could only be cruel to the animal, subjecting him to taunts by visitors, mistreatment from keepers, depriving him of any satisfactions he may have known in nature." In its place, and still under construction, was a model of display "that should suggest the *natural habitat* of the animal." The naked cage appeared on television as well. In a 1970 documentary on San Francisco's Fleishhacker Zoo, viewers digested its multiple incarnations: interior shots of a bird house with sparse foliage, metal scaffolding, and not a bird in sight; exterior shots of elephants adrift in the vast expanse of their concrete yards; an extended close-up view of a rhinoceros peering over its ramshackle barrier. Narration supplemented the visuals with news that "San Francisco Zoo is floundering: Her outdoor cages are small and packed so tightly in some areas that often the only animal that one sees is the barbed wire. Where there is no wire, vast spaces of cracked concrete meet the eye; a drab setting for the audience and the animal who must face that environment every day of its life." By the time *Science News* surveyed zoo conditions nationwide in 1976, the multifaceted image of bad zoo design had become a "heretofore immutable civic presence—the antiquated zoological park with its blocky, odorous animal houses, its small barred cages and its melancholy inhabitants." Renewal was an apposite and inevitable response to the decrepitude.[3]

This chapter considers the naked cage as a pivotal and emotionally charged figure of U.S. zoo renewal. Depictions of prerenewal zoos as a series of animal cages and caged animals helped construct the postwar zoo as a civic institution riddled with shame, much of which centered on design itself. It was not insignificant that proposed solutions to the naked cage centered on giving animals more cover. As Sarah Ahmed notes, in shame "one desires cover precisely because one has already been exposed to others. Hence the word 'shame' is associated as much with cover and concealment, as it is with exposure, vulnerability and wounding."[4] In its semiotics and its somatics, the naked cage underlined precisely this condition of an animal's damaging display and the need for protection. The critique often hinged on the aesthetic nakedness of the display proper, a direct or indirect skewering of architectural modernism that stressed, in Elspeth Probyn's more general terms, "the rupture when bodies can't or won't fit the place—when, seemingly, there is no place to hide."[5]

At the same time, much naked cage discourse gained momentum by connecting zoo animals' condition of nakedness to the condition of other urbanites in the 1960s and 1970s, mirroring white middle-class shame over racial injustice in American cities. The *Design and Environment* article profiling positive change at the Bronx Zoo, for example, was the same article that opened by asking, "Do bears at the zoo find life more bearable than men in the city? Yes, if the Bronx Zoo is an indicator." Likewise, the environmental writer Julia Allen Field asked in the 1967 pages of *Landscape Architecture*: "Why is there thought to be a mass appeal in caged animals when the city itself is increasingly regarded as an intolerable cage for human beings?" Four years later, Susan Pressman of the Humane Society of the United States told the press that many of the country's zoos were "little more than 'animal ghettos.'"[6] Provocative comparisons like these alluded to a potent context of meaning for midcentury zoo criticism—namely, a climate of crisis that placed the city in a state of moral, cultural, and physical decline. This sense of crisis was marked by region and race. Midwest and East Coast urban centers experienced the brunt of what Christopher Klemek calls "that seemingly ubiquitous concatenation of crime, social problems, physical decay, disinvestment, and abandonment that fell over so many U.S. cities beginning in the 1960s." To this chain of misfortune, other urban historians add the demographic concentration, suffering, and rebellions of poor African Americans in the nation's urban cores, all of which contrasted with the exodus of comparatively affluent whites from the city and other racial and ethnic groups who were able to conform to new forms of suburban whiteness.[7] Expressions of the naked cage reflected, augmented, and reconfigured the culture of shame that surrounded this sharp disparity. These expressions did not necessarily conflate caged animals with African Americans below the poverty line—animals were enlisted into a range of representations through naked cage discourse—but it did entail that problems of space at the zoo and race in the cities were intimately related aspects of postwar urbanism in the United States. The naked cage gave urban shame zoomorphic form, heightening it through images of once noble animals stripped of their dignity and suggesting that the shame of the American city was marked by species as well as racial difference. These affective entanglements not only enabled an urgent call for zoo renewal but also laid the discursive groundwork under which revitalization would be experienced by humans and animals alike.

The naked cage had its groundwork as well. I begin this chapter by situating how the figure was constructed and made unbearable within a longer history of urban shame of which zoos have always been a part. Synthesizing existing critical zoo history together with urban and environmental histories that have addressed the relationship between cities, nature, and race, I am particularly concerned with illustrating the roots of post–World War II zoo renewal's white bourgeois consciousness. These studies suggest that while the industrial city made many reform-minded Americans feel bad about urban life, early zoos were conceived and operated as points of civic pride, countrified oases amid the depravity. Critiques of zoo exhibits a century later revived this urban reform tradition and its politics of white shame across multiple fields and publics. Here I take up three specific instantiations of the revival: the design criticism of Desmond Morris, the photography of Garry Winogrand, and the animal advocacy of Peter Batten. Morris was the most influential of the three, mobilizing his prominence within the zoo community since the late 1950s. After earning his PhD at Oxford, Morris directed the television and film unit of London Zoo, worked as the zoo's curator of mammals, and coedited *International Zoo Yearbook,* a budding forum for professional exchange. More important perhaps, his output demonstrated a talent for pairing the enduring charm of zoos with a gravitas common to liberal social documentary, a compelling combination for his middlebrow audience. Quite differently, Winogrand's contribution to zoo renewal found its resonance in New York City and within the emerging modern art genre of social landscape photography. Winogrand's playful black-and-white images of public animal display in New York remain a reference point for photographers of the "street" and a model of how zoo watchers approached midcentury zoos not only as a problem of social content but also as a possibility of photographic form. As a former zoo director turned activist, Batten also worked as a photographer, focusing more squarely on the graphic documentation of animal hardship. His mission to track which and how institutions were failing produced one of the many obscure but gripping artifacts of American zoo history, titled *Living Trophies: A Shocking Look at the Conditions in America's Zoos*. Marginal within the zoo community when published in 1976, *Living Trophies* has gained some currency among contemporary zoo critics and offers an example of the persistence of naked cage discourse even amid its professed dismantling. To be sure, Morris, Winogrand, and Batten were distinct voices in the midcentury moment of zoo renewal. If their paths ever crossed, it was likely by happenstance. This disparateness, however, helps clarify the ubiquity with which an unfolding urban crisis gained carnal and racial intensity vis-à-vis zoos, demonstrating how once bucolic settings were now fully and problematically urbanized ones. Confronted with these and other naked cages, liberal middle-class Americans found mounting evidence for the need for large-scale zoo revitalization and converging animal exemplars of their racial unease.

URBAN SHAME IN THE INDUSTRIAL AMERICAN CITY

The shaming powers of the naked cage were tied to a longer history of urban shame. Since their beginnings, public zoos in the United States have been bound to their urban milieu and those Progressive Era reformers dedicated to its betterment. Early public zoos found their footing within the first crisis of American cities and became part of its proposed solution. The crisis revolved around massive demographic growth. In the second half of the nineteenth century, American cities swelled to a disorienting scale and number. In 1860, 20 percent of the total national population lived in cities. By 1910, the figure rose to 46 percent. The same years saw the number of cities with populations between ten thousand and twenty-five thousand people jump from 58 to 369, while the number of municipalities with populations of over one hundred thousand increased from 9 to 50. These populations were partly made up of American-born migrants who were leaving agrarian society, including African

American sharecroppers from the South, and Catholic and Jewish immigrants who originated mostly from Italy, Poland, Austria-Hungary, the Balkans, and other parts of eastern Europe. Newcomers went to work in an expanding urban factory system where oppressive labor conditions catalyzed violent strikes. They navigated new public services and infrastructures while enduring segregation and stratification along rural, racial, and ethnic lines. They made homes in an increasingly dense layout of poverty-stricken neighborhoods where tenement housing was dirty and dangerous. These daily struggles defined American cities as places of personal, familial, and community hardship for a multitude of people.[8]

The cities of the late nineteenth century were also shaped by a more affluent caste of inhabitants. Urbanites of predominantly Protestant faith, western European lineage, and middle-class means became a social force in city life. These crusaders understood the urban setting as a crowd-infested site of social, spatial, and spiritual ruin. With a mixture of sympathy and hostility, they took a keen interest in the escalating class warfare on the streets, the influx of foreigners into inner-city neighborhoods, and the unchecked activities of the bourgeoning brothels, saloons, and tenement housing. Social problems so defined surfaced in sensational newspaper coverage, crime magazines, dime novels, and documentary photography, in which reformers deployed realist strategies of show-and-tell to record the salacious details of the urban underbelly and construct it as such.[9]

What these muckrakers discovered in their urban odysseys generated widespread concern over the prospects for American civilization. Indicating their magnitude and reach, these concerns were shared by some within immigrant communities. In relation to fears of moral deterioration, for example, the historian Paul Boyer notes that Catholic and Jewish religious leaders were just as troubled as Protestant churchmen. But the latter had a greater impact on the period's discourse of decline, linking the city's problems to the waning of their particular faith and, by extension, to the immigrant presence itself. Urban reform literature also stimulated the exodus of many well-to-do residents to the new suburban peripheries, aided by the growth of private real estate developments and public streetcars. From the comfortable distance of the suburbs, affluent citizens could see the city as a strange and disorderly world in desperate need of social control, moral recentering, and physical rehabilitation. Indeed, as Boyer observes, the spatial relocation of the bourgeoisie helped produce this very perspective. On the city's pristine circumference there lacked a certain community cohesiveness, creating new worries about the possibility of civilization's collapse. Urban decline was, in this sense, a projection of suburbanites' own fears and longings onto those who continued to live in the urban core. It was also an invitation to exert organized control over precarious populations that posed a threat to reformers and their readers. In addition to their entertainment value, representations of urban disorder encouraged forms of genteel philanthropy and technocratic management to mitigate the risk of revolution.[10]

Shame was a prominent leitmotif in Progressive chronicles of urban vice, a feeling directed toward not only the socially disadvantaged but also well-heeled citizens who, as Richard Hoftstadter has argued, proved to be willing receptacles of Protestant responsibility, indignation, and guilt. Reformers themselves could be counted among the latter group, practiced as they were at self-accusation and a sense of personal involvement in their projects.[11] The shame of the city was to be shouldered as much by those with resources as those without, and the rhetoric of revealing what was otherwise hidden was critical to the process. For example, Lincoln Steffens's appropriately titled *The Shame of the Cities* took general aim at a liberal middle-class public with the weapon of disgrace. Intent on exposing municipal government corruption, Steffens wrote that his purpose was "to see if the shameful facts, spread out in all their shame, would not burn through our civic shamelessness and set fire to American pride."[12] What Steffens's journalism laid out for all to see, Jacob Riis's study of New York tenement housing identified as naked truths. In his last chapter of *How the Other Half Lives,* the Danish-born reporter-cum-photographer asked (and answered) on behalf of his readers:

> What then, are the bald facts with which we have to deal in New York? I. That we have a tremendous, ever swelling crowd of wage-earners, which it is our business to house decently. II. That it is not housed decently. III. That it must be so housed here for the present, and for a long time to come, all schemes of suburban relief being as yet utopian, impracticable.[13]

The exposed gap between decency and indecency—shameful in and of itself—was the spark that would implicate a certain caliber of Christian in the fate of others, igniting awareness and some form of nominal action. As Hofstadter notes, the emphasis was less on animating a need for structural change—too radical for the middle-class reader—than on inspiring a *feeling* that action was possible given this new and troubling information, "a sense that the moral tone of things was being improved and that he had a part in this improvement."[14] True to their burgeoning documentary form, reformers attempted to furnish that sense through the indexicality of their representations, stories and images that testified to, as Maren Stange puts it, "the existence of painful social facts and to reformers' special expertise in ameliorating them, thus reassuring a liberal middle class that social oversight was both its duty and its right."[15] That this sobering confirmation was achieved via an epistemological striptease is one irony of these cultural productions. Strategies of uncovering all this troubling knowledge could titillate as much as marshal calls for change.

Another irony is how these representations questioned the humanity of their subjects in the same breath that made humanitarian pleas on their behalf. The targets of bourgeois shame in the industrial city appeared as textually and visually "other" not only to Anglo-Saxon Protestantism but also to what was human. Riis's advocacy offered a particularly strong example of the technique by consistently relaying a New York City underclass of animal-like foreigners. Operating as a tour guide through text and image, the author led his readers through an undifferentiated mass of immigrant and migrant "hordes" and "colonies," living in increasingly "denser swarms" and "the big human bee-hives of the East Side." In a passage on "The Bend," where Mulberry Street "becomes the foul core of New York's Slums," Riis identified a more mammalian animality in the skulking, "unclean beast of dishonest idleness." Profiles of specific racial types may have complicated the image of animal squalor, but not enough to graduate the designated group to human status. The Italian was, for instance, "gay, lighthearted and, if his fur is not stroked the wrong way, inoffensive as a child." The "Chinaman" was "by nature as clean as the cat, which he resembles in his traits of cruel cunning, and savage fury when aroused." Alongside images of likeness to animals were images of animal practices that underscored the slum dweller's alterity. Riis reported on a staple scene from the Lower East Side's Jewish market that included "frowsy-looking chickens and half-plucked geese, hung by the neck and protesting with wildly strutting feet even in death against the outrage." Another tableau of beastly behavior surfaced in a "brawny [Italian] butcher, sleeves rolled up above the elbows and clay pipe in mouth, skinning a kid that hangs from his hook," a scene that dissolved into reports of a dead goat lying in the streets only to be hauled off by another Italian for "a wake or feast of some sort in one of the back alleys." Emanating from Riis's record of urban abjection was a shame that registered acute anxieties over the species identity of his target populations.[16]

The first public zoos were oriented toward clearing up the confusion by confirming the inalienable humanity of the American bourgeoisie and attempting to rehumanize the "other half." Opening in several large and midsized cities in the last four decades of the nineteenth century, zoos developed as recreational spaces dedicated to reflecting and reproducing white middle-class values and behaviors and extending them to a wider metropolitan populace.[17] Zoo makers envisioned their institutions as verdant antidotes to shameful urbanism, accessible within or nearby the city limits but distinct from the subhumanity of industrialization and its workforce. Mission statements emphasized scientific research, education, and wholesome entertainment through the exhibition of native North American and exotic animals on public park grounds. This three-pronged focus distinguished zoos from the spirited circuses, fairs, and street corner animal acts that were popular among the laboring classes and whose presence was already felt in places such as Central Park's zoo.[18] Zoo planners in cities like Philadelphia, Buffalo, Cincinnati, Cleveland, Rochester, and Washington considered these types of shows degrading for both humans and animals. In response, they attempted to create more respectable displays that encouraged, in the words of the Zoological Society of Cincinnati, "the study and dissemination of a knowledge of the nature and habit of the creations of the animal kingdom."[19]

The civic flavor of western European zoos was a trusted source of inspiration for constructing American zoos' white middle-class character. With their formal urban gardens, bustling scientific activity, and social events galore, European zoos struck American reformers as the apogee of refinement, especially for those who were touring the continent and could enjoy the sight of these thriving bourgeois cultures firsthand. William Hornaday, a founder of the National Zoo and first director of the Bronx Zoo, remarked on his own tour, "It is considered an honor as well as an advantage to belong to those zoological societies," for they were where "the aristocracies of intelligence, of wealth, and of birth" gathered to socialize. His reference to aristocracies that were, by this time, socially and politically irrelevant suggests that the primary appeal of European zoos was precisely their cultural cachet. For a citizenry to whom "Europeanness" itself conveyed status, the zoological gardens overseas invited admiration and, for some, homesickness.[20]

London Zoo in Regent's Park was particularly impressive to American zoo makers. After visiting in the 1850s, for example, William Camac, a physician by training, used the zoo as a template for the foundation of the Zoological Society of Philadelphia, which involved sending an engineer back to London to study the exhibitions.[21] The landscape gardener Andrew Jackson Downing also looked to London for the proposed zoo in New York's Central Park.[22] Led by Sir Stamford Raffles after a career of empire building in the East Indies, the British institution opened in 1826, dedicated to the social and spatial construction of its own elitism. By restricting admissions policies, using Latin nomenclature to label animals (many of which were royal gifts), and landscaping the park for an optimum promenade, the zoo in London sought out a cultivated, scientific class of zoo goers marked off from the "curiosity seekers" who were drawn to more popular animal displays.[23] The art of the German-born lithographer George Scharf expresses something of the London Zoological Society's early aspirations. Popular within the society, his work embodied and helped advance a new public of zoo enthusiasts and London Zoo's budding reputation as "the most delightful lounge in the metropolis."[24] Scharf's 1835 print of the Monkey House, for example, depicts Londoners in fine attire enjoying the full gamut of the prototypical zoo experience (Figure 1.1). More specifically, they engage in an exchange of looks that was central to the bourgeoisie's knowledge and appreciation of itself. As the historian Tony Bennett argues in his study of the museum's birth, exhibitionary spaces that emerged as part of nineteenth-century public culture were intensely self-reflexive:

> Relations of space and vision are organized not merely to allow a clear inspection of the objects exhibited but also to allow for the visitors to be the objects of each other's inspection—scenes in which, if not a citizenry, then certainly a public displayed itself to itself in an affirmative celebration of its own orderliness in architectural contexts which simultaneously produced that orderliness.[25]

Scharf's lithograph conveys these axes of inspection and order. In a leisurely arrangement reminiscent of a more formal classroom, a cluster of elegant visitors gathers near the ornate iron structure housing animated nonhuman primates. The animals are clearly visible through the cage, and curious visitors bend toward them for a closer investigation. Women in bright colors with parasols appear more occupied with their human company; they sit prominently on stools and nearby benches in light conversation and self-display. Meanwhile, youngsters are at mild-mannered play, and strolling couples make their way to and from exhibits designed on neoclassical principles of balance and proportion. The overall scene shows London Zoo as a decorous space in which to see captive animals and, in turn, in which to be seen by other zoo goers. By the 1840s the decorum would not have been as likely in Regent's Park, as more novel attractions in the city began to erode Londoners' interest in a genteel resort with scientific shadings.[26] Moreover, fiscal pressures required the zoo, like others in Europe, to relax its initial members-only policy, inviting a greater diversity of urbanites onto the grounds who could not perform civility with the same expertise.[27] But early constructions of the London Zoo had already made a lasting impression on Americans, for whom the prestige remained palpable and worth approximating in the United States.

Not all aspects of European zoos were well received. The future leaders of the American zoological societies did not identify with, nor could they afford, European architectural tastes. Many zoos overseas displayed their animal collection in elaborate buildings that glorified imperial conquest or extreme cultural difference.[28] Animal houses often appeared as exotic, ornamented, or otherwise stylized structures evoking the Near, Middle, and Far East. Between 1869 and 1873, for example, the Berlin Zoo's director oversaw the construction of the "bear and carni-

Figure 1.1. *George Scharf, "The Monkey House at the Zoological Gardens, Regent's Park," 1835.*

vore castle," the "antelope mosque" or "palace," the "pachyderm Indian temple," and the Moorish-style bird house. In 1897 architects designed a Japanese-style building with a pagoda entranceway to exhibit wading birds. Four years later, in consultation with a university Egyptologist, they built the Egyptian temple for ostriches, a structure covered in Egyptian paintings and hieroglyphs.[29] American zoo makers were not particularly opposed to these constructions as conspicuous displays of colonial power or racial fantasy, but they objected to their artificiality. Zoo architecture of this sort was excessive to American eyes, as conveyed in one visitor's observation that these were "rather pretentious buildings which fail to present the animals in a really effective manner." More specifically, the architecture detracted from an authentic, restorative encounter with the natural world.[30]

In ways that would shape mid-twentieth-century shame over the naked cage, the notion that a trip to the zoo could be a trip to nature "itself" became a definitive aspect of public animal exhibition in the United States and a source of civic pride. American zoos were initially designed as retreats from the city as much as upscale "Europeanized" slices of it. They were pieces of the countryside located within or on the outskirts of the urban core and praised by public officials for giving citizens representations of natural habitats and wildlife that minimized the human hand. As Jeffrey Hyson notes, this was the tone in one guidebook for Chicago's Lincoln Park bear pit, which, though recognized as "wholly artificial . . . closely resemble[s] the bear pits in the Rocky Mountains, built by nature." Similarly, one review of the Philadelphia Zoo's riverside site reported that the spot required "but a few touches of art to transform it into a fascinating scene of miniature forests, hills, ravines and mountain water courses."[31] The National Zoo was another facility that excelled at animal display through a naturalistic frame, though not in ways that disguised the work of the architect. William Ralph Emerson took his cues from the surrounding Rock Creek area to create uniquely rustic structures that were still recognizable as human architecture. The Buffalo House, built in 1891, was a two-level log cabin built of roughly hewn timber with the bark left on. Designed that same year, the Carnivora House (later known as the Lion House) was an unyielding tribute to the picturesque. Built atop the zoo's highest point, the building was constructed from massive, irregular stones quarried from the surrounding area and, with two corner lookout towers, gave visitors multiple hilltop views of the grounds. To some critics, the Carnivora House bordered on ostentatious; its large scale created concerns over the building's cost, while the architect's artistic sketches posed a challenge to the work of actual construction.[32] But in its attention to natural materials and cultivating the experience of being "in" nature, Emerson's design was faithful to a nascent American zoo aesthetic that developed independently from British and Continental models.

The preference for a naturalistic built environment was partly a manifestation of American zoos' associations with public parks. Most zoos in the United States began their institutional lives as zoological parks, not gardens. Most were divisions of public parks departments, drawing the bulk of their funds from these municipal sources.[33] Appropriately, planners built their zoos within the boundaries of the parks, on smaller budgets than European zoos but on much larger parcels of land at the edges of the city. Public parks sited on hundreds of acres became home to zoos that took advantage of the scale.[34] In 1890, for example, the Smithsonian Institution in Washington, D.C., reserved 166 acres of Rock Creek Park for the future National Zoological Park. The semirural South Bronx Park housed the 261-acre New York Zoological Park in 1896.[35] Planners in Boston, Columbus, and Chicago also placed their zoos in parks, each on city borderlands accessible by public transportation and, later, the automobile.[36] The public parks system gave zoos their institutional and physical location, but also their ideological coordinates. On par with tenement housing reform or calls for temperance, city parks were a social movement. Planners created expansive pleasure grounds on vast tracts of land, featuring meadows, foliage, and waterways, and promising to temporarily shield urbanites from the grime, velocity, and noise of the urban environment. This highly instrumental perspective framed parks as a check on the encroachment of the city rather than a feature of the city itself.[37] It entrusted their sylvan settings with the job of making city dwellers more civilized. Reformers like the landscape architect Charles Eliot looked to the "more natural and agreeable" space of the park to thwart the city's "confusion and excitement" and produce more "desirable types of humanity."[38] In the 1890s the movement turned its attention to building networks of parks, creating smaller patches of green to alleviate particularly congested districts in the central city. By the twentieth century, few American cities were without a parks commission, and most had a large municipal park supplemented by smaller ones to their credit.[39]

The success of the public parks movement can be traced to the influence of one of its leading figures and the founder of the profession of landscape architecture, Frederick Law Olmsted. In the 1850s, after already establishing his reputation as a vocal parks advocate, Olmsted and his design partner Calvert Vaux won the competition to design plans for a large park in New York City that they originally called "Greensward" but became known as "Central Park." The proposed grounds were envisioned as a naturalistic self-contained environment and inspired the creation of other urban parks around the country thereafter, many of which profited from Olmsted and Vaux's input.[40] Their creations took aesthetic cues from eighteenth-century English garden theory that stressed an uncultivated presentation of nature. A beautiful garden, according to this theory, was differentiated from the garden's surrounding landscape. It mirrored the natural world, but heightened its image into something still more natural and expressive of reason.[41] The American designers translated this principle to the new urban setting of the public park. They crafted unified landscapes of rambling pathways that followed the contours of the existing site and contrasted with gridded streets and rectangular row houses. They separated vehicular traffic from pedestrian traffic with curved roads and walks. They emphasized a succession of lookout points that offered verdant, complex tableaus in the "picturesque" style.[42] They placed trees and shrubs in informal formations that would "plant out" the city and others that would lead the eye from a darkened foreground to an undefined distant view.[43] They reserved broad areas of grass, broken occasionally by groves of trees on the edges of the open space.[44] These techniques re-created the informal, bucolic beauty of the English garden, recapturing, in the words of an early Central Park guidebook, the "delicate flavor of wildness, so hard to seize and imprison when civilization has once put it to flight."[45]

The landscapes of the first American zoos bore the stamp of Olmsted's delicate flavor of wildness. But the symbiosis between his naturalism and the medium of zoos was not immediate. Adding zoos to public parks introduced an element of risk by threatening to reduce the pastoral setting of these modified English gardens to the level of the popular animal show.[46] Olmsted's designs proposed animal watching as an elaboration of respectable encounters with rustic nature, partly to mitigate these concerns. For example, the centerpiece of a largely unrealized plan for the future National Zoo in Washington's Rock Creek Park was, in the architect's words, a "pleasure drive" that ran east–west through the grounds, with animal houses clustered together in the center of the property.[47] This design created "a parklike place" that was "distinguished less by the obvious qualities of the objects to be seen in it than by the manner in which they so combine, merge and blend in groups and masses as to become contributive to effects of scenery."[48] Animals here would not be the focus of any show, but an integrated and enriching part of a total pastoral scene. Moreover, exhibits would cater to both the animals' living requirements and visitors' imagined desires for restful views. Areas of animal display were viewable by foot, not from carriages, giving both animals and humans some peace and quiet. For areas beyond the displays and closer to the creek, Olmsted envisioned open sloping grass and scattered trees. Along the creek itself and beyond the zoo grounds proper, he proposed dense plantings of aquatic flora, to achieve another variant of the picturesque.[49] These were some of the ways that the zoo form adapted to the public park form, molding to its geography and subjecting humans and animals alike to the gentle discipline of urban green space.

Palates for the delicate flavor of wildness were not universal. The parks movement's naturalism was confidently white and white collar in orientation, aspects vital to a given park's pleasure and privilege. Rolling vistas, gentle creeks, and rounded walkways fed into a wider program of reform that sought to uplift the city's population of racial and ethnic minorities, industrial workers, and the poor. They catered to and exported the Arcadian longings of the metropolis's professional class with the beauty of what Elizabeth Hanson calls a middle landscape "situated outside the overstimulating city but short of primitive wilderness."[50] To this end, the public park was a variant of the national park, the summer camp, the country club, the wilderness novel, the suburban estate, and other sites of pastoral nature loving, consumed by affluent city dwellers and recent exiles, and promoted to those whose tastes and morals were considered vulgar by comparison. Like Olmsted's creations, these slices of nature also worked as built environments that exalted the recuperative powers of the outdoors and had little to do with rural places as they were routinely lived. As Peter Schmitt argues in his landmark environmental history of going "back to nature," the appeal of the so-called return was "living in the country without being of it," since to be of it compromised the cosmopolitanism that nature enthusiasts held dear.[51] Conjuring up and materially constructing a more delicate nature preserved urban sophisticates' social place, invited the less fortunate to rise above their ranks, while transporting everyone to "greener pastures."

The racial specificity of this broader nineteenth-century nature ideal worked in interrelated ways. Nature came to be known as pristine, placid, and uninhabited space, especially under its pseudonym of "wilderness." The years after the American Civil War witnessed a transformation of the idea of wilderness from the terrifying wasteland it had been for hundreds of years to a sacred and fertile zone appropriate for its new city-wary public. Wilderness, according to this new criterion, ought to be safe enough for recreational enjoyment and splendid enough to make the excursion worthwhile.[52] For national parks, this meant the removal or strict management of any unsettling elements of the wilderness experience, including people. Native Americans in particular risked disrupting the pleasant view with their resistant presence and upstaging the innocent wild animals that were a more welcome sight.[53] The attitude was echoed in proto-environmentalist John Muir's recurrent descriptions of the indigenous people he encountered on his Western travels as impure in contrast to the nature before him: "A strangely dirty and irregular life these dark-eyed dark-haired, half-happy savages lead in this clean wilderness."[54] The erasure of Native Americans from the national parks' landscape, both literally and symbolically, ensured nature's identity as unspoiled and free for communion. In a similar vein, urban park planners defined the whiteness of their "mini" wilderness against the unsettling element of African Americans and immigrants, who, as Riis and other reformers made clear, suggested wilderness of a more menacing ilk. Carolyn Merchant elaborates:

> In the minds of many Americans, the valence of wilderness had been reversed. The city had become a dark and negatively charged wilderness filled with blacks and southern European immigrants, while mountains, forests, waterfalls, and canyons were viewed as sublime places of white light.... Sublime nature was white and benign, available to white tourists; cities were portrayed as black and malign, the home of the unclean and the undesirable.[55]

Public parks in the city aimed to offer slices of the whiter wilderness, which conflated the aesthetic whiteness of a sanitized nature—pure and nonthreatening, bathed in light—with the social whiteness of Anglo and Nordic stock.

The promise of a good white nature within a bad nonwhite city faced challenges amid urbanites whose perceptions and practices of the middle landscape veered off script. African Americans' associations with pastoral nature, for example, were shaped by their collective experiences with slavery and the postemancipation oppression that took place on Southern lands. As a site of the destruction of black bodies and spirits through slave labor as well as the rapid degradation of soil in a cash crop system, this nature was far from sacred and fertile.[56] Vicious too was the practice of lynching, which claimed the lives of thousands and encouraged more to leave for the relative safety of industrial cities. For the literary critic Sandy Alexandre, lynching also stands as an acute case of "pastoral denial" manifest often as "a disturbingly limp black body conspicuously hung up on and against a backdrop of Arcadia's ostensibly innocent trees."[57]

Ethnic minorities and poor whites from rural communities also risked alienation from the nature ideal and its promise of white bourgeois citizenship. Like some Southern blacks, their use of the countryside for professional and subsistence hunting differed from the "gentlemen sportsman" who shot game for pleasure and with a sense of stewardship over it.[58] Members of New York's Boone and Crockett Club, for example, an elite organization of big-game hunters that helped establish the New York Zoological Park, singled out immigrant groups for their failure to abide by an ethic of fair play.[59] Hornaday, a member of the club, was especially incensed. In 1913 he published his popular pamphlet *Our Vanishing Wild Life: Its Extermination and Preservation* in book form through the New York Zoological Society. The book directed readers' attention toward Italian Americans who hunted songbirds for food, describing the practice with a twinned racism and moral outrage that circulated in much of the period's love of nature:

> The Italian is a born pot-hunter, and he has grown up in the fixed belief that killing song-birds for food is right! To him all is game that goes into the bag. The moment he sets foot in the open, he provides himself with a shot-gun, and he looks about for things to kill. It is "a free country"; therefore, he may kill anything he can find, cook it and eat it. If anybody attempts to check him,—sapristi! Beware his gun! He cheerfully invades your fields, and even your lawn; and he shoots robins, bluebirds, thrushes, catbirds, grosbeaks, tanagers, orioles, woodpeckers, quail, snipe, ducks, crows, and herons.[60]

For Hornaday, Italians were a threat to the tranquillity of open spaces and, specifically, the wildlife that enhanced those spaces through song. The "pot hunters"— from which the pejorative term *pot shot* derived—were figured as trigger-happy and indiscriminate in their kills. They perverted the liberal democratic principle of a nature accessible to all while inadvertently calling attention to the exclusivity of that very nature. Hornaday maintained an urgent sense that a zoo's grounds, like any other refuge, ought to be heavily guarded against these immigrant transgressions, which established the racial inferiority and beastliness of Italians.[61] Significantly, his account included a description of New York City's "war on the bird-killers," which was spearheaded by the New York Zoological Society. On the eve of the twentieth century, the northern half of the Borough of the Bronx, home to the New York Zoological Park, was becoming "a regular hunting-ground for the slaughter of song-birds." A volunteer and two members of the zoo's young police force spent every Sunday patrolling the wooded area, shooting at the poachers and making arrests—in effect, hunting the hunters.[62] Hornaday played with the insinuation that the culprits were something other than fully human: "It became known that those three men could not be stopped by threats, and that they always got their man—unless he got into a human rabbit-warren of the Italian boarding-house species."[63]

Hornaday's experience exhibiting one of the most revered animals in the industrializing United States offers another glimpse into the snags of a scripted urban nature. While African Americans underlined the possibility of pastoral denial, and Italian immigrants signified something akin to a vermin problem, the acquisition and display of American bison in the nation's first zoos demonstrated the precarity of using animals as a medium for becoming more human in the industrial city.[64] Of course, keeping the beloved native species in urban captivity was hardly discussed in these terms. The official rationale for bison display was wildlife conservation education and research. What was remarkable about the practice, however, was how concern for the state of wildlife overlapped with racial anxieties over the quality of urban life that it likewise, if more obliquely, expressed.

In 1886 a young Hornaday returned to Washington, D.C., from his two expeditions to the western plains and Rocky Mountains with a mere twenty-five bison of the last few hundred. The experience redirected his previous energies as chief taxidermist at the Smithsonian's National Museum toward the establishment of a federal zoo large enough to exhibit and breed the species and important enough to place conservation on the national agenda.[65] Hornaday and other National Zoo founders hoped such endangered animal exhibits would serve as a living lobby near government that could assert the value of wildlife to legislators.[66] In the years prior to the zoo's relocation to Rock Creek valley, the lobby was exceptionally close. Hornaday placed live bison on the national mall until 1891, in the south yard of the Smithsonian Institution Building and a short walk from the Capitol building. As one newspaper captioned in its illustration of the temporary exhibit, these were "almost the last of their race," alluding to the combined plight of the bison and those of its stewards who were worried over their own prospects in an era of civilization's decline (Figure 1.2).

Hornaday kept such connections near the surface of his own writing, despite the apparent contradiction of having participated in numerous buffalo hunts and feasts. In *The Extermination of the American Bison* (1889), a book that the historian James Andrew Dolph calls Hornaday's "bison memoir," the zoo man described a species threatened by "the descent of civilization," whose specific culprits ranged from inept government agencies to increasingly sophisticated firearms to men who had regressed into states of savagery and found "exquisite delight in bloodshed, slaughter, and death, if not for gain, then solely for the joy and happiness of it."[67] The critique grew more pointed, however, in Hornaday's account of a discrete period of "systematic slaughter" that reached its apex in the 1860s with the construction of the railroads and expansion of eastern markets. Like the Italian American in the Bronx woods, the American Indian had become the western case study in bad sportsmanship and lack of restraint, only in this case, with a death toll much higher than that of New York City's birds.[68] Mixed into Hornaday's diatribes against Native people is a record of affinity for "the great American bison."[69] For example, writing on his own hunting of "an enormous old bull" during his second expedition, Hornaday recalled a pivotal moment before the final blow. Having already shot the animal once in the shoulder, the easterner noted how the animal "then stood at bay, and halting within 30 yards of him I enjoyed the rare opportunity of studying a live bull buffalo of the largest size on foot on his native heath. I even made an outline sketch of him in my note-book."[70] Other stories positioned Hornaday closer still to the species, such as the account of a calf captured in Montana and taken into his improvised care. After struggling to feed the calf on the expedition, and transporting it by train back to Washington, D.C., Hornaday was deeply affected by the animal's death weeks later from clover poisoning, not the least because of his plans to house the calf at a future federal zoo designed explicitly to preserve and propagate threatened species.[71] Hornaday's attachment to bison carried over to his directorship of the New York Zoological Park in 1896. With twenty acres of Bronx grassland at his disposal, the former taxidermist displayed his animals in a setting that attempted to translate his signature dioramic style of a wilderness moment frozen in time.[72] Hornaday's exhibit was designed as a romantic image of frontier freedom that would ideally transport the viewer to the imagined integrity and wholesomeness of the Great Plains and its appropriate flora and fauna. Recalling his experience looking at the site before its construction, he wrote: "As I walked over the ground, again and again, and tried to imagine what would happen there if Noah should arrive with his arkful of animals and turn them loose, I saw the bison and the antelope seeking the

ALMOST THE LAST OF THEIR RACE.

Figure 1.2. *Bison pictured in South Yard of Smithsonian Institution Building, circa 1887. Smithsonian Institution Archives, Image 77–11420.*

rolling 20-acre meadow in the southeastern corner."[73] The expansive enclosure that materialized thereafter appeared to suit the bison well. Individual animals began to mimic behaviors in the wild, like wallowing in the dust, which added to the scene's authenticity as an endangered American way of life that was worth preserving.[74] This must have been a relief for Hornaday, given his worries about the effect that zoo life could have on the species: "In captivity he fails to develop as finely as in his wild state, and with the loss of his liberty he becomes a tame-looking animal. He gets fat and short-bodied, and the lack of vigorous and constant exercise prevents the development of bone and muscle which made the prairie animal what he was."[75] Like many zoo displays, however, the authenticity of Hornaday's scene and robustness of his animals was contingent on their cooperation as performers. The first group of bison died after developing intestinal disease from eating local vegetation. The ones that survived struck the keeper as embarrassingly shaggy when they shed their coats. Hornaday worried that the bison would seem more pathetic than noble, and took some solace in the production of paintings and drawings of the species, which the New York Zoological Society encouraged and Hornaday could more easily control.[76]

Thus, for all the investment in the democratic potential of an open nature, issues of control were central to the nation's early zoo makers and their ideal animal exhibits. The institutional lens of the first public American zoos in the United States was firmly fixed on animal display as a means of genteel self-fashioning and racial uplift: both highly regulative modes of urbanism and both subject to the power of zoo makers to direct *anything* about the zoo experience. Any civic pride that a zoo could inspire in its shamed public relied on human life adhering to the tenants of gentrified nature appreciation and animal life appearing natural in natural surroundings. As the figure of the naked cage came into visibility a hundred years later, critics revisited these measurements of self-respect and the degree to which American zoos had fallen indefensibly short of them.

DESMOND MORRIS'S DESIGN CRITICISM

Before the naked cage emerged as evidence of both shameful zoo and urban life, American zoos witnessed several decades of Olmstedian zoo naturalism followed by a sustained period of modernist design. From the 1930s forward, the dominant aesthetic for public animal displays shifted from unstructured rusticity and placid wilderness to clean lines and clarity of structure. Architects reveled in a different kind of nature by exploring the physical properties of concrete, glass, and steel, and the attendant advantages for basic animal care in an era predating widespread antibiotics. With an emphasis on abundant air and light, minimalist buildings emerged as the ideal spatial conditions for beauty and biological health. These axioms of zoo modernism found expression in the 1934 Penguin Pool at London Zoo whose impact was felt across the Atlantic (Figure 1.3). Designed by Berthold Lubetkin's U.K. firm Tecton, the exhibit was a model of streamlined, sanitary space, establishing Britain's credentials in high modernist architecture and becoming the gold standard for three more decades of zoo design.[77] The structure featured two sloping ramps in white concrete that interlaced in a double-helix formation over an elongated ellipse of water. Nesting boxes were tucked neatly into the pool's exterior walls, and observers stationed themselves along its perimeter. The exhibit was easy to clean, easy to see, and facilitated the swimming and waddling associated with the species. A shallow pool, lined with azure blue tile, allowed the animals to display their agility as seabirds while the cantilevered walkways exposed and accentuated their humor-

Copyright   Photo by F. W. Bond, F.R.P.S.
PENGUINS' POOL

Figure 1.3. *Postcard of the Penguin Pool at London Zoo designed by Berthold Lubetkin, Lindsay Drake, Tecton, 1933–34.*

ous gait, effecting what Pyrs Gruffud has described as the production of "penguine-ness."[78] The exhibit also worked as an elegant showcase for structural transparency and its technological achievement, illustrating modernism's full powers when given the optimum materials and plan. As the Bauhaus's László Moholy-Nagy framed it in his 1936 film *The New Architecture and the London Zoo*:

> The use of reinforced concrete has allowed Tecton, the London Architects, great freedom in designing forms specially suited to the housing of animals, and shelter-ing and regulating the circulation of the public. The animals for the first time are no longer housed in artificial reproductions of their natural surroundings. The new buildings provide a hygienic organic setting, the simplicity of which best displays the natural characteristics of the animals.[79]

For all its nakedness, indeed because of it, modernists understood these concrete ribbons and tiled waters as an intelligent zoo display sensitive to both animal and human spatial requirements.[80] Moreover, the Penguin Pool was initially touted as not only a stage for avian life but also, in Hadas Steiner's view, a "stage for structure," advertising a dynamic, shell-like spectacle of circulation itself, even if compromised by the circulators' visibly awkward walks along the ramps.[81]

By the late 1960s U.S. zoos had become tangible proof of the popularity of elemental, biomorphic forms.[82] But while many American zoo designers had found inspiration in the clean, organic setting offered through zoo high modernism, Desmond Morris's vision of a naked cage reframed modernism's core concepts as inappropriate architecture for animals. Minimalist designs were the antithesis of what was natural and the bane of an animal's life in captivity. Wrote Morris: "A rare and exotic beast, costing $10,000, that is sitting dully in its gleaming, hygienic, beautifully proportioned, architect-designed, and yet denuded cage, attracts less attention than a common little creature—costing $10—that just happens to be busily solving some 'trivial' behavior problem." Showcase modernism did not help actualize an animal's animality; it impeded it by eliminating the chance for stimulating activity. The same could be seen in more humble municipal zoos that "cram[med] the animals" into a smaller area to "give the public its money's worth" and received Morris's denunciation as "scruffy little animal slums." Making modernism look dated, dirty, and cruel, the zoologist predicted a turn away from a once-esteemed aesthetic, particularly in light of other contemporary modes of animal display: "Through television, books and films we are becoming more and more conscious of the shortcomings of the naked cage. We are becoming not so much sentimental as sympathetic. We understand the animals' true problems better and find the old zoo cages more worrying than stimulating, more depressing than exciting."[83]

Morris's account of life in the naked cage came on the heels of his best seller *The Naked Ape,* a book that had familiarized American readers with Morris's quirky brand of sociobiology. Sociobiology named a new wave of scientific inquiry in the 1960s and 1970s that used biological knowledge, and evolutionary theory in particular, to explain the social life of invertebrates and vertebrates, including humans. Its watershed work was Edward O. Wilson's *Sociobiology: The New Synthesis* (1975), in which the author offered genetic explanations for human social behavior including war, rape, and genocide. The claims precipitated a prominent, multivocal critique from scientific, social scientific, and activist communities. But judging from his copious and positive press reviews, Morris's claims were less hostile to progressive American sensibilities, focusing on "those aspects of our lives that have obvious counterparts in other species," at the comparatively mild risk of offending "some who will prefer not to contemplate their animal selves."[84]

"The Shame of the Naked Cage" relocated Morris's musings on human–animal similitude to contemporary zoos, beginning with a cover image of a concrete-framed orangutan hunched over with hands clasped and eyes closed (see Plate 1). Captioned as a zoo animal that was "inert and morose," the primate's pose was also discernible as a sign of human disgrace, echoing the midcentury psychologist Sylvan Tomkins's thinking on the signification of shame. Describing shame as "the affect of indignity, of defeat, of transgression, and of alienation," Tomkins observed how the shamed subject is prone to hanging his head. This posture effects a concealment of the face that coincides with a figurative loss of face. Paradoxically, the shamed face also draws attention to itself, and the self that resides within it, at the precise moment when the face attempts to be hidden from view. The ensuing "torment of self-consciousness" makes feeling ashamed akin to a feeling of exposure, or nakedness.[85] Taken in this intensely humanistic sense, whereby shame violates-yet-emphasizes an intrinsic human subjectivity, the cover image set the necessary affective tone for Morris's critique of contemporary U.S. zoos by representing the appropriate reader response to the animal's circumstance. Covered but also hypervisible, the orangutan appeared as the reflection of a shamed human spectator.[86] In a subsequent issue of *Life,* the Cincinnati Zoo's public relations director confessed: "We are not feeling at all 'Simon pure.' Particularly in our older buildings, some of which go back to 1875, cage space is far from ideal. Although never by choice, we do have examples, such as 'Sammy' our orang, of animals living a solitary life." Meanwhile, other zoo professionals openly refused to be goaded by the call to feel bad. Larry Hanes of the Indianapolis Zoological Society was one holdout: "Through your desire to present an article steeped in sensationalism, you have neglected to mention the achievements of the world's zoo in the fields of recreation, education, research and conservation."[87]

As a centerpiece of its sensationalism, the first layout of Morris's article put readers directly in front of a naked cage and massaged its connotations (Figure 1.4). Taken by the *Time Life* photographer Arthur Schatz, likely at the Boston Zoo, a black-and-white image spanning two pages depicted the interior of an enclosure with a small steel door, an iron-barred window, a corner unit (possibly for food), and a raised wooden platform supported by metal brackets.[88] Overwhelming the image in their sparseness were the concrete floor and white walls. Dingy and crude, they converged midway up the page at a horizontal line of no escape, confirmed by the occasional scratch mark along it that might have once tested the possibility. Three baboons inhabited the display with a quiet disregard for each other and the camera's presence. Morris's essay that followed delivered the textual version of this miserable scene, detailing the bleakness of zoo spaces in the United States and a roster of abnormal activity that they engendered: a chipmunk circling wildly in a tiny, otherwise empty enclosure; a solitary monkey resorting to self-mutilation in its wired quarters; a sexually frustrated male hyena attempting to mate with a food dish; a

Figure 1.4. *"The Shame of the Naked Cage,"* Life *magazine, November 8, 1968. Photograph by Arthur Schatz, Time & Life Pictures, Getty Images.*

mongoose mimicking a kill by shaking a lump of meat. This was the naked cage in all its indignity, underlined by *Life* editors with the gray prison-wall typography spelling things out as such along the bottom of the introductory pages.

Morris's own use of the term surfaced halfway through his piece to distinguish between the possibilities of living in the wild and the limits of "old-style zoos." Whereas wild spaces are highly specific to an animal's range of needs—sleeping places, feeding points, escape routes—the naked cage was "bleakly simplified" and catered to the needs of caretakers.[89] This misdirected functionalism, oriented to the wrong species, privileged efficiency over animal comfort. Shrunken living quarters meant keepers could fit more animals in less room. The standardization of cages meant a reduction in building costs. To reduce the costs of maintenance and health care, surfaces were made as durable as possible and objects within enclosures were kept to a minimum of "perches, tiles and slabs of concrete." Describing the units as "small, uniform, hard and empty," the zoologist's economy of words reinforced the sense of austerity that others recognized in their own institutions and sought to rectify, only now with a more fully articulated image of the trouble.[90]

The argument for spatial overhaul took its affective power from a generalized knowledge of who else endured physical and psychic confinement in the modernist city circa 1968. The naked cage was highly and negatively racialized, fusing the shame over captive wildlife with the shame over those other city dwellers subjected to urban renewal schemes, especially public housing. By the late 1960s, inner-city government housing projects were on their way to becoming one of the most stigmatized places in the United States, evidenced partly by their emphasis on enclosure—as in, to live "in" public housing.[91] The brunt of the stigma was shouldered by low-income African Americans who had been displaced from their former neighborhoods through slum clearance and highway construction and were barred from white residential areas. Often erected in the same spot where clearance had occurred, public housing met the immediate needs of this population but also re-confined poor blacks to urban enclaves that had existed since the 1910s.[92] Like urban zoos, these projects took their inspiration from modernism's ethic of "form follows function" and the perceived integrity of industrial materials. Multistory apartment dwellings in superblock formations became the model, epitomized in Chicago's Robert Taylor Homes (1960–63), where designers Shaw Metz & Associates created twenty-eight virtually identical sixteen-story structures that ran along 3.2 kilometers of cleared land. Optimistically conceived as towers of light, ventilation, and social harmony amid density, the projects echoed elements of Le Corbusier's skyscrapers-in-a-park vision of urban planning.[93] But as architectural historians have shown, planners and designers were also committed to their bottom lines, selecting cheap building materials and eliminating amenities like usable play areas for children and ground-floor bathrooms.[94] Journalists were soon reporting on the physical deterioration of these structures—broken elevators, lighting systems, and windows—along with the social deterioration called "high-rise crime."[95] The nationally televised demolition of Saint Louis's Pruitt-Igoe development in April 1972 was the climax of this coverage; an acute moment of shame over public housing that, for its suburbanizing viewership, highlighted the purported failure of architectural modernism to address the needs of vulnerable urban populations and the lives that were damaged in the attempt (Figure 1.5).[96] In this climate, Morris's critique of naked cages was able to strike particular chords with its readers, wherein the inhumane functionalism of existing animal enclosures bore the marks of shunned black spaces in the central city.

White middle-class anxiety over the zoo problem grew more overt in Morris's

Figure 1.5. *Part of the Pruitt-Igoe development demolished on national television, April 21, 1972.*

book-length follow-up to his article in *Life*. Titled *The Human Zoo*, the 1969 study approached the urban crisis from a zoologist's perspective, situating the design dilemma of the naked cage firmly within a landscape of midcentury urban planning and its social fallout. Bad zoo design and its victims were considered reflective of and continuous with some of the human degeneracy that Morris and other reformers saw in the modernist planned city.[97] Morris began by refuting the description of urban space as a "concrete jungle." This popular metaphor within urban crisis discourse coded blackness as depraved wildness and underlined the sense in which sections of the American city were unfit for human habitation, without ever making reference to the racial identities of those who actually inhabited them.[98] By a contrast more superficial than substantial, Morris based his analysis on the premise that wild spaces and creatures were good and modern civilization was the problem:

Under normal conditions, in their natural habitats, wild animals do not mutilate themselves, masturbate, attack their offspring, develop stomach ulcers, become fetishists, suffer from obesity, form homosexual pair bonds, or commit murder. Among human city-dwellers, needless to say, all of these things occur.... The comparison we must make is not between the city-dweller and the wild animal, but between the city-dweller and the captive animal.[99]

With eight vivid sketches of deviance practiced by both zoo animal and urban human, the zoologist set the rhetorical tone for an analysis of multispecies pathology in the contemporary city. Much like the figure of a concrete jungle, the trope of the human zoo placed race within the discussion without ever having to name it as such. American readers were invited to engage the core connection between human urbanites and zoo animals as a way to work through a national conversation on the crisis in the cities and the escalating despair of a black urban "underclass."[100]

Discussion points were typically inflammatory. They combined a postwar scientific literature on animal behavior with the preoccupations of other midcentury urbanists: the antiseptic isolation of high-density, high-rise designs, a lack of accessible green space, and, as Jane Jacobs put it, "general social hopelessness."[101] Morris argued that the conditions of human life in the city matched those of "the animal zoo inmate [that] finds itself in solitary confinement or in an abnormally distorted social group. Alongside, in other cages, it may be able to see or hear other animals but it cannot make any real contact with them." The curtailment of physical space compounded this sense of detachment, violating most species' evolutionary needs for a set minimum. Still, city dwellers made attempts to "fight against the unnatural spatial cramping" with urban parks and weekend car trips. These coping techniques were reminders that "we should be thankful that we can do more than pace back and forth across our living-room floors." For those who could not, Morris offered yardsticks from contemporary zoo space by which to measure the depth of human misery, a disproportionate number of which involved primate sex. On hypersexuality: "One male orang-utan living in an empty cage, when provided with a female, mated with her and embraced her so persistently that she temporarily lost the use of her arms and had to be removed." On prostitution: "Female monkeys in captivity have been seen to offer themselves sexually to a male as a means of obtaining food morsels scattered on the ground, the sexual actions distracting the male from the business of competing for food." On developmental abnormalities: "Monkeys reared in total isolation ... find it almost impossible to adapt in later life to any kind of social contact. Placed with sexually active members of their own species, they do not know how to respond. Most of the time they are terrified of making any social contact and sit nervously in a corner."[102] By marshaling these and other scientific observations of captive animals living under zoo modernism, *The Human Zoo* built critical reference points for bad urban design more broadly. These inventive analogies gave credence to concerns that urbanism had become something other than human while paradoxically assigning blame to humanity's most recent achievement, the modernist city.

The book's concluding pages brought zoo criticism closer to the racial dynamics of urban planning. For Morris, planners of the human zoo were repeating the same mistakes as animal zoo planners, capitalizing on advances in medicine, hygiene, housing, and food production to create "efficient homogeneity." But whereas some zoo directors had begun to recognize the limitations of these modernization strategies—foregoing, for example, the use of sanitary tiles in enclosures—urban designers at large continued the architectural trend "towards austere design-simplicity." Morris pointed to the proliferation of "huge tower blocks of repetitive apartments" to meet the needs of the "swelling super-tribal population" and the creation of modernist "superslums" where slums alone once stood.[103] The critique of high-rise housing was well positioned to ramp up white liberal discomfort over urban space, particularly when paired with Morris's sociobiological terminology. While the concept of the super-tribal recalled the book's early discussion of an ancient (Sumerian) phase of urban development whereby social life became irrevocably impersonal, its deployment to explain current cities shifted its meanings considerably. After 159 urban riots during the summer heat waves of 1967, and another period of street-level rebellion sparked by the assassination of Martin Luther King Jr. in 1968, "swelling super-tribal populations" could be taken as a reference to those African American poor who were most alienated in U.S. cities and whose impact was most recently felt.[104] Ever aware of his target audience, the British zoo man warned that bad urban design at its present scale and intensity sowed the seeds for (more) unrest, anticipating that "tomorrow's super-tribesman" will fight hard to change the conditions of his own captivity. "They will have the training and the time and the exploratory energy to do so, and somehow they will manage it. If they feel themselves trapped in a planner's prison they will stage a prison riot." Not incidentally, super-tribe also tapped into a long-standing white European interest in the primitive with which the zoologist was uniquely acquainted and that kept the racial register of his analysis in full play.[105] The concept of the human zoo was Morris's naked cage writ large and racialized with dexterity.

The preemptive response to another outbreak of violence was a more instinctual approach to design, one that reclaimed the territorial quality of human activity shared with other animals and was expressive in children. Riot-free cities needed more spatial complexity, contingency, and opportunities for primal play. For Morris, the twisting country lane was the ideal playscape, but "rubbish dumps" and "derelict buildings" worked too. At their best, planners would abandon modernist aesthetics altogether and embrace a particular geography that took the zoo metaphor to a pastoral conclusion.

> The politicians, the administrators and other super-tribal leaders are good social mathematicians, but this is not enough. . . . they must become good biologists as well, because somewhere in all that mass of wires, cables, plastics, concrete, bricks, metal and glass which they control, there is an animal, a human animal, a primitive tribal hunter, masquerading as a civilized, super-tribal citizen and desperately struggling to match his inherited qualities with his extraordinary new situation. If he is given the chance he may yet contrive to turn his human zoo into a magnificent human game-park. If he is not, it may proliferate into a gigantic lunatic asylum, like one of the hideously cramped animal menageries of the last century.[106]

In hyperbolic prose, Morris's parting thoughts on the "super-tribal citizen" deftly conflated the plight of poor blacks in the city with a white professional class dedicated to addressing it. Peeling back an architecture of urban alienation, the zoologist exposed a mixed creature at once different from and similar to a midcentury concerned public, and whose "extraordinary new situation" deepened the shame over the state of U.S. cities while advancing the project of studying biological needs and tendencies to fix the crisis. The solution of a human wildlife preserve delivered the final antiurban thrust of *The Human Zoo,* which by this point had extinguished any of architectural modernism's historical specificity by connecting it to the gothic horrors of Victorian institutions. The game park was presented as a refuge from an urban milieu rendered utterly uninhabitable. That it mirrored the choices of many Americans who were abandoning the cities for suburban peripheries only strengthened the shaming power of Morris's branch of reform. His critique of zoos and the cities in which they were located found emotional traction in these demographic shifts, experienced so differently between middle-class Americans who took to their game parks and poor African Americans who became further ghettoized in the cities that remained.

GARRY WINOGRAND'S ANIMAL PHOTOGRAPHY

Newly recognized within the New York art world, Garry Winogrand and his treatment of bad zoo design circulated through channels different from Morris's popular sociobiology. Along with Lee Friedlander and Diane Arbus, Winogrand's images gained acclaim through a 1967 exhibit called "New Documents" at the Museum of Modern Art, heralding a new generation of photographers who used small snapshot cameras as their tools and the "social landscape" of 1960s America as their subject matter.[107] Winogrand held an interest in modern human–animal relations throughout his career, but it was in a series of photographs, ultimately published as *The Animals,* that he expertly exploited the unspoken truths of urban living in American zoos. Taken mostly between 1962 and 1963, and published as a modest forty-four-image art book in 1969, the series is the product of Winogrand's family visits to the Central Park Zoo, the Bronx Zoo, and the Coney Island Aquarium. What is striking about this imagery is its uneasy relationship to, and production of, white liberal shame.

On the one hand, *The Animals* did convince New Yorkers that their city's zoos were in a bad state. To one *New Yorker* writer in 1975, for example, the book showed the Central Park Zoo "for the dirty prison it was, focusing on the bars, the concrete floors, the dispirited ugly animals, the dumb (for thinking they are enjoying themselves), ugly people, and the grubbiness and meanness, conveying an atmosphere of nakedness and brown-soap harshness." For another, the images were about "exposing an animal world full of depression, frustration, and rage, not unlike the modern world around it." Later appraisals offered more of the same. In 2005, for example, the Museum of Modern Art's curator of photography, John Szarkowski, applauded Winogrand for an "unsentimental eye that doesn't shy away from the bars of the cages." Similarly, *New York Magazine* described his pictures as a "time-capsule document of very antiquated notions of zoo design."[108]

On the other hand, Winogrand's series disrupted its documentary genre—a disruption signaled by the artist's own insistence that his work was less social concern photography than a concern about photography, empty of commentary and executed as "a game to play."[109] Regarding the symbolic power of his pictures, and the ethics of taking them, the photographer was patently noncommittal:

> I make the contest [between content and form] difficult, let's say, with certain subject matter that is inherently dramatic. An injury could be, a dwarf can be, a monkey—if you run into a monkey in some idiot context, automatically you've got a very real problem taking place in the photograph. I mean, how do you beat it?[110]

Winogrand's remarks are telling not only in their implied relegation of zoos to an "idiot context" but also in their refusal to participate in a larger climate of urban crisis along its well-established visual conventions. Despite a nakedness akin to Morris's "Shame of the Naked Cage," there was something self-consciously shameless about Winogrand's approach. His photographs were capable of disabling viewers from feeling too bad at the zoo and from taking much responsibility for its poor condition.

Winogrand's references to his "game" were more of an aspiration than any adequate account of process. As he recalled in a 1981 interview: "The animal pictures came about in a funny way. I made a few shots. If you could see those contact sheets, they're mostly of the kids and maybe a few shots where I'm just playing. And at some point I realized something was going on in some of those pictures, so then I worked at it."[111] The shift from leisure to labor was made possible through a technology effective for both spontaneous play and the new work of photographic modernism. Winogrand's 35 mm camera with a wide-angle lens was especially nimble and extroverted, resulting in what critics have described as "sharp-focussed, fast-shutter, action-freezing picture[s]" that are "packed with astounding quantities of incident and 'information.'"[112] *The Animals* gave social landscape photography some of its most expansive examples of midcentury urban life. New York City is multi- and interspecies space: a dynamic, imperfect, and heterogeneous public sphere open to the unexpected and constituted by it.

To Cold War viewers, scenes looked spontaneous and mildly chaotic, and could be consumed in semirapid succession, similar to a walk through a midcentury zoo: the smiling woman awkwardly thrusting her baby in front of an iron-barred mother and baby orangutan, the small monkey apparently miffed by the human hand tapping at its glass window, the brown bear and young man locked in an absurd showdown between an outstretched tongue and a (toy?) gun (Figures 1.6–1.8). Several other photographs emphasized this sense of mutual defiance, like the gorilla who gazes directly back at his spectators, and the viewer, with elbows resting firmly on knees, or the lama engaged in a staring contest with a woman in fur—neither flinching. Other images reveled in ineptitude. In one photograph, a large cassowary, a bird known for being habitually aggressive, stands frozen in place behind a slack wire-mesh fence while a visitor fusses with his camera, fumbling in the scripted activity of taking pictures. Critics of modernist design could find some traction in these pictures: for example, the outdoor tank with a partially submerged sea lion against the backdrop of high-rise apartment buildings under construction, or another sea lion whose fleshy whiskered face addresses the viewer from a tiled and concrete pool, while a curved row of spectators peers over, matching a curved row of iron bars.[113] But other photographs took exhibits from the early twentieth century as the stage for degeneracy, like the outdoor elephant display with a pachyderm's trunk reaching over a rustic stonework perimeter, as if sniffing for the litter lining the site (Figures 1.9–1.10).

Figure 1.6. *Garry Winogrand,* New York, ca. 1965. *Copyright The Estate of Garry Winogrand. Courtesy Fraenkel Gallery, San Francisco.*

Figure 1.7. *Garry Winogrand,* New York City, 1964. *Copyright The Estate of Garry Winogrand. Courtesy Fraenkel Gallery, San Francisco.*

Figure 1.8. *Garry Winogrand,* New York, 1961. *Copyright The Estate of Garry Winogrand. Courtesy Fraenkel Gallery, San Francisco.*

Winogrand's attraction to tilted lines heightened the impulsiveness of these violated barriers. Human and animal, however similar, were rarely rendered so through the steadiness of a horizontal composition: no equivalence through spatial equilibrium here. Instead, the photographer accented slight but potent angles, consulted vertical edges, explored the possibilities of teetering. Straight fences, bars, windows, and railings cut diagonally across the picture plane or receded into photographic space at an incline. Curved barriers in stone and concrete snaked through in gentle undulation. These elements made for unstable viewing, exemplifying what the critic A. D. Coleman notes of the 1960s' new documentary style generally: "Increasingly asymmetrical, unbalanced, fragmented, even messy, especially in contrast to the photography that had preceded it, this work demanded of both photographer and viewer an openness to radically unconventional formal structures."[114] Similar to Friedlander and Arbus, Winogrand used a heightened formalism and troubled boundaries in the same gesture that revealed their ubiquity. Literal and figurative lines between observer and observed became at once acutely visible and elastic,

Figure 1.9. *Garry Winogrand,* Aquarium at Coney Island, 1962. *Copyright The Estate of Garry Winogrand. Courtesy Fraenkel Gallery, San Francisco.*

Figure 1.10. *Garry Winogrand,* New York, 1963. *Copyright The Estate of Garry Winogrand. Courtesy Fraenkel Gallery, San Francisco.*

such that any photographic subject at the zoo could seemingly be matched, jux-taposed, or intertwined with any other: interspecies bedlam. What emerged was a pronounced disorder of relations between human and nonhuman, rehearsing the sense of perversity that had characterized American urbanism since Progressive Era muckraking. In *The Animals,* this perversity manifests as a recurrent breach of Enlightenment-style subjectivity, a failure to appear entirely human mixed with the morbid delights of viewing animals without much dignity themselves. Winogrand's figures appeared in states of nakedness born from their surroundings, a nakedness that the critic Ben Lifson notes of the artist's urban subjects in general: "Did he photograph animals? . . . The wild look in the eye of a young woman being kissed and the snarling face of a man on a street corner tell us he did."[115] Perversity in *The Animals* was intensified by the medium of photography—or, what Allan Sekula describes as its "obstinate bit of bourgeois folklore." The photograph, even when expressionistic, enjoys the status of naked truth, of a realistic world picture autono-mous from human intervention.[116]

While *The Animals* reproduced a kind of naked city, it did so without the conventionalized sense of shame. For every photograph that risked conveying something very bad through its disquieting content and jarring forms, two or three more kept the jokes flowing and the snapshot style light. Winogrand's critics have put stress on this sense of levity. Szarkowski, his staunchest advocate, argued early on that Winogrand's naked cages were masterful in their progressive social commentary for their ability to render the urban condition "funny looking." When the curator assessed the animals therein, he betrayed the modernist project of making timeless, universal art and alluded to their similarities to poor blacks: "They are underemployed and overly-sociable; they are deprived of the chance of both success and failure, and receive their food, their shelter, and their mates as welfare handouts." Other critics have identified Winogrand's humor as a strategic device to avoid any meaningful critique and to secure his artistic credentials. Martha Rosler, for instance, argues that the photographer (and his peers) engaged in a "connoisseurship of the tawdry" that kept him and the viewer aloof from what was caught on film and free to engage the nuances of formalism. From this angle, Winogrand's photos appear off-center, ironic, and indifferent, a space of permission to gawk and chuckle, the urban crisis minus shame and/or incitement to action. Winogrand's imagery, in this reading, becomes a soft critique of zoo modernism, where the dutiful response of white liberal shame over depicted conditions was filtered through the pleasures of odd angles, disjunctive shadows, unexpected cropping, and so forth. Still others suggest Winogrand's privileging of form over social content was never quite true. Andy Grundberg, for example, stresses the disavowals of Winogrand's humorous games. "If we laugh," writes Grundberg, "it's as if to dispel something left unexplained and unresolved."[117] Grundberg's intimation is that there is indeed something to dispel here, that the photographer's disinterested eye cannot quite maintain the distance required to be convincingly modern.

The extent to which this "something" in Winogrand's zoo pictures was a form of white middle-class anxiety is a complex question, posed most vividly perhaps in a print from 1967 that was exhibited independently in the Museum of Modern Art's 1969 traveling show "New Photography USA" (Figure 1.11).[118] Distinct from the other images of animals and humans behaving badly across barriers, the photograph featured a "family" of four, smartly dressed and conducting their public selves among dark shadows, bare trees, and a crowd of other zoo goers. The visual punch line, soaked with fears over racial miscegenation, lay in the makeup of the foursome: a black father, a white mother, and two chimpanzee children. It is unclear whether Winogrand was the accomplice to a joke already under way in this scene (he rarely discussed the contexts of his work and left no record of the circumstances surrounding

Figure 1.11. *Garry Winogrand,* Central Park Zoo, New York City, 1967. *Copyright The Estate of Garry Winogrand. Courtesy Fraenkel Gallery, San Francisco.*

this picture). Winogrand would have likely preferred us to believe that this was a moment in the making, captured by his lens in midplay of the game. But others, such as Victor Burgin, argue that it is his camera lens that is *making the joke here*—and one that is, as Burgin puts it, "not only closed but hostile" to the social change that might otherwise have emerged in an image of racial mixing at this point in U.S. history. Burgin notes how a white observer's identity and social position is never adequately challenged in the picture—nor, it can be said, is an observer's position as human, who is invited to take in and spit out this family farce, keeping their own human subjectivity intact.[119] Carrie Mae Weems's (1995–96) appropriation of the image underscores the point with another variation of closure and hostility (Plate 2). By using the text "Some Laughed Long and Hard and Loud" and a red-tinted spherical crop, the piece literally targets Winogrand's playful ways of seeing race and species, calling him out on his game.

But if Winogrand's game in this family portrait was to rehearse a racial joke, it was also, in the same whimsy and in conjunction with his other photographs, to place the discourse of bad zoo design, even at its most aestheticized, into the urban politics to which it firmly if not exclusively belonged. With its averted gazes and high tonal contrasts, the image fantasized the uncomfortable stakes of letting zoos continue on their path of decay—namely, the corruption of a once-esteemed metropolitan space of Anglo-American decorum. The sentiment was reiterated in one travel writer's account of the Central Park Zoo in 1971: "It is an animal slum where the remarkable products of millions of years of evolution are condemned to an irrelevant, bankrupt, freak-show existence in buildings that are eyesores and nose sores." In Winogrand's pictures, the freak show had spilled out into the zoo's pathway, projecting the eye and nose sores of chimpanzees as children and the extinction not of wildlife but of a whiteness in the American public sphere discernible in Julia Allen Field's assessment that same year: "The whole concept of the zoo is a projection of amusement values instead of the life base of beauty, dignity and wonder which we find in nature, yet rarely deliver in visual terms to people."[120] Winogrand was at least partly to blame. His games toyed with the vocabulary of a city's decline, games that appeared alongside more sober threads of the urban crisis, and games that remind us who was inclined and at liberty to play.

PETER BATTEN'S ANIMAL ADVOCACY

When Peter Batten published his book *Living Trophies* in 1974, images of bad zoo design were already well and variously drawn. In addition to Morris's architectural sociobiology and Winogrand's playful obliqueness, critiques from animal rights and welfare advocates had been steady since the beginning of the 1970s. Organizations such as the Society for the Prevention of Cruelty of Animals, People for the Ethical Treatment of Animals, and the Ark Trust became active in their denunciation of zoos, bolstered by U.S. legislation that also put zoo practices under scrutiny. While the Marine Mammal Protection Act (1972) and the Endangered Species Act (1973) put pressure on acquisition protocols, amendments to the Animal Welfare Act (1968) emphasized the degree to which public animal display had become a point of national shame.[121] Enacted on December 24, 1970, and enforced by the United States Department of Agriculture, the revised law added the category of exhibitors to the existing roster of regulated animal facilities. Zoos, for profit or not, were newly required to follow "minimum requirements with respect to handling, housing, feeding, watering, sanitation, ventilation, shelter from extremes of weather and temperatures [and] adequate veterinary care."[122] The adaptable figure of the naked cage brought these minimum requirements—or more accurately, their violation—into troubling view. Media stories published in the wake of the act's passage outlined deficiencies with existing animal spaces despite new standards. At Lincoln Park, the *Los Angeles Times* reported on animal houses that "are dark and musty, and the great apes—the finest collection in the world—are confined to clean, sterile cages behind glass." In May 1972 the *Miami Herald* ran a lead story on West Palm Beach's Lion Country Safari's zookeeping after dark. Specific focus went to the hypocrisy and health hazards of allowing big cats to move freely during park hours and thereafter crowding "as many as 26 of the beasts . . . into one of five enclosures measuring 28-by-30 feet." Newspapers also covered the Humane Society of the United States' covert survey a year earlier, which reviewed seventy-one municipal and private zoos in twenty-eight states. According to the *Washington Post,* the society found "dilapidated old cages" at New York's Central Park Zoo, "wall-to-wall elephants in the elephant cage" at Pittsburgh's Zoo, and "clean but mean cages in Atlanta," with special mention of the "antiseptically clean, but small cell" for the zoo's black panther.[123]

Batten went deeper with the indictment. The former San Jose zoo director magnified the urban shame reflected in and incited by watchdog groups and media outlets with an inventory of exceptional horror. Gruesome-yet-matter-of-fact descriptions of zoo animals in crisis formed the foundation of his book, *Living Trophies.* The story began with the author's account of the end of his zoo career. After leading the short-lived San Jose Zoo for its first and only six years, Batten relocated his animals, including twenty-four individuals, to the Gladys Porter Zoo in Brownsville, Texas. Six weeks later, Batten learned of several deaths, injuries, mutilations, and unjustified trades. The discovery spurred a fact-finding tour of 104 zoos across the United States, described as "four months of depressing zoo viewing and photography." The ensuing document presented copious eyewitness accounts, documentary images, and elaborate appendixes that testified to the naked cage's longevity and racial meanings, but also to its capacity for multispecies authorship.[124]

Much of the material confirmed the need for revitalization that earlier zoo criticism had made urgent. But by appearing late in the public conversation, Batten's publication marked a uniquely shameful point in naked cage history. His identification of overcrowding, pacing, infections, and spatially induced disabilities and mortality read counter to the institutional shifts already under way by the time of his study, challenging optimistic affirmations that "a new zoo" was under construction in the United States. "American zoos," he wrote, "are desperately trying to change their public image to justify a continued existence and ensure future supplies of animals for exhibit." Sharply critical of wildlife conservation research and themed exhibits, Batten argued that zoos had disavowed their role in the disappearance of wild animals and were "preaching a doctrine of concern for those which remain." Evidence of this compromised concern could be seen in certain renovated displays, which he judged to be "purely for the benefit for the zoo visitor, although the animal may find temporary therapy in dismantling the man-made habitat." In a reversal of Dale Osborn's advice for dressing the naked cage, Batten used the example of the Erie, Pennsylvania, Zoo's primate house to show aesthetic naturalism as a form of "window dressing": "Two employees were fabricating quite elaborate fiberglass trees, complete with leaves, in front of the ape displays. When finished, visitors will be able to enjoy an instant safari by looking through the branches (which are on their side of the moated exhibit) to see the animals in their cells."[125] For Batten, any natural habitat exhibit that failed to consider an animal's preferred use of territory offered inhabitants less than a well-built cage; the naked cage could be modernist or naturalistic in design.[126]

Aside from its aesthetic elasticity, the disgrace of Batten's vision of the naked cage lay in its embrace of foreignness. In a complex statement that variously echoed the xenophobia of Jacob Riis and William Hornaday, Batten wrote:

> Years of hearing visitors call cassowaries "peacocks," toucans "frootloop birds," tigers "lions," and otters "beavers"—as well as frequent inquires from certain ethnic groups whose sole interest in animals is manifested in the question, "Are they good to eat?"—has convinced me that people who wish to learn about wild animals are, like the Siberian tiger, a vanishing species. . . . rare animals cannot be prostituted to supply family fun. The ultimate solution may be television; even the uncontrollable feeding impulse might be fulfilled by an exchange of snacks among viewers.[127]

For Batten, ethnicities who deviated from western European protocols of gentility inscribed within public zoos had not-quite-human curiosities and appetites, on par with animals who needed to be fed snacks. This negative animalization contrasted with the positive animalization in comparing good nature lovers to endangered species. Through this delicate imbrication of race and species, the animal advocate's order of things took a Progressive Era anxiety over the urbanized foreigner and concern for wildlife to its logical conclusion in the 1970s. For Batten, the simultaneous pandering to animal-like humans and sacrifice of actual animals spoiled the chances of a decent nature space, so much so that dismantling that space in favor of television seemed plausible, if only as a decisive way to excise the threat of uncivilized public animal viewing.

Living Trophies also alerted readers to the injustices of exhibiting animal species indigenous to North America. These species were identified as "second-class citizens" and extensively documented in text and image. Compared with extravagant enclosures allocated to, for example, the National Zoo's Chinese giant pandas, "native hawks and eagles do not fare as well, and the twentieth-century ghetto dominates cage design." Readers learned that bald and golden eagles were housed nationwide under "Spartan conditions" in undersized cages that were frequently without screening or overhead shelter. Hawks and owls were placed together in small quarters despite being natural enemies. Raptors lived behind glass and often flew into it. Batten's citation of poorly housed indigenous mammals was especially long, ending appropriately with a reform favorite: "Mountain lions, bobcats, cacomistles, raccoons, skunks, opossums, red and grey foxes, coyotes, wolves, otters, beavers, brown and grizzly bears, deer, pronghorn antelope, elk, moose, and buffalo are commonly used to fill run-down cages in our zoos." Advocacy for these animals was less a code for nativism than its frank articulation: "American animals should enjoy at least equal status in housing and care to that of their foreign cousins, regardless of comparative market values." Pandas and other "glamorous tenants" from abroad might currently be more desirable, but they were not intrinsically so. Batten insisted that native species were also of strong visual interest, but suffered disproportionately in naked cages and beyond. The inequality prompted a reassessment of the very idea of wildlife conservation: "To preach conservation of foreign animals by placing them on 'vanishing species' or 'endangered' lists while the native animal is so poorly treated, both as a captive and in its wild state, is blatant hypocrisy."[128] Thus, in varying inflections and strengths, Batten's aversion to foreigners marked another distinct feature of his call for change, reviving shame over the inadequacies of zoo goers and the spatial devaluation of national icons like the bald eagle and North American bison.

Still, while *Living Trophies* continued to flex the figuration of the naked cage along the logic of race and urban space, it also announced itself as something irreducibly different from these procedures. Much of Batten's tour involved him approaching captive animals as singular creatures living under extreme physical and psychological stress. In this sense, the "shocking look at the conditions in America's zoos" (the book's subtitle) was a sustained investigation into the biology of zoo design, the spirit of which recalled Heini Hediger's renowned zoology in *Wild Animals in Captivity*. Published in English in 1950, Hediger's research as a Swiss zoo director unsettled many zoo world assumptions by foregrounding the importance of an animal's quality of captive space over its quantity.[129] While there is some evidence that Batten was interested in Hediger's writing—the zoologist is briefly cited in *Living Trophies*—more telling is that Batten mobilized the same antianthropomorphic sensibility that allowed Hediger to ask: "What does limitation of space (iron bars, cages *etc*) mean to the animal?"[130]

Figure 1.12. *"Coyote huddles in rain storm—floor drains into den, leaving animal without dry refuge* (Bridgeport, Connecticut)," *in Peter Batten,* Living Trophies, *1974.*

Batten's iterations of the question involved wide-ranging descriptions of functional failures in exhibit design: slippery or poorly selected floors, dangerous projections, insufficient light, dirty water, absence of security barriers, inadequate heating and cooling, poorly planned moats, and so on. Sixty-five photographs offered what laundry lists could not: an eyewitness, denotative view with lighting and composition as dreadful as the life of its subjects. One poorly focused outdoor image showed a coyote standing oddly atop a cinderblock structure, captioned as "Coyote huddles in rain storm—floor drains into den, leaving animal without dry refuge. *(Bridgeport, Connecticut)."* Visible across the picture plane was a tall wire-mesh fence through which the camera looked into the enclosure and established its point of remove (Figure 1.12). Another photograph, taken from Racine, Wisconsin, gave a clumsily framed look at hoofstock standing within a grotto-style display, with the caption "Aoudads cannot walk, much less climb their synthetic mountain" (Figure 1.13). Twenty-four other versions of the question appeared in the book's penultimate chapter, posed to help evaluate a reader's local zoo and translate shame into activism. These included: "Can the animals walk at least four times their own length?"

Figure 1.13. *"Aoudads cannot walk, much less climb their synthetic mountain. Animals' hooves need prompt attention* (Racine, Wisconsin),*" in Peter Batten,* Living Trophies, *1974.*

"Do 'daytime' animals have adequate light and/or sun? (Or are they in dark interior cages with no access to outside runs or U/V light?)" "Are the animals at the front of the cage, and do they appear alert and relaxed? (Or are they curled up near the back of the exhibit, or pacing nervously?)" "Do cages or dens have artificial heat or cooling installed; on a warm day do animals breathe normally?"[131]

These lines of visual and textual inquiry offered readers a different way to look at the zoo and indications of the lived experience of animal captivity irrespective of racial meanings. Batten's questions suggested that visibly suffering wildlife in urban centers were just that and should be engaged on these other-than-human terms. More specifically, his attention to an animal's physiological responses turned zoo goers away from the subtle semiotics of zoo design that aligned animals with representations of other urbanites. Instead, zoo goers were urged to consider the fuller sensory problem of animal urban space in this period. The book's recurrent sensitivity to an enclosure's smell, temperature, lighting, floor materials, water quality, and room to move fashioned a critique that did not rely on the racial connotations created through other versions of the naked cage, including his own. It pointed rather to a formulation of bad zoo design that was open to a captive animal's participation in the production. Batten's questions could be posed and re-posed by zoo goers, but answers were at best speculative without the epistemological involvement of zoo inhabitants—that is, the presence of an animal who consents to coproducing kinds of knowledge furnished by a photograph, a written description, a sense of shame. This attention to a nonhuman actor in and of itself produced hints of a reform project more expansive and radically democratic than Morris's liberal sociobiology or Winogrand's obliqueness. It sketched out a politics affectively organized in relation to the creatures that have always inhabited American cities, a kind of reform that not only shamed white middle-class zoo goers and marginalized human viewing publics into some call for change but also allowed for the possibility that animals could signify and be discernible as city dwellers in their own sense and situation. The extent to which that possibility was developed is another chapter in the history of American zoo renewal.

2

Zoo Slum Clearance in Washington, D.C.

In 1952 the *Washington Post* reporter Chalmers Roberts embarked on a mission to redevelop downtown Washington. Armed with statistics, graphs, and maps, his eighteen-part series "Progress or Decay?" diagnosed the metropolitan center as a site of acute blight marred by escalating traffic jams, waning business districts, and growing slums. Reversing this downward spiral, he argued, was urgent, given that "the critical civic problem in Washington today—as in every other major American city—is the flight to suburbs." For Roberts, the ultimate cost of a declining downtown was the loss of particular forms of residential and commercial life to the District's outer edges. The outward migration of predominantly white families was allowing Washington to become the nation's first black-majority city, or in Roberts's thinly veiled vocabulary adapted from the New York City urban developer William Zeckendorf, "to rot at the core or be abandoned altogether."[1]

By equating civic vitality with an urban population that was not black, the *Post*'s series reflected and advanced a vigorous movement for urban renewal in the nation's capital that was buzzing with white racial anxiety. Substantiating the historian Thomas Sugrue's assertion that "in the postwar city, blackness and whiteness assumed spatial definition," Washington planners, developers, politicians, and pundits changed the physical landscape of the Federal City with an eye to bringing middle-class citizens who qualified as white back from the flourishing fringes of suburban Maryland and Virginia.[2] Redevelopment, argued renewal advocates, would create appealing new communities within the city limits and offer white Washingtonians a "positive urban choice" over suburban living.[3] Redevelopment would also reinforce the federal stature of a city whose urban decay, within clear sight of the Capitol, amounted to a national disgrace.[4] This second aspect of the District's renewal was also highly racialized. The history of constructing a built environment that was attractive to visiting tourists and government professionals was also a history of ignoring the city's poor, most of whom were African American.[5] The area southwest of the National Mall became a major target of these joint objectives to improve urban space. Between 1954 and 1958, planned "superblocks" of modernized apartment buildings, town houses, commercial strips, parking lots, and highways emerged as the dominant landscape in Washington's Southwest sector. A 1965 film by the American Institute of Architects editorialized on these changes with upbeat shots of middle-class whites living in the new River Park housing development and narration that "there are times when only complete renewal can answer the need" (Figures 2.1–2.2).[6] As urban historians have documented, the results of this complete renewal were devastating to the Southwest's largely black and low-income original residents.[7] A lack of affordable housing in particular pushed more African Americans out of the area, permanently displacing them from their well-established, if "blighted," communities and inaugurating two more decades of renewal in other sites of the Federal City. The neighborhoods of Foggy Bottom and Capitol Hill, for example, were of special interest to investors and white residents, but were spared a demolition and redesign on the scale of the Southwest.[8] The same cannot be said of a mixed community located on 164 sloping acres of Rock Creek Park in Washington's Northwest sector.

Granted, the redevelopment of the National Zoological Park was never formally included in the roster of federally sponsored and municipally executed neighborhood regeneration projects. The animals of 3001 Connecticut Avenue, Northwest, were widely understood as residents of a deteriorating city zoo, not of a deteriorating city. At the same time, the revamping of the National Zoo between 1958 and 1976 gave public expression to the very concept of urban renewal in ways that routinely rehearsed its racial dynamics. Much like other urban reformers, zoo management, concerned citizens, architects, and architectural critics were preoccupied with the liabilities of blackness and the prospects of whiteness in and around their target area. Master planning of the grounds was equally geared to making urban space palatable again for white-collar middle-class Americans who had escaped to the suburbs, and a civic showpiece for tourists of the nation's capital. What made the National Zoo's renovation exceptional to most Cold War renewal schemes was the pronounced emphasis on nonhuman life, whereby differences of species—whether one was human or not—became as important an axis of civic belonging or estrangement as differences of race. In Washington, D.C., the "Shame

Figures 2.1 and 2.2. *Screenshots of River Park development in Southwest, Washington, D.C., from* No Time for Ugliness *(1965).*

of the Naked Cage" lay in architectural, photographic, and textual representations of zoo animals as the city's black poor, and with them, zoo workers and visitors.[9] Much preferred were representations of the National Zoo as a verdant space of white bourgeois civility for animals and humans alike, a naturalistic landscape that brought all living beings into harmony and parity, and suggested living conditions conducive for species survival.

In this chapter, I chart intersections of racial and species difference over the two decades of the National Zoo's renovation, from the rhetoric of the "zoological slum" to the antiurban thrust of citizen activism, to the architectural modernism of 1960s animal displays and, finally, the "humanistic" naturalism of animal exhibition in the 1970s. Each phase racialized zoo grounds and occupants in a different way, mirroring larger shifts in the Federal City's redevelopment and giving it zoological shape. Key exhibits under consideration include the old Lion House, the Bird House, the

Great Flight Cage, and the Mann Lion–Tiger Exhibit. My readings of the National Zoo under renewal attend to its distinctly urban framework while suggesting ways to rethink urban renewal as a multispecies endeavor.

ANIMALITY AND BLACKNESS: THE RHETORIC OF A ZOOLOGICAL SLUM

In his 1965 sociological study of the federal urban renewal program after World War II, the city housing and planning expert Charles Abrams meditated on the rhetorical force of the word *slum*:

> Unlike words such as substandard, tenement, and insanitary housing, it is short, electric, and suited to newspaper headlines. From the day slum entered the language of social reform, its mere mention was enough to revolt the good citizen, win the support of the crusading press, and dedicate official action to its extinction.[10]

A blending of *slop* and *scum*, and close to other disparagements like *slump, sludge,* and *slut,* the word *slum* proposed, in a visceral way, a space of material and moral deprivation. It described, from an outsider's point of view, uninhabitable living conditions that were inhabited all the same. The slum, noted Abrams, was "the shame of the cities" and by the mid-1960s had become the impetus for reform measures that included public housing and other renewal projects.[11]

But in stressing that the slum was "easier to revile than to remedy," Abrams's rhetorical analysis gave way to a discussion that blended its signifier with its signified. Alan Mayne notes that to "conflate 'slum' (an imaginary overlay that is properly studied in relation to urban popular culture) and the actual social geography of urban disadvantage" is a common habit within urban studies.[12] For Mayne, slums are better understood as myths. They exist exclusively, and effectively, as representations. Initially depicted through the written pleas and pictures of nineteenth-century bourgeois urban reformers and popular entertainment genres such as the pulp novel, slums are replete with middlebrow fears and fantasies that are removed from the lived realities of inner-city inequality. Their power to shape public attitudes and agendas is rooted precisely in this remoteness, since slum myths "subsume the particularities (and underlying human scale) of actual places with an abstraction of urban disequilibrium and menace."[13]

Dating from the turn of the twentieth century, visual images of slums in Washington, D.C., were especially potent, particularly when they could be juxtaposed to the grandeur of the city's federal architecture. The spectacle of decrepit neighborhoods near the Capitol became something of a trope in the urban reformer's repertoire of social documentary photography, as recognized in Roberts's "Progress or Decay?" series. "In 1953," he predicted, "the bulldozers will go to work on some of Washington's worst slums, and photographers will have one less place to take pictures of slums in the shadow of the national Capitol."[14] Lewis Hine was one of those photographers, having documented a ramshackle back alley in the District's Southwest section with the neoclassical top of the Capitol building towering in the background (Figure 2.3). When republished in Scott Nearing's 1916 study of wealth and poverty, the photograph's caption underscored the sharp differences between the two sites with a brief nod to the bestial character of slum living: "In this rich land the avenues of wealth and the alleys of poverty lie side by side. With ease, comfort and luxury in abundance, poverty lurks and snarls."[15] Few other representations of the slums conveyed the misery of the immediate surroundings, the wider context in which they were produced, and the threat that they posed to a law-abiding citizenry. High contrasts between dark and light were pivotal to the image's power. The rotting wood and dirty bricks of the alley dwellings captured in the sight line of the Capitol's gleaming marble dome literalized the conviction that, in Washington, D.C., slum life and civic life was the difference between black and white. The racial undertones of the spatial gap were made more explicit when reinterpreted in the 1960s. In a 1965 photo book, *O, Say Can You See? A Bifocal Tour of Washington,* readers were asked to consider "a tourist's view of the Capitol" with images of black ghettos on alternating pages. Photos by George de Vincent moved between white marble buildings and monuments and filthy yards and interiors populated only by seemingly idle African American children.[16] A UPI wire photograph from 1967 by Emil Sveilis raised the stakes by picturing another shadowy corridor of District slums with the Capitol dome shining in the distance, adding in its caption that "to many residents of Washington, this city appears to have all the ingredients for a racial riot; sixty-three per cent of the city's residents are Negroes and most of them live in rundown areas such as the one shown here" (Figure 2.4). The possibility of a riot was particularly threatening, and realized a year later. In April 1968, after some twenty-thousand African Americans burned and looted their city in the wake of Martin Luther King's assassination, a self-identified black revolutionary clarified why: "[Riot is] just a term used to make us look wild, you know, like we're a bunch of savages."[17] Indeed, representations of the Capitol juxtaposed with the riot-ready slums implied that substandard living spaces in Washington, D.C., were sites not only of black social unrest but also of animality, and that both ought to be remedied in the Federal City.

Figure 2.3. *Lewis Hine's photograph of Southwest, Washington, D.C., republished in* Poverty and Riches, *1916. The full caption reads: "A NOTORIOUS ALLEY SLUM NEAR THE NATIONAL CAPITOL. This remarkable photograph shows the capitol at Washington two blocks distant from one of the worst districts. It illustrates literally some of Dr. Nearing's statements. 'In this rich land the avenues of wealth and poverty lie side by side. With ease, comfort and luxury in abundance, poverty lurks and snarls. What is poverty? Poverty is found wherever a family is living on an income that will not provide for physical health and social decency.'"*

It would take Dr. Theodore Reed, the new director of the National Zoological Park, to more fully enunciate what these representations, and the slum clearance they endorsed, could only suggest. Without question, Reed's language of urban renewal was rooted in the well-being of his zoo charges and held little interest in the welfare of impoverished black residents of the District. A veterinarian by training, Reed was foremost an animal man with expertise in the health care of ranch cattle and creatures common to postwar zoos. Upon assuming the directorship of the National Zoo in 1958, however, he began to recognize the rhetorical promise of labeling the aging institution a "zoological slum":

I had been giving a number of talks around Washington. I'd talk to anybody that asked me, church groups and rotary clubs and all that sort of stuff. I wanted to get the message out and get myself known. The Cleveland Park Citizens Association,

Figure 2.4. *UPI wire photograph of Southwest, Washington, D.C., 1967. Reprinted with permission of the D.C. Public Library, Star Collection; copyright* Washington Post.

which is up by the zoo, asked me to talk to them and asked me to tell it like it was. So I did! I was pretty discouraged about things, and I felt like telling it like it was. . . . I said it was a zoological slum.[18]

Among his audience of "very education do-gooders," the descriptor produced results. Select members of the Cleveland Park Citizens Association banded together to form another citizens' group called the "Friends of the National Zoo" (FONZ), which began to generate widespread interest in and federal funding for zoo revitalization, including a master plan and two more in the decades that followed.[19] Years later, Reed reflected on the meaning of his effective term by recalling a typical example:

I have to admit we were a zoological slum. We were bad. I had forty cages that could not hold animals [and] that were abandoned. We had 12 [mountain] goats. They were up at the end of the zoo by the Connecticut Avenue entrance. The first thing a keeper did in the morning was chase those goats back in the pen because they could get out. They'd stay in the pen all day and when the zoo locked up at night they'd get out and walk around the whole zoo.[20]

For Reed, a slum meant broken cages and unmanageable animals, a deplorable combination that suggested a certain degree of professional incompetence from a staff of keepers who were largely uneducated and African American.[21] But what initially amounted to a routine embarrassment for zoo management and inconvenience for employees became a city tragedy when a white toddler visiting from Chilliwack, British Columbia, crossed the guardrail at the Lion House and was fatally mauled by two African lions.

On May 16, 1958, Julie Ann Vogt, aged two and a half years, arrived at the zoo with her four-year-old sister, Judy, and grandfather, Harry Jackson. The trio had taken in the zoo the previous day and this time went directly to the exterior cages of the Lion House. Initially holding both children's hands, Jackson let go when the youngest said she wanted to hold her own hand. Julie then attempted to feed peanuts to the male and female lions, Ceasar (also known as Pasha) and Princess. Eyewitness accounts were vague on precisely how she managed to get beyond the guardrail that formed a three-feet-high barrier of square iron bars. From there, it was an eight-foot walk to the front of the lions' cage, enclosed by vertical round iron bars and divided periodically by horizontal bars of flat iron (Figure 2.5). Jackson testified to suddenly noticing the female lion grabbing his granddaughter by the shoulder and pulling her against the cage. Other witnesses swore it was the male lion that first attacked. Harry then climbed over the guardrail and took hold of Julie's arm and head, creating a tug of war between him and now two lions. A white women interviewed on the scene reported seeing the child's head separate from the body and the female lion carrying the body deeper into the cage. She noted that the grandfather was "hysterical" as he carried the child's head in his hands, prompting her to give him a paper bag to put it into "to get it out of sight of the school children."[22]

The death of Julie Ann Vogt was not the only human fatality at the National Zoo in these years, but it was one that mattered. In a 1992 interview Reed recalled that "we had two or three drownings in the Creek. But you don't get excited about that. When a lion kills, you get excited. Little black boys fall into the Creek. That doesn't count."[23] That Vogt was a white victim of an animal attack factored heavily in the intensity, and variety, of responses, each of which constructed the National

Figure 2.5. *Police photograph of the National Zoo's Lion House with zookeeper Michael Brown, 1958. Smithsonian Institution Archives, Image SIA2007–0135.*

Zoo's status as a slum not unlike the slums that civic-minded people had come to call "the Other Washington."[24] Shared among these responses was the sense that conditions in Rock Creek Park's sixty-nine-year-old zoo had become acutely unsafe and required both emergency corrective measures and long-term renovation. The question of fault was more contentious and threw the racial and species politics of this newly dubbed slum into still sharper relief. As much as finger pointing became a way to ensure that Julie's death would not be repeated, it also fleshed out who or what was the menace in this zoological slum. Just as the District could be framed as a "haven for Negroes" as late as 1947, and so ripe for a planning strategy of "black removal," the tragedy at the Lion House exposed undesirable elements at the zoo that demanded a corresponding purge.[25] Who to blame was key to the revelation.

The National Zoo, under the administration of the Smithsonian Institution, accepted immediate responsibility. Two days after the accident, zoo officials began surveying all facilities for safety, posting warning signs to alert visitors of danger, increasing police and keeper patrols, and covering guardrails with protective wire-mesh fencing.[26] Exhibits that could not be reinforced with additional barriers were abandoned and those that could were identified as being unsightly and visually obstructive. Four months later, management shut down major sections of the zoo from public view. These included a hazardous Monkey House; the Antelope House, considered "beyond restoration"; the Elephant House, since a river hippo had learned to lunge up onto the barrier rail; and two areas of the Bird House that had falling plaster and roof rot.[27] Each closing was an admission of culpability and a cost to the zoo's reputation. The ensuing civil suit filed by Julie Ann Vogt's aunt was more exact, pricing accountability at $100,000. Management settled out of court for a more forgiving $13,500, but not without the shame of having failed in its duties as a public zoological park.[28]

Institutional blame also found its way to the zoo's black labor force. In a letter to management one year after Julie's death, Francis Richards of Kensington, Maryland, shared her own story of braving the zoological slum, in which she accused two black keepers of endangering young zoo goers. Upon noticing her boy had gone through a gate in the Small Mammal House, the distraught mother retrieved him and exchanged words with Keeper Roberts. By Richards's account, Roberts was "a stocky colored man with a mustache" who refused to take responsibility for leaving the gate open, countering that it was Richards's responsibility to watch her child more closely. Richards invoked the death of Julie Ann Vogt as a consequence of such carelessness, to no effect. The two were joined by another black employee, who agreed with his colleague. Zoo management did not entertain Richards's subsequent suggestion that the men be fired for their negligence and insubordination toward a guest.[29] Reed, for his part, drew different conclusions after an investigation, speculating that the gate was in fact closed and the visitor's indignation was because "she accused a colored man of leaving the gate open and he denied it, and a second colored man entered the picture and tried to vindicate the first one."[30]

Blame also fell on the lions. Lawyers filing the civil suit on behalf of Vogt's aunt placed legal responsibility with the zoo, but also suggested that the animals were not quite innocent either. While the lions, since their acquisition four years prior, had not displayed any tendency to attack humans "greater than that found in the normal beast of their species and age under zoo conditions," the male had a less than spotless record.[31] In November 1953 Ceasar had injured another girl in Aspen Hill, Maryland, who was petting and handling the chained animal in a partially closed trailer. The girl took a fall in front of the lion, which reached out its paw and scratched her face, neck, and shoulders.[32] A District newspaper compounded the profile of dangerous beasts by restaging the more recent tragedy in a photograph. Published in the *Washington Star,* the image showed a local child placing her foot inside the same ironwork that Julie negotiated "to demonstrate how youngsters can slip between the bars" (Figure 2.6). The animals were beyond the photographic frame, perhaps absent from the shoot altogether. The omission may have been a practical choice given how unreliable a lion's display of ferocity could be in captivity circa 1958. As the zoologist Desmond Morris noted in this period, captive animals in prerenewal zoos were prone to abnormal behaviors. They could not be counted on to routinely act like animals.[33] The vulnerable gaze of a youngster, dressed in a pale-colored dress and shoes, meeting the viewers' own gaze, was a more stable shot. Overdetermined in her innocence, the toddler conveyed the subhumanity of a zoo predator by appearing as its visual opposite, a disquieting reminder that extreme peril awaited on the other side of the barrier, but without ever visualizing the specific species identity of that period. "What is dangerous for a little white girl?" the picture asked viewers of a racially polarized urban region, and left the question suggestively open. Reed was well aware that his animals were being criminalized and rose to their defense: "There was some cry that I should kill the cats and I said I wasn't going to do it. They hadn't done anything wrong. They were cats."[34] Many agreed, including one Sunday school class of fifth- and sixth-grade boys who "unanimously opposed destruction of the animals," since "the animals did what came naturally."[35]

The boys would have been less likely to agree with Reed's contention that the most liable of all parties in this tragedy was the zoo-going public. In the midst of asking a Senate committee for an emergency fund of $86,000 to improve cages and fences, the director singled out an "irresponsible public" as the major problem with

Figure 2.6. Washington Star *photograph re-creating the Vogt accident at the National Zoo, circa 1958. Reprinted with permission of the D.C. Public Library, Star Collection; copyright* Washington Post.

National Zoo safety.[36] Reed was already skeptical that the accident at the Lion House began with the girl slipping through one of the spaces of the guardrail, a physical impossibility by his estimation, and others.[37] It was more plausible, to him and others, that her grandfather had lifted her over the barrier, which had become familiar zoo-going practice.[38] Indeed, since the girl's death, eight adults and sixty-five children had been removed from the zoo for crossing (wire-mesh) guardrails, indicating to Reed that visitors had "sad disrespect for potential danger."[39] The *Washington Post* suggested that Reed's efforts to refortify exhibits were ultimately driven by a desire to protect the animals from the dangers created by such public misbehavior. In a short article headlined "Zoo Mending Its Fences to Save Beasts from Us," the newspaper related how the director was trying "to keep the people away from the animals."[40] Reed was not shy to admit that at the zoo "we have more trouble in front of the bars than we do behind the bars."[41]

Conscientious zoo goers had more personal ways of articulating the sense that visitors required rehabilitation as much as animals and their surroundings. After the lion mauling, the zoo received guilt-ridden letters from parents who confessed to letting their own children wander off, however momentarily, and discovering them precariously close to elephants, bears, and the big cats. Letter writers were candid in their self-admonishment, especially for having failed to report the incidents to the proper authorities: "If I had reported twenty-six years ago that our son went through the bars of the lion safety section, [Julie's] life may have been saved."[42]

All these accusations—of bad keepers, bad animals, and bad zoo goers—amplified the cry for zoo redevelopment. The physical conditions of this zoological slum had degraded all participants at the zoo, mirroring the deprivation and depravity that white Washington felt to be pervasive among the black population of the city's ghettoized neighborhoods. The sports broadcaster Phil Wood's recollections of the District in the 1960s articulate those sentiments:

If you lived in Fairfax County or Arlington County or Montgomery County or PG County . . . you saw black people, but you didn't see them in big numbers. . . . you'd hear people talk about "Well, that's a colored neighborhood now" or "We don't go there anymore." . . . I remember driving through the District at times with [my mother] and she had lived in the District back in the 40s into the 50s, and she'd say, "Well this used to be such a *nice* neighborhood" and by that she was essentially saying, "This used to be a white neighborhood." And again I guess there was that fear factor that, well, the black people in some way mean us harm . . . it wasn't an unspoken thing. I mean people would bring it up, people would talk about it. But . . . it was more out of ignorance than any actual experience.[43]

If car rides into town could stimulate racial anxieties for a self-exiled class of whites, so could the National Zoo's annual Easter Monday event. A ritual of family picnics and egg rolling for thousands of African American Washingtonians, Easter Monday at the zoo was a response to the traditional whites-only policy for the holiday at the White House. While cherished by members of the black community, the event also became a day marred by youth assaults and vandalism in the immediate postwar years, prompting zoo officials to fortify the grounds and many city residents to associate the day with slum-related delinquency. In a 1957 memo to Smithsonian officials, for example, Reed requested "permission to limit the admittance to the

National Zoological Park on Easter Monday, 1958, to children under 12 years of age, accompanied by adults," adding that "I think we should get some information as to what we can do about the limitation of certain groups in a public park." Secretary Leonard Carmichael responded with "yes, but do it now."[44] Given these sensitivities, the Vogt incident, and all that it uncovered, risked defining zoo space, negatively, as black space year-round.

The comparison between the zoo and the slums gained some currency in the local press as zoo renewal unfolded during the 1960s and 1970s. In a sharp critique of the zoo's cages in 1971, Nancy Ross of the *Washington Post* likened the animals to "slum children," citing the deaths of sixty-seven primates and twenty parrots from lead poisoning, the same problem faced by poor children in the District who were eating the leaded paint chipping off of walls.[45] In an editorial letter that same year, Marian Newman, a resident of Bethesda, Maryland, and volunteer with the Committee for Humane Legislation, juxtaposed the figure of suffering animals with the figure of insufferable humans. Newman complained about a recent zoo visit where "animals in small, dark and barren cages were subjected to a barrage of marshmallows and peanuts." She voiced her frustration with the pace of change at the zoo, adding, "these suffering animals serve as a reflection of our attitude towards other living creatures."[46] Wolf Von Eckardt, the *Post*'s architecture critic, continued the analogy when he mobilized the term *slum* a year later in his assessment of the zoo's current state. While the recently acquired giant panda pair, Hsing-Hsing and Ling-Ling, were housed in quarters that were "perfectly adequate," most other animals were "unconscionably crowded in surroundings that . . . range from barely adequate to downright ugly."[47] Supplementing these direct comparisons was a steady stream of complaint letters addressed to the zoo that itemized its troublesome state. Cockroaches were in full view, reckless cyclists were running into children, pedestrians were falling into holes in the sidewalk, tourists felt shocked and frustrated by decrepit, underlabeled animal exhibits.[48] Perceptions of the National Zoo were spiraling downward.

In 1961 the authors of a report to Smithsonian Institution executives, including Secretary Carmichael, offered one of the more vivid accounts of the zoological slum. Still sore from the tragedy at the Lion House, these concerned Smithsonian employees included a photographic essay on zoo conditions that was more distressing than any editorial. The sequence of images echoed the "slum tours" that city officials had been conducting since the turn of the century, and with renewed vigor in the postwar period.[49] Each 8.5-by-11-inch black-and-white image, twenty-one in total, was overlaid with a typewritten caption to frame the view. Current views of the zoo focused initially on racially mixed crowds negotiating congested and

A normal busy day overloads the roadways and sidewalks.

Figure 2.7. *National Zoo street scene, 1961. Smithsonian Institution Archives. Record Unit 50, Box 127, Folder: NZP Report of 1961.*

garbage-filled grounds, insinuating that going to the zoo was akin to visiting the city's condemned Southwest. One photograph, captioned "A normal busy day over-loads the roadways and sidewalks," pictured a car-filled street cutting right through the grounds (Figure 2.7). The scene appeared all the more unappealing for the vo-luminous trash littering the adjacent lawn and the pedestrian routes packed with visitors on foot and on benches.

A second image, while aesthetically pleasing in composition, provided more evi-dence of the zoo's deplorable conditions (Figure 2.8). "Sidewalks designed in 1910 for pedestrian traffic" made a visual parallel between the iron bars of the outmoded bear cage and the iron railing that snaked along the visitor pathway. Near to the cage itself, the railing displayed the recent installment of raised fencing, from the

Sidewalks designed in 1910 for pedestrian traffic.

Figure 2.8. *National Zoo sidewalk, 1961. Smithsonian Institution Archives. Record Unit 50, Box 127, Folder: NZP Report of 1961.*

traditional 32 inches to 45 inches, angled outward to prevent unauthorized crossings. Farther back, unsightly safety mesh kept pedestrians in check in a manner that echoed the bears' appearance of being incarcerated. The sight of barren trees, either dormant from the winter or dying from rot, underlined the feeling that the current zoo was a space of urban decay. Smithsonian executives viewing the picture would have been acquainted with recent activity at the zoo to cull its many dead or diseased trees, at least one of which was the cause of a serious accident. In June 1958 a large tree limb fell in front of the wolf cage and injured a visitor from Seat Pleasant, Maryland, and the visitor's elderly relative from neighboring Calvert Street.[50]

Later photographs in the series took officials closer to the animal shelters, associating zoo dwellers with residents of the inner city. An interior shot of the Antelope House showed a structure that, while closed to visitors, remained home for, in the

This non-fireproof wooden structure, built in 1898 and second oldest in the Zoo, was closed to the public as a health hazard.

Figure 2.9. *Antelope House at the National Zoo, 1961. Smithsonian Institution Archives. Record Unit 50, Box 127, Folder: NZP Report of 1961.*

Washington Post's words, "a few animals that can't be crammed elsewhere" (Figure 2.9).[51] A barren corridor housed creatures in partial silhouette against iron-barred enclosures with cement floors. The enclosures' outer wall appeared to have peeling paint; two wooden support beams appeared overly worn.[52] The more prominent animal, a mangy striped hyena, stood upright at the front of the bars, as if to address the viewer. Another animal lolled in its corner. Outdoor views of animal housing delivered more bad news. Wild horses and zebras were relegated to structures identified as nonfireproof (Figure 2.10). Small quarters with horizontal wooden slats bore some visual relationship to postwar pictures taken by the local press of dilapidated house exteriors in the Southwest section of town. Described as a "row of condemned negro shacks 100 block of P St., S.W.," the grassless terrain and shabby building

These non-fireproof wooden shelters for wild horses and zebras are unsightly. Their size and construction make caring for the animals difficult.

Figure 2.10. *Quarters for hoofstock at the National Zoo, 1961. Smithsonian Institution Archives. Record Unit 50, Box 127, Folder: NZP Report of 1961.*

facades in one *Washington Star* photograph could have sheltered exotic hoofstock (Figure 2.11). Likewise, in another image of run-down houses on F Street, S.W., a small gathering of black children occupied an area roughly equivalent to the zebra yards (Figure 2.12). Three standing figures, including a woman in a doorway, made a more obvious and unsettling connection to the standing zebras. As zoo photographers saw it, zoo animals were, in their present environment, on residential par with poor black Washingtonians.

The idea of a zoological slum was thus highly versatile. It garnered citizen support for improvements both material and behavioral, it made an otherwise senseless act of animal violence seem meaningful and accountable, and it won over governing bodies that held the purse strings for large-scale reconstruction of the zoo's physical plant, administrative buildings, and animal exhibits. Key to the idea's utility was an

Figure 2.11. Washington Star *photograph of 100 block of P Street Southwest, circa 1955. Reprinted with permission of the D.C. Public Library, Star Collection; copyright* Washington Post.

Figure 2.12. Washington Star *photograph of F Street Southwest, 1949. Reprinted with permission of the D.C. Public Library, Star Collection; copyright* Washington Post.

association that few postwar zoo lovers would find comfortable condoning, however true it rang for them. Constructing the National Zoo as a slum elaborated on a quiet, persistent link between animal space and black space in the District's urban core. In so doing, it enabled zoo redevelopers to excise the double stigma of wild animality and blackness that plagued the old National Zoo, and to envision the new zoo in more promising terms.

FROM CITY TO NATION: ANTIURBANISM AND THE FRIENDS OF THE NATIONAL ZOO

FONZ was the first audible voice to recognize the implications of the zoological slum concept, defuse its racial connotations, and propose a program for renewal that appeared race blind. The organization was initially composed of well-educated, civically active men and women who held "a special feeling for wildlife" and made their homes in the nineteenth-century "streetcar suburb" of Cleveland Park, adjacent to the zoo.[53] Founding officers included its first president, Max Kampelman, an attorney and political scientist whose personal real estate dealings with the zoo's associate director, J. Lear Grimmer, sparked interest in the zoo's own housing issues.[54] Mrs. L. Noble Robinson was another FONZ original. Robinson had formerly worked as president of the Connecticut Avenue Citizens Association and went on to chair the D.C. League of Women Voters. Dr. Malcolm Henderson was a professor of physics at the Catholic University of America and previously director of Atomic Test Operations with the U.S. Civil Defense Administration.[55] These and other similar initiators understood that their nonprofit, nonpartisan group was in a unique position to "develop the potential" of the zoo and secure "its rightful place in this Capital."[56] Pressuring Congress, speaking as concerned citizens, and maximizing personal and professional connections, FONZ leaders were able to put the National Zoo's revitalization on the public agenda in ways that only nongovernmental elites could. Reed acknowledged this advantage early on when he refused at one meeting to comment on the group's intentions because they were "so near to lobbying."[57] FONZ ran on the energies of affluent white Washingtonians familiar with the workings of District politics and invested in the redemptive promise of a revitalized zoo. Throughout the 1960s and 1970s, its growing membership list would continue to reflect this demographic, as the group attracted the city's white bourgeoisie to its cause and alienated other racial and ethnic groups.[58] A 1968 newspaper piece on a typical FONZ member was one example. Profiling Mrs. Gilbert Grosvenor, the *Washington Star* asked its readers, "Do you know her?" The wife of a National Geographic Society executive appeared taking close-up photographs of a tortoise at the revitalizing zoo. Described as "a native Washingtonian who feels flexibility is the spice of life," the piece included a list of her favorite things at the moment: favorite furniture, eighteenth-century English; favorite fashion designer, Pucci; favorite city, Kandy, the ancient cultural capital of Ceylon; favorite charity, the Friends of the National Zoo. "It was through her activities with the Friends that the zoo's new baby giraffe was named after her."[59]

Eight years earlier, newspapers were considering another FONZ showpiece: a twenty-page position paper titled "The Crisis at Our National Zoo." Its publication on November 13, 1960, represented a pivotal step in clearing the zoological slum. Taking a wide-angle look at the problem, in terms of its institutional history and its comparative status with other zoos in the United States and Europe, the "Crisis" paper prescribed a return to the zoo's original mission, as conceived by Smithsonian secretary Samuel P. Langley in his 1888 appeal to Congress:

> Here not only the wild goat, the mountain sheep and their congeners would find the rocky cliffs which are their natural home, but the beavers brooks in which to build their dams, the buffalo places of seclusion in which to breed and replenish their dying race; aquatic birds and beasts their natural home, and in general all animals would be provided for on a site almost incomparably better than any now used for this purpose in any other capital in the world.[60]

For FONZ members, Langley's vision was full of possibility but had yet to be realized. The image of a natural-looking zoo, peppered with home-building wildlife, recast the urban facility as a respectable conservation outlet that was scientific for researchers and educationally enriching for its visitors. The new National Zoo would be wise to foreground its role as "a city of refuge for the vanishing races of the continent" that were losing their native habitats and, for some, nearing extinction.[61] The first FONZ logo visualized these stakes by centering an American bison on an open plain at sunset (Figure 2.13). With an aquiline nose, furrowed brow, and hairless face, the animal displayed remarkably human features, possibly western European in origin, that subtly constructed likeness between bison and their human advocates.

Implicit in the revival of Langley's ideal was indeed a suggestion of equivalence between animal species endangered by the ravages of industrial growth in the nineteenth century and well-to-do Washingtonians threatened by a struggling bourgeois urban culture in the twentieth. The National Zoo's founding pastoral scene held a special appeal for FONZ in the face of a strong regional and nationwide discourse of postwar urban decline. In his history of that discourse, Robert Beauregard argues that American antiurbanism, which traditionally pitted the beauty and moral

Figure 2.13. *Friends of the National Zoo logo, 1958. Smithsonian Institution Archives, Image SIA2014–01212.*

goodness of the waning countryside against the degeneracy of the expanding city, experienced a second life after World War II. For the newly prosperous middle class and those located on its economic edge, the postwar city represented a continued estrangement from the perceived innocence and authenticity of nature, both animal and human. Simultaneously, with the rise of the suburbs, pastoralism found renewed cultural purchase. Social critics and reformers framed the countrified landscapes of the urban periphery as the inner city's aesthetic, spiritual, and fiscal opposite. Like Americans of nineteenth-century suburbs, mid-twentieth-century suburbanites were pursuing and occasionally achieving the exalted intangibles of private lawns and expansive gardens that city dwellers could not.[62]

Living on the outskirts of the District's urban core, FONZ members, and their ideas for a new zoo, reflected some of this optimism. But specific invocations of Washington's contemporary suburbanism—by this time located farther afield in Maryland and Virginia—were absent in the "Crisis" paper. The hallmark of FONZ antiurbanism centered instead on a denunciation of the zoo's municipal funding source. Since its inception, the zoo had been financed by the District of Columbia, an arrangement that FONZ argued was out of step with the zoo's national identity:

"Washington, a city of 800,000 people, could afford to maintain a modest munici-pal zoo. It cannot conceivably, from its city finances, provide for a truly national zoo." The evidence was that "the zoo we call 'national' is well on its way to be-coming a second-rate municipal zoo."[63] Such was the gist of the crisis according to FONZ: the zoo's current status as a city zoo would devolve even further.

The specter of a "second-rate municipal zoo" was a watered-down version of the more racially pointed zoological slum. Hovering near the idea of second-class citi-zens, the term gave journalists, who widely quoted it, a euphemism for the zoo as a space of black and animal subjugation, mixed with the sting of a damaged national reputation.[64] The term also gave the Smithsonian Institution the impetus to take full financial responsibility for the facility.[65] Nationalizing the zoo in this way trans-formed revitalization into a federal project on par with other programs of renewal in the District, which likewise sought to reverse Washington's urban decline without ever specifically mentioning the racial identities of those citizens believed to be at the root of it. Beauregard suggests that the perceived root of urban decline was the expanding presence of African Americans in U.S. cities, rendered visible through a declining number of whites and continued practices of segregation: "Decay and race would be thrown together in a discursive unity, and this flow of [black] people to the cities, despite the glaring need to replace the loss of the white population, was not cause for celebration on the part of civic boosters."[66] Developing FONZ's "truly national" National Zoo through civic will and federal funds was one response to these racialized laments over urban decay. A national zoo would be impervious to slums and slum dwellers, lending weight to Sugrue's broader observation that, in the postwar period, "to be fully American was to be white."[67]

The transition from a city zoo to a national zoo was aesthetic as well. Following the publication of their position paper, FONZ presented "A Master Plan for the National Zoo" to Secretary Carmichael and Dr. Reed. The plan was developed by the landscape architects Meade Palmer, of Warrenton, Virginia, and Morris Trotter, of Washington, D.C., who were retained by FONZ in May 1959 with fund-raised fees.[68] Palmer and Trotter's combined experience included designing parks, college campuses, memorials, towns, and residential subdivisions. Absent of much inter-est in animal architecture, their proposal for the zoo left out specific building de-signs and the technical details of exhibiting animals, focusing instead on a general framework for immediate and long-term renovations. The designers were, however, more specific about the beneficiaries of these renovations: "Well-educated families, accustomed to good contemporary planning and design, familiar with the attrac-tive techniques of popular education, do not happily accept zoological exhibits that have not been modernized for a generation or more." For Palmer and Trotter, these visitors of "sophisticated and discriminating tastes" were the primary clients for zoo revitalization in Washington, D.C., not the animals. This included locals who could see themselves reflected in the ideals and composition of FONZ as well as tourists who would prefer and benefit from a truly national zoo.[69]

Palmer and Trotter's scheme eliminated the current road that cut through the property and designed in its place a circular road and parking areas that were situated along the grounds' circumference (Figure 2.14). Their zoo was a pedestrian-friendly space, emphasized by the enlargement of the existing Connecticut Avenue entrance into an oval plaza. Pedestrians would embark on their visit there, but also be able to access a new information center and auditorium, as well as a terraced restaurant surrounding the plaza, all designed to "introduce the visitors to the Zoo through a handsome and important 'gateway of buildings.'"[70] Converting the Connecticut Avenue entrance into a plaza also solidified the zoo's connection to its upscale neighbors living on the other side of the avenue, in the expensive houses and apartments of Cleveland Park. By contrast, the neighborhood east of the property, identified by one zoo analyst in 1961 as "a transition area from whites to non-whites [predominantly African Americans and Latinos]," received no formal entranceway.[71] Rather, the Harvard Street entrance brought visitors straight into the path of the circular road and a pickup point for cars and buses.

The Palmer–Trotter plan made visitors entering from Connecticut Avenue still more welcome with a broad central path of grass and shrubbery starting from the plaza. This "Greenway" served zoo goers on foot and those who rented small mechanical "scooter-chairs." It followed the route of the existing road, leading past current buildings and areas for exhibits that had yet to be built: a moated hoof-stock habitat, a monkey island exhibit, and facilities to replace the destroyed animal houses. Complementing the Greenway were two offshoot footbridges, which took visitors to and from an expanded and redecorated Bird House located in a deep gully. Meanwhile, the architects reserved a major open visitor area on top of the knoll where the antelope and lion houses used to stand. Modest in comparison with the plans that would precede it, the Palmer–Trotter plan was a loose vision of an integrated landscape that relegated regular vehicular traffic to its margins and highlighted the topographical variation of the property. Changing the zoo's built environment along these lines was the necessary physical reconditioning to realize FONZ's conservationist thrust and dreams for a truly national zoo. It held out the promise of a physical plant "updated" to a higher standard and one that could operate "as a vigorous, informal educational institution."[72]

FONZ imagined the most drastic physical reconditioning offsite. As the ulti-

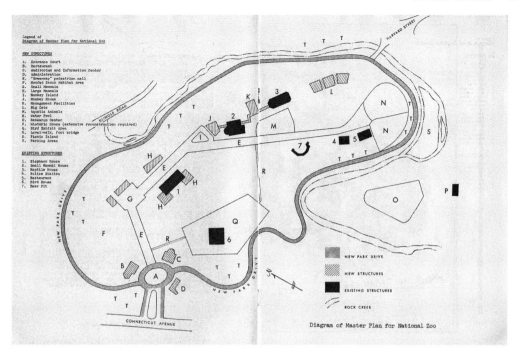

Figure 2.14. *Master plan for the National Zoo by Palmer and Trotter, 1959. Note sections A (entrance court), E ("Greenway" pedestrian mall), F (hoofed stock habitat area), I (Monkey Island), R (Level-walk footbridge), and Q (bird exhibit area). Smithsonian Institution Archives. Record Unit 326, Box 51, Folder 11.*

mate expression of the organization's antiurbanist longings, presenters of Palmer and Trotter's work concluded the "Master Plan" document with a call for an out-of-the-city breeding zoo to complement zoo revitalization in Rock Creek Park. The aesthetics of this second zoo—a plan B of sorts—were vague, but the urgency was fierce and specific:

> Some limited breeding is being done today in the industrialized nations. There are several successful projects of this kind in the United States. But the depletion of choice species is so rapid, and the number of animals necessary to assure the survival of a breed in captivity so great, that a large breeding zoo has become an imperative need today. Fittingly, such an "open" country zoo, dedicated to the preservation of animals threatened by extinction, should be operated in conjunction with the National Zoo itself.

The concept of a breeding zoo focused exclusively on developing an animal conservation program of national standing and dispensed with the urban tradition of a zoo for animal exhibition.[73] Reproducing endangered animal species in an "open country" zoo was a definitive way to rescue the National Zoo from its second-rate municipal status and erase any vestiges of a zoological slum. It bypassed the city altogether and embraced rural space as the answer to the ambiguous wildlife concerns of FONZ's particular membership. "Choice species" became a metaphor for Washington's white professional class, who, if all else failed, would seek their refuge in the country.

THE ARCHITECTURE OF URBAN SANCTUARY

By the 1960s Washington's zoo enthusiasts grew more confident that a breeding zoo north of the city was not the only recourse in revitalization. In their 1961 master plan, the architectural-engineering firm of Daniel, Mann, Johnson and Mendenhall (DMJM) took elements of FONZ's master plan for the urban campus and adapted them into a comprehensive vision for renovated grounds, this time, with renovated animal exhibits as well. With offices throughout the world and a portfolio that spanned recreational facilities, public buildings, high-rise apartments, and aerospace research centers, the L.A.-based firm was a large organization that, as the *Los Angeles Times* phrased it, "is exerting a direct or indirect influence on the lives of millions."[74] Such aptitude and authority proved attractive to the Federal City's new zoo makers, who had big dreams for their zoo, fueled by other large-scale planning projects in the District and the desire to eradicate slum conditions in Rock Creek Park. An agenda of an open session meeting of the National Capital Planning Commission in 1962 gives a sense of projects that were active in this period. Scheduled for discussion in addition to the National Zoo's recent master plan was the Washington International Airport Access Highway, a Howard University Area Urban Renewal Feasibility Study, "Street and Alley Closings," and "Changes in the Permanent System of Highways Plan."[75]

The DMJM scheme directly invoked the memory of Frederick Law Olmsted and his contribution to the National Zoo by reproducing his original 1890 drawing in the published plan and framing it as the zoo's finest moment.[76] DMJM drew attention to Olmsted's construction of "a pleasant and easily accessible landscaped area" coherently designed to create a "quiet pedestrian atmosphere."[77] By 1961 Olmsted's mark on the zoo had all but disappeared thanks to design choices that upset the coherency of the grounds. The firm singled out the proliferation of cars cutting through the central exhibit area as a primary example of the zoo's misdirection, along with the general physical and educational impoverishment of animal displays. As stated in the plan's introductory passages, "Despite the impression of beauty and awe which watching activities of the different species engenders, the overall appearance is one of sadness and neglect."[78] DMJM's plan resulted in a four-year construction program geared to reclaiming a more naturalistic, Olmstedian zoo. Specifics included the redevelopment of the Bird House in 1965, a new area for hoofed animals in 1967, and an animal hospital and research building in 1969.[79] Renewing the experience of bird-watching, however, was the signature accomplishment of the 1961 plan and a milestone in the zoo's long-range modernization program.

The opening of the remodeled Bird House on February 11, 1965, was black-tie and by invitation only. Minibuses carried distinguished guests from the Elephant House parking lot to the Bird House, where they were hosted by the Smithsonian's new secretary and trained ornithologist, Dillon Ripley. The Marine Corps enlivened the atmosphere with a jazz ensemble. Staff served canapés straight from the kitchen area that was designated for bird food preparation, while U.S. army engineers provided lights to illuminate the soon-to-be-opened Great Flight Cage, built on the steep hillside of the Bird House's western face.[80] Walks through the refurbished facility and glimpses of the enormous outdoor structure by its side revealed a new approach to displaying avian life that delighted Washington's high society and encouraged them to, as Reed hoped, "smell and hear, and almost feel, those birds."[81] What they saw was a modernized exhibition space in two parts: an architecture of urban sanctuary, designed to return white citizens not unlike themselves to the metropolis with the experience of a tangible human–animal proximity. With the renovated Bird House and the original Great Flight Cage, Washington's new zoo makers sought to lure back people who had experienced their own form of flight. Several elements of each structure collaborated to produce the effect of both getting back to nature and getting back to the city.

The first structure was a reinterpretation of its initial design in 1926 by Municipal Architect Albert L. Harris. Originally, the building stood as a palatial Italian Byzantine–Romanesque edifice that used nature more as ornament than environment. Harris aligned large building blocks and a raised central portion in classical symmetry. A concrete portico of two supporting columns stood as the Bird House's centerpiece, defined by a gabled top and a decorative door depicting birds and flowers in a colorful mosaic (Figure 2.15).[82] The architect Richard Dimon, of DMJM, decided to leave the sturdy outside walls intact. In keeping with a more nationally oriented zoo, he also accommodated the patriotic addition of a fifty-seven-hundred-pound granite eagle placed in front of the house, which had sat atop New York's Pennsylvania Station since 1910.[83] But he removed the building's impressive front

Figure 2.15. *Bird House at the National Zoo designed by Albert L. Harris, 1926. Smithsonian Institution Archives, Image 97–3040.*

section, including its mosaic door. Dismantled in eight sections and hand cleaned, the mosaic reappeared as an interior entranceway, leading bird-watchers to a new centerpiece, the Central Flight Room.[84]

The Central Flight Room was a free-flight aviary designed to immerse visitors in the sensory pleasures of tropical nature. It replaced the older interior flight cage containing, by the late 1950s, birds that would not breed, a leafless perching tree, and a large still pool (Figure 2.16).[85] The new flight room was a bright and lush corrective to the inanimateness, painted with graphic tree silhouettes on its primary walls that evoked a stylized equatorial rain forest and formed a striking contrast to the relocated mosaic (Figures 2.17–2.18). Formerly the central hall of the original building, the room spanned thirty-two feet in height, seventy-two feet in length, and fifty-one feet in width. Construction crews converted the old ceiling into a double-layered clear plastic sunroof with water sprinklers, giving birds and flora plenty of natural light and periodic rain showers. One wall of artificial rockwork with a twenty-foot recirculating waterfall added humidity and dynamism to the

Figure 2.16. *Original interior exhibit in Bird House at the National Zoo, circa 1936. Smithsonian Institution Archives.*

Figure 2.17. *Central Flight Room of renovated Bird House at the National Zoo, circa 1965. Courtesy of the Smithsonian National Zoological Park.*

Figure 2.18. *Central Flight Room of renovated Bird House at the National Zoo, reproduced in* The Torch, *February 1965. Smithsonian Institution Archives, Image SIA2014–01214.*

room, while trees rooted in the soil-filled holes of the floor foundation added green-ery. A low coral rock wall defined a visitor walkway on the ground level. Two gently angled ramps that joined at one corner of the room to form a nine-foot-high viewing platform gave additional vantage points. From there, zoo goers could stand "eyeball to eyeball" with a variety of nonaggressive birds flying and perching in their verdant environs: tanagers, fruit pigeons, mynahs, bulbuls, rice sparrows, saffron finches, cowbirds, doves, thrushes, francolins, rollers, toucans, orioles, nuthatches, and many other species.[86]

Complementing the immersion experience of the Central Flight Room were twenty-seven other exhibits and two indoor–outdoor cages. These displays followed principles that helped differentiate the renovated space from a predecessor that, in Reed's eyes, was "just row after row after row of little square cages with little birdies in it."[87] Dimon designed the new exhibits to be viewable at the eye level of a twenty-eight-inch-high child; he minimized visual barriers between birds and visitors through the use of fine stainless steel vertical wire, and glass in curved or straight forma-tions; he placed labels just above the floor at a commonly legible angle of 45 degrees; he managed crowds by widening public areas and placing exhibits on only one side of the walkways; and he included ramps wherever possible instead of stairs. Bird curators played a role in the redesign as well by dispensing with the tradition of dis-playing individual species and stressing instead "community groups of compatible birds."[88] Each enclosure attended to the particular needs of these groups through flexible features like independent temperature control, removable plastic wall pan-els, customized plantings, and individually heated perches. With this heightened adaptability and these animal-friendly innovations, zoo promoters hailed the mod-ernized Bird House as a place "*for* the birds" and "a deluxe bird hotel."[89] Bill Henry of the *Los Angeles Times* was more audacious in his report of the renovations' appeal, straddling both the metaphorical and material conditions of human residency in the District: "Experts who have seen plans for the completed structure say the birds at the zoo will have the best housing in town."[90] Aspects of the improved Bird House did reiterate some upscale residential spaces in Washington's redeveloped urban areas and suburban outskirts. The building's new glass entryway with a vaulted, curved canopy in white concrete, for example, bore a loose architectural relation to the aluminum barrel-roofed and plate-glass River Park townhomes in the redevel-oped Southwest, and a roster of other lesser-known variations on the theme (Figures 2.19–2.20; see also Figure 2.1).

Despite its modernizations, the Bird House was upstaged by the edifice that stood beside it as the new zoo's first architectural wonder and its program of deslumming the grounds (Figure 2.21 and Plate 3). The Great Flight Cage was not the first out-door bird exhibit at the zoo, though in materials and form it was the most extravagant in its construction of a nature compatible with postwar middle-class whiteness.[91] Designed and built as a circular outdoor enclosure that visitors could enter, the cage stood a generous 130 feet in diameter, with a towering ninety-foot-high central steel mast. Wire cables radiated out from the mast to support six parabolic arches of steel, each painted white and pitched out at an angle of thirty degrees and a height of sixty feet. Vinyl-coated wire mesh, also in white, draped over the top of the hillside cage and appeared to vanish against the sky. Black wire on the "sides" of the struc-ture was, like the Bird House's wire, comparatively invisible, blending in with the cage's backdrop of trees and foliage. Visitors accessed the cage by crossing an arched bridge from the second floor of the Bird House, which in proportion and shape echoed Washington's budding system of freeways. The most prominent of these sys-tems was the Capital Beltway, completed in 1964, which linked most communities of the outer suburbs to central Washington and included two major bridges across

Figure 2.19. *Bird House entryway at the National Zoo, 2013. Photograph by Jen Cohen.*

Figure 2.20. *Aluminum contractor advertisement featuring Kent-Lincolnia Apartments in Alexandria, Virginia, circa 1965.*

the Potomac River.[92] The Flight Cage's bridge was a smaller 115 feet in length and led to an organically shaped double set of glass doors that formed a "bird lock." Once inside, a pathway took people uphill to the opposite side of the cage before exiting from a second bird lock, thereby sealing all escape routes for any birds with an urge to leave. The cage's interior, however, attempted to mitigate those types of urges by creating an ultranaturalistic setting of (artificial) rock mounds, cascading waterfalls, small pools, and a variety of hardy plantings, including four twenty-foot-high trees.

The birds were likewise a hardy range, numbering approximately eighty individuals of forty-three species, such as jays, ornamental ducks, ornamental pheasants, trumpeters, gulls, terns, ibises, egrets, and turacos. The engineering to keep the birds comfortable year-round exceeded that of the Bird House, from heated rocks for nonperching birds to infrared heat lamps and pockets of forced warm air heating.[93]

In these ways, the Great Flight Cage was true to its name. Its oversized form created an all-encompassing feeling of being close to wild nature and away from the city through a monumental style that civic-minded Washington held dear. In Reed's judgment the enclosure belonged to the city's panorama of other great architectural works:

> In the wintertime, if you go up to the top of the Washington Monument, up on the far right is the Shrine of the Immaculate Conception, the far left there is the Washington Cathedral, and then the center is the Great Flight Cage. . . . I took somebody up there in the wintertime, some visitor, relative, and looked up there and said, "My God, I've changed the skyline of Washington."[94]

For Reed, the new outdoor aviary could hold its own with other colossi in the urban landscape, illustrating Norma Evenson's observations that monumental schemes are largely based on "an architectural conception of vista and the abstract relation of sculptural masses, rather than on human use."[95] An accident of sightseeing, Reed's scheme was considerably more improvised than those that had been worked out on Washington's Mall since the McMillan Plan of 1901. But his appreciation for the trinity of buildings at a physical remove was characteristic of a monumental gaze as well as a desire to maintain Washington as a stately "city in a park." Such figurations of the Federal City were typical of the moment. In a 1965 report released by the National Capital Planning Commission, for example, urban planners recommended building "an open and horizontal city, replete with broad vistas and extensive parks, its buildings of low or moderate height and well sited on tree-lined streets and avenues."[96] The focus on producing a "monumental statement" at the zoo was loyal to this direction, if somewhat off its chosen path of the Mall and Washington's diagonal and axial streets. As the first entirely new exhibit to emerge from the 1961 plan, officials at the Smithsonian "wanted a statement, and this is about as good a statement as you can get. . . . It is a statement that we're remodeling the zoo."[97]

The statement of the Great Flight Cage was more polysemic than Reed's narrow interpretation. It inspired a set of associations that, like all monuments, was communal in spirit and, like this monument in particular, gave avian expression to white middle-class fears and fantasies in 1960s Washington. Constructions of the cage as

Figure 2.21. *The Great Flight Cage at the National Zoo designed by Richard Dimon, 1965. Courtesy of the Smithsonian National Zoological Park.*

a space of sanctuary were simultaneously layered with other references to flying birds. As Dimon said to the *Washington Star,* "we want you to have a feeling of bird flight . . . from the shape of the arches and from the hilltop site."[98] Reed concurred, referring to the cage as "the beautiful floating one with the outstretched wings of the birds."[99] Publicists for the steel industry were equally drawn to the cage's bird-related form, using lofty language that highlighted the importance of its primary material and presented it as a medium of flight. The enclosure was understood as "soaring 90 feet into the air" with slender steel arches that were likewise "soaring." Its steel cables "sweep to the arch tops, then drop earthward." Its steel mesh's "white, lacy appearance" was "not unlike the clouds into which the birds seem to soar." For Washington's new zoo makers, the Great Flight Cage emerged partly as a spatial metaphor for air travel. It offered its visitors the pleasure of transcending their urban condition through the aesthetics of flying birds, to "see exotic feathered friends against the universal sky so natural to all" and ultimately become "free as a bird."[100]

The zoo's newest exhibit shared its aesthetics with another achievement in regional architecture. Dulles International Airport opened in 1962 in Chantilly, Virginia, as a large-scale homage to modern aviation (Figure 2.22). Designed by Eero Saarinen, the airport had a striking, massive terminal building composed of two leaning rows of forty- to sixty-five-foot pylons that supported a concaved roof suspended between them.[101] Like "the sweep of an airplane wing," according to the local historian Margaret Peck, the roof's curved shape visually conveyed a feeling of flight for Washingtonians who came to use the airport as a gateway for international travel.[102] By the time of the Dulles design, Saarinen was fluent in its primary gesture, having designed the 1960 TWA airport terminal at Idlewild, New York. "Eero's Bird," as *Architectural Review* named it, was an engineering daydream with a strongly avian character.[103] While under construction, *Architectural Forum* documented the TWA terminal's progress with reports that "the concrete bird stands free" and "will soon be ready to 'fly.'"[104] The Dulles design reiterated some of this sensibility and, in the process, gave future visitors of the zoo's Great Flight Cage a reference point for appreciating their new bird enclosure.

But while the sweeping upward lines of Dulles airport encouraged users to fly up and away, the zoo's monument worked in the inverse. Parabolic arches pointed downward, creating a transparent shelter to protect a zoo-going public from the dangers of city space, and commune with bird life at a naturalistic, antiurban remove. An early draft of the design pointed to this fortification wish by envisioning the cage as a geodesic dome of tubular metal, similar to Buckminster Fuller's signature design

Figure 2.22. *Dulles International Airport, Chantilly, Virginia, 1958–63; expanded by Skidmore, Owings & Merrill, 1998–2000. Photograph by Balthazar Korab. Library of Congress, Prints and Photographs Division, Balthazar Korab Archive. LC-DIG-krb-00175.*

and safe from exterior harm.[105] Closer to its debut, Smithsonian publicity and the local press emphasized the cage's "tent-like" shape with ground-level photographs of arches anchored firmly and elegantly in place, a "grounded mobile" equipped with "wind shelters and heated shelters" and so ready for any adversity the surroundings might produce.[106] Moreover, as much as Dimon aimed for feelings of flight, he and his colleagues also "wanted a structure that would enclose happily both the people and the birds."[107] The sentiment was reproduced nicely in a 1973 *Post* article that photographed the Washington's Travelers Aid Society dinner dance against the towering backdrop of the cage. Covering the activities of a "vanishing breed" called the charity ball goer, the article reported that "a lot of people who might easily have had to spend the evening caged up in a hotel ballroom were set free to roam the National Zoological Park last night."[108] Dimon's structure thus towered as a double symbol of white urban flight and fortification erected within a city that had become predominantly African American in composition and concerns. Moving between an architecture of avian-inspired mobility and civic sanctuary, the Great Flight Cage became an imaginative monument to a Washington beyond its slums.

HUMANE NATURALISM

On March 28, 1974, Dr. Reed supervised the demolition of the old Lion House. The operation was swift and decisive, reducing most of the 1891 structure to "dusty rubble and twisted bars" in twelve minutes of bulldozing.[109] The operation's brevity would have suited the director, who was concerned about the possibility of architectural preservationists in the city making a bid for the building's survival. Reed initially made an effort to imagine a place for it in his new zoo, but "no matter what you tried to do with that Lion House, it was still the old Lion House."[110] William Ralph Emerson, a New England architect hired for his talent in rustic and picturesque constructions, designed the building as the first large permanent animal house at the zoo. The finished structure stood as an example of good zoo naturalism, particularly for its use of gray gneiss quarried locally and two watchtowers for appreciating the hilltop views. But, as Heather Ewing notes, the building's austere facade of cages together with the towers also carried accidental connotations of a prison.[111] By the early 1960s these connotations were a point of fixation amid the racialized rhetoric of a zoological slum. "Massive bars and cramped cages represent the old-fashioned menagerie-type display," read the caption to an unflattering photograph of the Lion House in the Smithsonian's May 1961 report (Figure 2.23). The image emphasized the stone structure's horizontal facade with shadowy watchtowers on either end and an exterior overwhelmed by heavy ironwork. The dearth of visitors and invisibility of animal denizens underscored the building's aura of incarceration. Interior photographs of the House often reinforced the connection by showing rows of exposed cats confined in small spaces behind bars, or individuals up against the bars (Figure 2.24).

How Smithsonian officials responded to these particular images is unknown. Worth noting is the larger archive of barriers alongside which any representations of the Lion House would have circulated. As much as urban reformers rehearsed value contrasts between the District's federal and slum architecture, they also reveled in the wire and steel that defined ghetto space in the District. Haynes Johnson's 1967

Massive bars and cramped cages represent the old-fashioned menagerie-type
display. The modern zoo uses moated open-type exhibits.

Figure 2.23. *Lion House exterior at the National Zoo, 1961. Smithsonian Institution Archives.
Record Unit 50, Box 127, Folder: NZP Report of 1961.*

series about poverty for the *Washington Star,* for example, featured photographs of
black youth silhouetted against storefront gates and neighborhood chain-link fences
(Figure 2.25). The series aimed to profile life in Anacostia, where black Washingtonians from the Southwest relocated after urban renewal. By 1967, this neighborhood southeast of the Potomac River was largely African American, featured most
of the District's public housing projects, and experienced regular clashes between
police and residents.[112] More generalized portraits of urban internment likewise embraced the barrier motif, such as a 1969 press photograph of six boys on foot, and
one on a bicycle, racing playfully down a cobblestone street directly toward the
camera, but also toward the coarse wire fencing that stood before and constrained
their play (Figure 2.26). Commonplace to media portrayals of black poverty, these
and other images of confinement informed the view of anyone considering the fate
of zoo buildings in these years and helps explain how, despite decades of minor

Figure 2.24. *"Existing Conditions," in* Master Plan Report, National Zoological Park, *circa 1974. Smithsonian Institution Archives. Record Unit 365, Box 14, Folder 17.*

refurbishments, an exhibit once admired atop the zoo grounds' highest point disappeared from the landscape.

The symbolic significance of razing the Lion House was not lost on Washington's zoo lovers, who took it as a positive step in the long and often-stalled process of zoo renewal. According to Reed, "By the time we got . . . to the Lion House, people were accepting the fact that we were going to be done, that something was happening to the zoo, the zoo was alive, it was going ahead and moving ahead."[113] Much of the zoo's future vitality hinged on removing this public site of death. Along with its penal atmosphere, it remained the traumatic spot of Julie Ann Vogt's death. The Lion House

Figure 2.25. Washington Star *photograph from "Across the River" series on poverty, 1967. Reprinted with permission of the D.C. Public Library, Star Collection; copyright* Washington Post.

had no comfortable place in Washington's new zoo, even as a monument to Julie's life, or, for that matter, the animals that lived and died in its enclosures. In fact, by the second decade of renewal, monuments of any sort were no longer welcome in designs for a revitalized National Zoo.

The new National Zoo makers were disappointed with architectural monumentalism; it had done little to prevent transgressions of proper visitor behavior. Slumlike conduct persisted among zoo goers despite efforts to create a more uplifting setting that would inspire people with the wonder of nature. Memos passed among management, for example, noted a general increase in animal stonings and theft. Dimon's modernist masterpiece in particular posed a problem, with "daily occurrences of kids climbing rocks in the Flight Cage and otherwise being out of order."[114]

Figure 2.26. Washington Star *photograph of children at play in the Federal City, June 29, 1969. Reprinted with permission of the D.C. Public Library, Star Collection; copyright* Washington Post.

The head of zoo police, for his part, was skeptical, speculating that the higher number of incidents might be a result of more intensive reporting and documentation; if visitors were still acting badly, management was also responding with renewed anxiety.[115] As part of that anxiety, deputy zoo director and former FONZ president John Perry proposed a range of remedies to tighten up security, including deploying uniformed boys from the Youth Opportunity Corps to supervise vulnerable areas. Reed was receptive to the idea and honed it further: "Perhaps you could use the boys in the great flight cage to police it, keep it clean, and do certain keeper work in that area and also be doing patrol and observation work."[116]

In addition to exhibit vandalism, the partially renewed zoo was not immune to the civil unrest that had come to define life in Washington, D.C., in the mid-1960s. Zoo officials were aware of this possibility and prepared accordingly, meeting in February 1968 "to discuss problems should civil disturbances occur in Washington."[117] Two months later, the head of Operations and Maintenance thanked the D.C. Police Department and other administrators for their assistance in shutting down zoo buildings and gates on April 2, 5, 6, and 7 "in conjunction with the emergency declared by Mayor Commissioner Walter Washington."[118] After the riots, officials were still on guard when members of the Black Army of Liberation and the Moorish Nation arrived on the grounds on June 5 to conduct a demonstration march, put on an acrobatic performance, and play dance music. The roughly three-hundred-strong group began its procession from the bus parking lot to the east side of the cafeteria before being stopped by zoo police. A follow-up report on the confrontation shared one informant's tip that the gathering "was to be a meeting to plan the peaceful take over of Washington D.C."[119] Public activity of this sort was not only prohibited in the revitalizing National Zoo but actively feared. That management restricted access to their newest animal exhibits during these incidents showed a certain lack of faith in the new zoo architecture's civilizing power.

The turn away from monumentalism was also evidenced in Reed's growing discomfort with his collaborators. In the wake of the bird exhibit design, he complained that Dimon had become too inflated by the experience and had overstepped his authority. A joint trip to tour the hoofstock displays of several European zoos found the young architect more vocal than usual. As Reed recalled, Dimon "now began to tell me what was going to happen, and so we were getting into an area of conflict."[120] When the Commission of Fine Arts, the District's aesthetic watchdog, turned down Dimon's other plans for the zoo, the director was relieved: "I was glad to see him go, because, you know, you don't tell me what to do with animals."[121] Subsequent rejections of other zoo designers by the Commission of Fine Arts as well as the National Capital Planning Commission added to the unpopularity of having "too much architecture" at the National Zoo, a euphemism for buildings that celebrated the designer's ego and technological prowess at the expense of creating an immersive urban nature experience.[122] These designers submitted plans that, according to the architectural historian Suzanne Fauber, ignored the atmosphere of Olmsted's original plan and converted the grounds into "a totally modern showplace using the sixties technology."[123] Reed's solution was to create a new position for a staff architect "to keep the architects under control and keep things moving."[124] Norman Melun was hired in 1970 with experience in other public building projects in the city. He joined the local firm of Faulkner Fryer and Vanderpool and the landscape architect Lester Collins in executing a new master plan for the zoo.

The new plan was formally approved in 1971 by the Smithsonian, the Commission of Fine Arts, and the National Capital Planning Commission, and informally approved that same year by the Friends of the National Zoo.[125] Directors of FONZ applauded the proposal, citing how "it plays up landscape architecture and plays down building architecture. . . . Of particular interest [is] the logical process of elimination of the solutions of more recently modernized zoos." To FONZ's taste, those solutions were overbearing and would not fit "the particular needs" of the National Zoo, which included the need to enhance the grounds' natural features.[126] The defining feature of the 1971 plan was precisely an aversion to overly modern design solutions, following through on an aesthetic naturalism that previous plans had attempted but could not deliver. The DMJM plan, for example, sought as the seventh of eight design principles "to minimize or suppress 'architecture' in the conventional sense; subordinate buildings and other structures to the primary need for proper animal background."[127] The ensuing Great Flight Cage, however, betrayed this intention, even to the point of betraying the new zoo's emergent emphasis on captive reproduction. As Reed recalled, the exhibit "is a show cage. It's not a cage for breeding . . . but the idea is people want to see a lot of birds, and we have a lot of birds in there."[128] Ten years after DMJM's designs, the master plan developed by Faulkner Fryer and Vanderpool bumped the concept of nonarchitecture to number two on their list of fifteen, second only to the related aim of preserving the natural character of the Rock Creek Park site. As quoted in this later plan:

> Landscape is to be the dominant visual factor in designing animal exhibits. Earth bermes, heated caves and underground structures are to be used wherever possible in lieu of conventional buildings.[129]

The firm's drawings of animal exhibits in cross-section illustrated how spaces were sunken into the ground, merging with the landscape (Figure 2.27). While these spaces

Figure 2.27. *Drawing of Lion–Tiger Exhibit at the National Zoo designed by Faulkner Fryer and Vanderpool, 1971. Smithsonian Institution Archives. Record Unit 365, Box 14, Folder 17.*

represented an expansion of physical terrain for inhabitants and spectators alike, they also conformed to the land's gradations and often were partially concealed by them. In the 1971 plan, the optimum exhibit minimized the appearance of any human construction, took maximum advantage of outdoor surroundings, and used "unobtrusive forms of animal containment" such as moats, hidden fences, and glass.[130]

The rejection of big architecture at the National Zoo reflected wider shifts in the District's urban renewal after the mid-1960s. The experience of slum clearance and redevelopment in Southwest Washington taught developers and city dwellers about the pitfalls and racial injustices of unmitigated urban planning. Planners demolished important landmarks, replaced them with suburban-type commercial centers and freeways, and displaced thousands of low-income and African American residents from their neighborhoods.[131] Washingtonians of many racial and ethnic identifications came to understand this process of modernizing the urban landscape as a process of alienating citizens from their collective environs and each other.[132] Built in the late 1960s, the vacancy of I. M. Pei's L'Enfant Plaza spoke directly to such failures. The office and shopping center situated south of the Mall promised Washingtonians their own Rockefeller Center, an agora, and "modern America's most beautiful 'outdoor salon.'"[133] By 1973, however, the plaza's pronounced absence of civic life rendered it another mistake in Southwest's comprehensive renewal: a contrived communal space that was physically and psychologically cut off from its community.[134]

The *Washington Post*'s Wolf Von Eckardt took note of the changing season in renewal efforts. In the 1970s "citizens' opposition and a new public attitude" were "in favor of historic continuity rather than cataclysmic urban renewal."[135] Writing on the District's built environment, Eckardt took part in shaping this attitude, proposing a movement away from "militant Modern architecture" that was embodied most vividly in civic structures like the Kennedy Center and the FBI building. Both, said Eckardt, were "dangerously stretching the human measure."[136] Worse still was the brutalist architecture of the Third Church of Christ, Scientist, erected two blocks from the White House and designed by I. M. Pei & Partners' architect Araldo Cossutta (Figure 2.28). Since Washington was "essentially a garden city," Eckardt believed that this largely windowless and concrete-heavy octagonal bunker with an attached brick plaza was a "rude, utterly inappropriate faux pas" that would "disrupt the order and integrity of a fine street as though you were in suburbia."[137] It belonged to an "architecture of enormity" whose technophilic creators claimed "deep, mystical meaning in the often bizarre concrete sculptures."[138] Eckardt advocated instead for more "humanistic" architecture and planning schemes that extended the neoclassicism and civility of the Beaux Arts movement in France and its incarnation as the City Beautiful in Washington, D.C.[139] In addition to reviving these aesthetic prescriptions for good citizenship and social betterment, urban redesign, according to this critic, should approach the natural environment as a participant in the built world: "It is part of the new humanist architecture to design with nature, to make our buildings part of the natural ecology instead of letting them pollute the earth."[140] Eckardt's post-1960s planning preference was a restorative one in this sense, returning Washingtonians to an ideal of public space that exchanged the often concrete oppressiveness of 1960s modernism for the human sensibility of turn-of-the-century naturalism.

The suggestion that naturalism was somehow more humane than modernism was a racially loaded proposition that Eckardt and his ilk were not prone to acknowledge. If the fallout of 1960s modernism in urban renewal was spatial inequality between poor blacks and the rest of the District's social fabric, the return to a gentler and greener architecture represented a form of soft white power, invoking Anglo-American discourses of racial uplift that were prevalent among nineteenth-century urban progressives and their aesthetic partners. In the vocabulary of urban renewal, "human" had never been race neutral and nature had never been innocent.[141]

The 1970s generation of new zoo makers in Washington excelled in the project of "humanizing" the urban landscape through nature. With the design and construc-

Figure 2.28. *Main entrance to Third Church of Christ, Scientist designed by Araldo Cossutta, Washington, D.C., 1970. Photograph by Matthew G. Bisanz, 2009.*

tion of a new lion and tiger exhibit, zoo renewal became a more muted expression of white urbanism. As the only animal structure in the 1971 plan that was built from scratch, the exhibit was the hallmark achievement of the second phase of National Zoo revitalization, and opened in May 1976. Built on the former site of the original Lion House, the three-acre exhibit was also a reinvention of its 1891 predecessor's rustic aesthetic. Whereas Emerson's design integrated with the surrounding environment through natural materials and hilltop vistas, Avery Faulkner's vision for a big cat display became an inextricable part of the hill itself (Figure 2.29). Save for two glass-faced interior enclosures for intimate female and cub viewing, and a small audiovisual room for screening educational films, the Lion–Tiger Exhibit was an outdoor viewing experience.[142] Three multitiered outdoor theaters in an irregular curvilinear structure fit into the hill's natural topography. Faulkner allotted space for two tiger exhibits and a larger lion exhibit, each variously composed of straight lines and curved segments that conformed to the existing hill. Zoo goers stood on a visitors' walk that outlined the circumference of the entire structure and gazed across a twenty-five-foot-wide watered moat. From there, they could see the cats on four terraced levels with multiple protective dens built into the retaining walls, each with radiant heated floors. The terraced levels featured grass and bamboo, a few large trees, tree trunks, and clusters of rock for terrace steps and decoration. Meanwhile, engineers planned for dangers that the exhibit's aesthetic naturalism might present, including heated moats to prevent a frozen path for animal escapes, electric wires on the shorter surrounding walls should the cats leap onto them, and ladders and safety ropes if anyone fell into the water.[143]

For Reed, it was paramount that the setting did not dwarf the view of the cats with an excess of concrete. Other new animal displays in Europe and the United States had overwhelmed their exhibit with concrete backdrops that were overly sculptural and monolithic in appearance. Critiquing the lion exhibit at the Louisville Zoological Gardens, for example, the director wrote to one museum colleague:

> It gave me the feeling of the awesome proportions of man and some of the ancient Egyptian temples. Of course, I have some violent disagreements with the treatment of the moats. I think they are much too brutal, a little too deep, a little too wide, and give the impression when seeing them of a tremendous brutal barrier.[144]

The Louisville exhibit was an example of what not to build in Washington, D.C. (Figure 2.30). It represented a zoological version of the Third Church of Christ, Scientist, or the Smithsonian's own brutalist "temples" that Eckardt identified as the Hirshhorn and the Air and Space Museum.[145] In Louisville, imposing concrete masses privileged abstract architectural forms, and the egos that created them, over human comfort and intimacy with the natural world. Severe moats, also of concrete, compounded the problem by creating an unpleasant chasm between man and beast. Builders of the National Zoo's big cat display responded to these concerns by softening up the appearance of their primary material. They cast their concrete against irregular board forms that created a rough wood look to all the exhibit walls. The Commission of Fine Arts recommended still more modification: "The random width board form-work should be used in conjunction with the concrete slightly

Figure 2.29. *The Mann Lion–Tiger Exhibit at the National Zoo designed by Faulkner Fryer and Vanderpool, 1976. Smithsonian Institution Archives, Image 92–1787.*

tinted with a warm buff color. Every opportunity should be taken to stay away from the stark gray of raw, untreated concrete."[146] Additionally, gardeners planted ivy vines in a four-foot ledge just beyond the visitor railing, so that greenery would creep downward along the walls toward the moats.

Efforts to naturalize the exhibit as such were in step with other current work in landscape architecture. Reed condemned the Louisville exhibit and others like it, but he applauded the work of Julian George, the Los Angeles landscape architect who designed lakes and cliffs in Southern California with hybrid materials like "soil cement."[147] The director was especially impressed with George's contributions to the San Diego Zoo's Cascade Canyon. The canyon exhibit was built in 1973 to display two different species of African antelope, Lear's macaws, and Malayan

Lion Exhibit Under Construction

SOURCEBOOK

Figure 2.30. *Construction at Louisville Zoological Gardens, 1974. Smithsonian Institution Archives, Image SIA2007–0140.*

tapirs. Central to its appeal was an artificial stream that passed through two artificial waterfalls and a series of rapids before ending in a small lake, from which water was pumped back up a ninety-four-foot landscaped hill to the top of the falls. Cascade Canyon also contained over twenty-thousand feet of sod, transplanted palm trees, and several hundred bushes and ferns "aesthetically placed to simulate a forest glen."[148]

But while George's forest simulation used "picturesque Africa" as its model, the

National Zoo's Lion–Tiger Exhibit represented nature from a domestic perspective.[149] Lester Collins was instrumental in this regard. The landscape architect who was brought in for this second phase of renewal, "to lessen the visual impact of architectural building forms," had a strong nativist streak in his work.[150] Though appreciative of other cultures' interpretations of natural landscape, particularly seventeenth-century France and contemporary Japan, he believed that American landscapes of all kinds were best designed with their Americanness in mind, sensitive to the "heart" of their specific regions.[151] For the creation of domestic outdoor space, for example, Collins praised the West Coast: "Nowhere has the style of outdoor living and swimming pools or backyard eating been done as well as in California. California gardens serve their culture."[152] Designs for the Lion–Tiger Exhibit observed this homegrown ethic by keeping the cats on soil that was recognizably Washingtonian. This was an overall strategy in National Zoo renewal. Planners avoided organizing exhibits around "zoogeographic" regions, that is, the continental origins of animal species. Melun in particular was explicit about the aim to keep displays explicitly related to their locality:

> While the landscape here already exists, we have no plans to alter it drastically or to attempt to create bits of Asia, Africa or other places that differ radically from our Middle Atlantic environment. Our objective is to maintain an informal American park with an air of studied negligence.[153]

The regional focus gave visitors a chance to appreciate the reworking of the historic Lion Hill on its own bucolic terms. Visual and textual material that accompanied the inverted hill reinforced its nativism with photographs of the old Lion House, accounts of the *ex-situ* breeding program, and information about Dr. William Mann, the National Zoo's previous director, after whom the exhibit was formally named.[154]

The softer and more self-reflexive renewal embodied by the zoo's new lion and tiger complex created an environment that eventually blurred the identities of its feline inhabitants with distinguished members of white Washington. Dedicating the exhibit to Mann went some way toward the conflation, a process that was itself marked by a good-humored confusion between man and beast. As Reed conveyed to other planners in a 1973 memo:

> The homonymous problem arises between his name "Mann" and the common generic name, homo sapiens, for "man." They both have the same pronunciation but "man" has many different connotations in relation to the animals on exhibition. We must therefore think of a good title for the new feline exhibit that will explain

definitively that this exhibit is named for Dr. William M. Mann. Suggestions are earnestly sought; however the suggestion that it be called the "Mann Cat House" is forthwith rejected.[155]

That visitors might confuse the species identity of the exhibit occupants was a real possibility and best avoided if zoo renewal was to maintain its legitimacy. Officials settled on "The William M. Mann Lion and Tiger Exhibit," but its attempted division between human and animal did not hold. Local press at the exhibit's opening ceremonies promoted the collapse. Under the headline "Kings of the Jungle Are Pride of the Hill," Judith Martin at the *Washington Post* played with the double meaning of "pride": "A pride of Smithsonian officials is a small group that can show off a spectacular new exhibit facility, completed within its budget and deadline." Also on the hill that evening were "three lions, four white tigers and several hundred of their or the institution's friends." This second group was, if not quite interchangeable, highly comparable. Martin reported that the lion and tigers, "leaping playfully in the grass," had a late supper, while "other participants were . . . promptly given picnic baskets and bottles of wine and told they could wander wherever they liked." Beyond the shared behavior of leisurely roaming the zoo's greens, the animals and guests also appeared to share an appreciation for high-end city living: "The tigers, especially have been wallowing in luxury in their new quarters, heading for the moat like a bunch of singles to an Arlington roof pool."[156] In-house photographs of the cats that circulated in Smithsonian publications of various kinds emphasized the feeling that in their new living complex, the animals had something in common with other affluent citizens in the Federal City—namely, a restored look of ease in and ownership of urban space. The big cats were frequently depicted in states of active play that only spacious quarters could facilitate. They also appeared in states of repose that stressed the tranquillity of their new urban settings, complete with shady trees, grassy terraces, a large pool, and pleasant views of their genteel neighbors across the way (Figures 2.31–2.32).

The National Zoo's second period of redevelopment thus offered city dwellers a more tempered vision of urban improvement from a decade prior, one disenchanted with monumental architecture and responsive to the dashed hopes of artificially imposed bourgeois public space in the city. The preferred form of revitalization was ultimately one that could resurrect the aesthetic power of an understated naturalism for its zoo-going public and correct the dehumanizing fiascos of an earlier generation of urban renewal schemes. Only then could planners adequately clear the zoological slum, expunge its blackness from the District's civic imaginary, and secure a physical and figurative place for a less beastly Washington.

Figures 2.31 and 2.32. *Residents of the Mann Lion–Tiger Exhibit at the National Zoo, circa 1976. Courtesy of the Smithsonian National Zoological Park.*

3

Mohini's Bodies

In a 1977 letter to Dr. Porter Keir, director of the National Museum of Natural History, National Zoo director Dr. Theodore Reed expressed doubts that the zoo's rare female white Bengal tiger would survive the following year. Mohini, a Hindu name meaning "enchantress," was approaching nineteen years of age—old for the species—and had begun to experience kidney problems, vision problems, and a lack of coordination with her hindquarters. Reed's letter inquired if the museum would be interested in taking the beloved animal, posthumously:

> Would you please assess this unusual color phase of tiger and determine if you want all of her, parts of her, and what you plan to do with her. Let us make plans before we are faced with a crash decision of having a carcass on our hands. (What a hell of a way to talk about such a lovely animal as "Mohini.")[1]

Reed's discomfort was understandable. His inquiry divided the popular matriarch of the National Zoo's white tiger collection into a collection of body parts, a crude way to describe a tiger that had contributed much to the institution in her lifetime and assumed the status of a nearly human subject. The zoo acquired her in 1960 from an Indian maharaja. In Washington, D.C., she took up residence in the old Lion House, became the public face of the Friends of the National Zoo (a private citizens' group responsible for zoo revitalization in the District), and was the focus of concerted efforts to reproduce a white tiger line, with success in 1964, 1969, and 1970. Two years later, she was temporarily boarded at Chicago's Brookfield Zoo with her white offspring, Rewati, before returning home to a remodeled lion–tiger complex where she lived out the rest of her days until her euthanization on April 2, 1979.

Predating a civic fixation with giant pandas, Mohini was the Federal City's mid-century pride and joy, and the first white tiger exported to the United States. Born from a white-colored male and an orange-colored female, the great cat was considered a partial albino, a genetic mutation marked in tigers by a white coat with black or ash gray stripes, a pink nose and pads, and blue eyes.[2] The combination was a statistical anomaly that connected Mohini to a longer history of human fascination with animal albinism and associated conditions. People from across cultures and generations have given white creatures—from deer to pythons to whales—special spiritual, recreational, legislative, and scientific attention. Many of these curiosities have lived in modern zoos: for example, the Victorian exhibition of Toung Talloung, a white elephant from Rangoon, at the London Zoo; the thirty-seven-year career of Snowflake, the albino Western Lowland gorilla, at the Barcelona Zoo; Blizzard and King Louie, a white bison and white alligator currently on exhibit at the Assiniboine Park Zoo in Winnipeg and Louisville Zoo in Kentucky, respectively. White tigers have also lived in zoos, as well as in circuses and, since the early 1980s, on the Las Vegas strip.[3]

Against a familiar tenet that these and other atypically blanched animals are inherently and unanimously wondrous, this chapter considers how the enchantments of Mohini revolved around and were directed toward the particularities of midcentury zoo renewal in Washington, D.C. Mohini was bought, exhibited, and bred for her white phenotype and the white racial identities of her adoring fans. She gave her zoo public a positive reflection of themselves and their prospects as bourgeois nature-loving citizens through shifting representations of what a female white tiger's body could look like and mean. These representations were seemingly contradictory, they occasionally overlapped with each other, and they helped produce a whiteness that became integral to the renewed National Zoo and its mandate of wildlife conservation. Through them, Mohini corrected the zoo's shameful reputation as a "zoological slum" and became part of an antiurban campaign to restore the institution to its original stature as truly national. Such was the wonder of this white tiger's whiteness.

Two of Mohini's most discernible and complicated representations are my focus here, particularly as they circulated in the National Zoo's discursive apparatus of popular, scientific, and in-house media, and in Washingtonians' recollections of the tiger: Mohini as a foreign body and Mohini as a domestic body. Both highly gendered and classed, one body was also fiercely exoticized and eroticized, while the other appeared as a familiar, desexualized model of motherhood. The disposition of whiteness in both these bodies was not the same either. Toward the same revitalizing ends, each drew on, and fetishized, Mohini's physical characteristics and their associated behaviors quite differently. Viewers of the foreign body registered the color of her fur and facial features as signs of noble Indian birth and esteemed cultural heritage; viewers of the domestic body took them as signs of American normalcy and health. As an uneven pair, these two primary forms of bodily representation enabled the tiger's spectators to tentatively fashion their own white subjectivity in a period that saw American recolonization of developing nations and a shrinking confidence in the future of racial whiteness within the United States. But neither was stable. When unruly animality and genetic illness forced itself into the picture, Mohini's bodies took a sharp and unexpected turn, suggesting that if animals participated in the National Zoo's reconstruction as a breeding ground for racial identities in the 1960s and 1970s, they could also throw those identities into disarray.

THE FOREIGN BODY: MOHINI AS BENGAL TIGER-WOMAN

Washington's new zoo makers were initially enamored with Mohini for her exotic pedigree. The white tiger's courtly Indian origins infused her with much prestige, which by 1960 the National Zoo badly needed. Residency with an Indian maharaja constructed the big cat as an exotic royal treasure and, when adequately anthropomorphized, as Indian royalty itself. Both inflections worked well for zoo leaders and members of FONZ, who were increasingly vexed about the National Zoo's position on the totem pole of cultural enrichment. Reed, the zoo's director since 1958, had already labeled the zoo a slum that was unable to satisfy its original mission. John Perry, a former president of FONZ turned assistant zoo director, took a more positive spin, arguing that while the National Zoo had an inescapably "municipal character," it was also a "tremendous potential resource" for public nature education.[4] The zoo's experience with a new orange-colored tiger was another example of status anxiety. Obtained from India in the early days of Reed's directorship, the male cub traveled around to the stores of a local food chain on a borrowed circus wagon while zoo staff conducted a publicity-seeking contest to name him. Smithsonian officials admonished Reed for his lowbrow antics, suggesting that it violated the "proper spirit" of the institution. Reed himself was disappointed with the list of suggestions from city youth, particularly the persistent bid to name the tiger Mighty Mo, after the company's hamburger. "There was one Shere Cam. Somebody had read [Joseph Rudyard] Kipling. And Kitty, and Pussy, and Yellow, or Stripsey—all sorts of stupid, crazy names."[5] Reed was hoping for an Indian moniker "that would mean something. But the American high school kids in Washington D.C. ain't got no couth."[6] Judges conceded to the popular will and named the new cub Mighty Mo.

The National Zoo's acquisition of its first white tiger began to correct the provincialism by operating as a classic Orientalist undertaking with 1960s American flourishes. Edward Said's concept of Orientalism is a fitting frame for understanding the event. For Said, Orientalism is a mode of both representing non-Western geographies and, in turn, materially shaping Western ones: a "mode of discourse with supporting institutions, vocabulary, scholarship, imagery, doctrines, even colonial bureaucracies and colonial styles." Said further emphasizes that Orientalism was born from, though is not exclusive to, a specific nineteenth-century relationship between France, England, and what was understood as "the Orient," including India and the Bible lands. American versions of Orientalism flourished after World War II, styling itself after its European predecessors.[7] More specifically, Mohini's relocation from India followed a cultural script of white heterosexual men traveling to colonial peripheries for encounters with exotic otherness. These encounters were almost always eroticized and often worked out through the bodies of non-Western women. They enacted what Griselda Pollack describes as the Orientalist siting of sexuality, which drew on the social and economic exploitation of nonwhite people by white people to conjure up European male heterosexual representations of erotic femininity. The effect, Pollack notes, was a mixed economy of signs, wherein race stood for sex and vice versa.[8] By the mid-twentieth century, the colonial peripheries had changed, at least politically, and so had their visitors. India, in this case, had achieved sovereignty from England, and its aristocracy was attracting another imperial power in the form of American businessmen, thereby ushering in a new era of colonial relations between the United States and the Republic.

One of these men was Ralph Scott, a Washington attorney, realtor, and avid safari goer. Known to fellow hunting enthusiasts as "one-shot Scott," Scott was responsible for the capture of Mighty Mo and the cub's transformation into a colonial symbol under American capitalism, which included, in addition to the fast-food naming contest, a press-friendly picnic on Scott's Maryland farm for a group of children from India. The photojournalistic combination of Indian children and an Indian tiger brought a little bit of the subcontinent to readers of the *Washington Star* while allowing the foreign youngsters "whose parents are on various missions here" to experience a white colonial engagement with the natural world. Dressed in smart Western clothing, the children were shown eating ice cream and petting the young cub in the firm hands of the zoo's senior keeper of cats, Burt Barker.[9] For his next act, Scott proposed to Reed over cocktails that they obtain a white tiger for the National Zoo. Scott had seen one of these animals after staying with Martand Singh, the last maharaja of Rewa, as a paying guest on a hunting trip.[10] Reed, tired from his dealings with Scott over Mighty Mo, was wary at first. But the account of a white tiger proved irresistible to the director, who had never heard of such a creature, and initially assumed it would be "some washed out, light yellow thing, probably [a] scroungy, mangy, crazy thing."[11] Upon seeing film footage of Scott's travels, Reed was re-educated on the beauty of these animals and agreed to pursue acquisition.

The maharaja of Rewa was the only known private keeper of white tigers. Living a princely existence in a now-independent country, the aristocrat and his animal collection were, to his American guests, a final gasp of traditional India, a means, as Said observes of postwar Orientalism at large, to "carry on as if nothing had happened."[12] There was no shortage of colonial nostalgia in Reed's eventual visit to Singh's palace in the town of Govindgarh: "The only thing out there were some chikaras and the white tigers. . . . It was very, very nice, lots of marble, big banyan tree out in front, right of Kipling."[13] Singh began breeding white tigers on his family estate after supervising the capture of a rare white male cub in 1951 from the jungles of Central India. In 1958, the tiger, named Mohan ("Enchanter"), mated with an orange-colored female tiger and subsequently sired a litter of white cubs, of which Mohini was one. With diets of sixty pounds of goat meat a day, the two-year-old cubs were reportedly a drain on the maharaja's depleting resources, prompting him to agree to donate two other whites, Raja and Rani, to the New Delhi Zoo and sell Mohini to the National Zoo.[14] The $10,000 acquisition was made possible through corporate money. John Kluge, president of Metromedia Broadcasting and an acquaintance of Scott's, agreed to fund the purchase and donate the rarity to the National Zoo as a gift to American children.[15] Mohini's acquisition was also made possible through the permission of President Dwight Eisenhower, who had seen one of the maharaja's white tigers at an agricultural exhibit in India and was willing to overlook raised eyebrows over what amounted to a big business donation to a Smithsonian organization. On October 18, 1960, with traveler's checks tucked into a newly purchased Abercrombie & Fitch money belt, Reed embarked on "his flight to the Orient" in the company of Barker.[16]

Reed narrated his Indian experience most prominently in the pages of *National Geographic*.[17] A May 1961 article, titled "Enchantress!," began with the zoo director's foray into a staple site of exotic otherness, identified by Singh himself as "the harem courtyard":

> The door creaked open—revealing a gorgeous creature with inquisitive gaze focused on us. She stared with calm curiosity, then walked slowly toward us with the dignity of one to the palace born.
>
> As she came closer, I was astonished by her perfect development. Her ice-blue eyes were peculiarly aloof, yet inquisitive. I extended my clenched hand in the

experienced animal handler's form of greeting. Daintily, she licked my knuckles. Fortunately, bars separated us—her fangs were three inches long.[18]

So described, Reed's first encounter with his future zoo resident was sexually charged. It followed the familiar narrative structure of the white European gentleman entering into the forbidden and intimate space of Oriental femininity. The revelation beyond the door anticipated Malek Alloula's 1981 meditation on the courtyard visitor as he who "having lifted the curtain . . . roams openly throughout the harem, undisturbed, observing at leisure the life that is hidden from indiscreet eyes."[19] The subjects of Alloula's reading were women who posed as harem dwellers for postcard photographers in French Algeria. Drinking coffee, smoking hookahs, these women appeared in a state of perpetual languor that spoke of both their sexual availability and remoteness. In the maharaja's courtyard, Reed's introductory description of harem life expressed a similar movement, centered on the figure of the as-yet-unidentified white tiger. Her slow approach, aloof yet inquisitive looks, and tongue that reached through bars established an aura of simultaneous proximity and distance that defines Oriental allure. But unlike Alloula's subjects, the species identity of the Maharaja's harem dweller was mutable. Features of the "gorgeous creature" under Reed's gaze were not specific to animal or human. Made possible by the enigmatic setting, the confusion was sequential, provocative, and heavily gendered. At first, Reed's referent appeared human, exceptional in her physique and composure. But the extended appendage of the animal handler—clenched in a gesture of phallic power—marked a turning point in the scene, human blended into tiger, replete with licks and fangs. Thus Reed's opening passage constructed his chosen animal as a woman of posh Eastern origins while also inscribing the profile of that imagined woman with a distinct animality. Both were enticing to the American zoo man.

The photographs in "Enchantress!" supported the textual representation of a seductive Bengal tiger-woman. In seven short pages, the staff photographer Thomas J. Abercrombie gave readers penetrative views of the National Zoo's newest cat and the palatial quarters she had previously inhabited. The extent to which these images amounted to a form of visual penetration was suggested in Reed's own commentary on the photographer's practice. Reed doubted in the article if "the tiger ever saw [Abercrombie's] face—she thinks he has a telephoto nose and range-finder eyes."[20] Such dedication produced pictures that satisfied the magazine's largely middle-class American readership and orientalized their sense of white tigers. The crowning image of the piece, large and opposite the graphic of Singh's family crest bearing a white tiger, was the portrait of Mohini (see Plate 4). Like other portraits in the *National Geographic* portfolio, the photograph gave perceptual and conceptual access to an unfamiliar subject, humanizing it through a face-to-face visibility while keeping its strangeness intact. Catherine Lutz and Jane Collins elaborate on this staple strategy for the magazine:

> The portrait allows for scrutiny of the person, the search for and depiction of character. It gives the ideology of individualism full play, inviting the belief that the individual is first and foremost a personality whose characteristics can be read from facial expression and gestures.[21]

By giving the animal's face over to the viewers' inspection, Abercrombie's portrait of Mohini accomplished this humanization and elevated the tiger to regal status. The cat appeared more magnificent than the domestic cats of American households and the tigers of most current American zoos. Against the cat's black stripes, light gray fur veered closer to the nobility of white. Blue eyes, pale and clear, loosely referenced the blue blood and gemstones of royalty, while pink tear ducts, nose, and tongue signified a fleshy vulnerability, as if still human despite her rank as *Panthera tigris*. What interrupted this otherwise straightforward anthropomorphic production was the subject's snarling facial expression. An open mouth laid four gleaming white fangs bare along with Mohini's identity as a tiger. Whether the snarl was prompted by aggressive handling or otherwise induced, Abercrombie had captured an instant of the cat's animality that troubled any uniform understanding of Mohini as an Indian highness, matching Reed's textual blurring between foreigner and feline.

Subsequent photographs added to the complexity of Mohini's exoticism by situating tigers in various scenes of India before its independence. Some depicted the maharaja's palace riches, including a state coach and a lavish throne room decorated with mounted tigers. Another page featured images of white and yellow cubs at play and an orange mother tiger guarding over them, as palace matriarch. Still other images showed the harem quarters, pictured deep within the palace recesses, and looking decrepit (Figure 3.1). Shot from above, these courtyard photographs displayed white tigers roaming partitioned spaces with deteriorated walls and soiled floors, and feeding on dropped meat "where veiled beauties once lounged."[22] The top-down perspective recalled what Mary Louise Pratt identifies as common in Western travel narratives: a "monarch-of-all-I-survey" scene that has historically established a relation of dominance between imperialists and their "others." Travelers after decolonization, however, looked down over unfamiliar places and saw landscapes and cityscapes of disorder, absence, and ugliness, aesthetic evaluations that helped negate national struggles for independence.[23] This was the view offered in these courtyard photographs, but not without the satisfaction of having taken one

Figure 3.1. *The maharaja of Rewa's harem quarters in* National Geographic, *May 1961. Courtesy Thomas J. Abercrombie/ National Geographic Creative.*

of India's remaining treasures back to the United States. Mixed in with other photographs in the article, readers could see the repeated image of a caged white tiger ready for transport.

Representations of the National Zoo's female white tiger on American soil continued to seduce the zoo-going public through appeals to the animal's royal roots and harem upbringing. In visual images especially, Mohini most often appeared as a body in languid repose. Shortly after the cat's arrival in Washington, D.C., the *Washington Star* staff photographer Paul Schmick circulated an image in the popular press of the feline stretched out in her new home at the National Zoo's Lion

New knowledge about wildlife reveals that

Zoos Drive
Animals Psycho

A zoo orangutan
inert and morose

NOVEMBER 8 · 1968 · 40¢

Plate 1. *Cover of* Life *Magazine, November 8, 1968.*

Plate 2. *Carrie Mae Weems,* Some Laughed Long & Hard & Loud, *1995–96. Copyright Carrie Mae Weems. Courtesy of the artist and Jack Shainman Gallery, New York.*

Steel for Strength

Steel for the birds

This Great Flight Cage houses a variety of exotic birds from all over the world. Opened last summer at the National Zoological Park in Washington, D.C., the imaginative structure was built of steel for beauty as well as for economy. It was cited for "excellent engineering" in the 1964 Design in Steel Award Program sponsored by the American Iron and Steel Institute.

Visitors can enter the cage through covered walkways and observe a variety of birds. The aviary is built of six steel arches, a central steel mast, two miles of steel cable, and a 'web' woven from vinyl-covered steel wire. The web

alone is strong enough to withstand a 100 mph wind.

Bethlehem supplied the structural steel for the arches and mast. We also furnished the supporting steel cables.

Bird cages or gymnasiums . . . schools, skyscrapers, bridges . . . steel is the ideal structural material for strength and economy. Bethlehem research is developing better and stronger steels for tomorrow's needs.

Architect: *Daniel, Mann, Johnson and Mendenhall*. General Contractor and Steel Erector: *Edrow Engineering Co., Inc*. Structural Engineer: *Donald J. Neubauer*. Consulting Detailer: *Rick Engineering*. Fabricator: *Fabricators' Steel Corp*.

BETHLEHEM STEEL

Plate 3. *Bethlehem Steel Corporation national advertisement featuring Great Flight Cage designed by DMJM, 1965. Smithsonian Institution Archives, Image SIA2014–01213.*

Enchantress!

QUEEN OF AN INDIAN PALACE,
A RARE WHITE TIGRESS
COMES TO WASHINGTON

By THEODORE H. REED, D.V.M.
Director, National Zoological Park, Smithsonian Institution

Photographs by THOMAS J. ABERCROMBIE
National Geographic Staff

"THE HAREM COURTYARD lies beyond this
door," said His Highness, the Maharaja of
Rewa, as he handed a servant a big brass key.
"In my grandfather's day you would have been in
trouble just for standing here—fanatic retainers,
razor-sharp swords, and all the traditional amenities."

The door creaked open—revealing a gorgeous creature with inquisitive gaze focused on us. She stared
with calm curiosity, then walked slowly toward us
with the dignity of one to the palace born.

As she came closer, I was astonished by her perfect
development. Her ice-blue eyes were peculiarly aloof,
yet inquisitive. I extended my clenched hand in the
experienced animal handler's form of greeting. Daintily, she licked my knuckles. Fortunately, bars separated us—her fangs were three inches long.

Here at last was one of the rare white tigers for
which I had come halfway around the world. Her
stripes were black, shading into brown, but her main
coat was eggshell white instead of the normal rufous
orange. Exotic coloring and magnificent physique

628

Plate 4. *Portrait of Mohini in* National Geographic, *May 1961.*

Plate 5. *Scenes from "White Tiger in My House" in* National Geographic, *April 1970.*

Southern California needs a wildlife refuge. For humans.

Remember Southern California? The place people used to go to get away from it all. Now, it all is here:

Traffic.

Factories.

Ghettos.

Ticky-tacky housing.

Unbreathable air.

Unpalatable water.

All the wonderful by-products of progress.

The rush West didn't give Southern California a chance to get organized. It grew up too fast. Bulldozed hill by bulldozed hill. One stucco-lined street after another.

Whatever happened to the San Fernando Valley?

Enough of history. What about today? After three decades of heaping civilization upon the land, perhaps we're wising up. Thinking things through. Planning for tomorrow. Before it's too late.

Unfortunately, compared to what we once had, there's precious little good land left. Livable land that's never been black-topped or super-developed or defoliated. The kind of land young men used to go West for. The kind of rich California ranchland Walter Vail bought in 1904 to establish a giant cattle empire.

But, this is 1971. Nostalgia is about as useful as hindsight. Isn't it a little late to close the barn door?

No.

Thirty-five miles due east of Laguna Beach, about halfway between Los Angeles and San Diego is the very land Walter Vail kept from the clutches of progress. One hundred and forty square miles of it. For sixty years, while Southern California boomed and suburbanized, no one but the Vails, their ranch hands and their friends set foot on the property. Until 1964, all those miles of gently rolling grasslands, oak-studded hills and mountain plateaus were the exclusive domain of Black Angus cattle and their brethren.

Rancho California

For the past six years, this 95,000-acre chunk of yesterday has been Rancho California; a very carefully planned refuge for people who want to take another crack at living. This time, with a very real sense of knowing what *not* to do. And a plan for tomorrow that says *no* to a lot of things that ruined a large part of Orange and Los Angeles Counties.

How big is 95,000 acres? You could get three and a half San Franciscos in it. You could spend all day at Rancho California and only see a quarter of it. You could stand on its northeastern border and be fifty miles from Palm Springs, or climb a hill on its western edge and see the Pacific Ocean only twelve miles away.

What's happened to the Vail Ranch since it became Rancho California? We know what you're thinking and you're wrong. It hasn't been mindlessly bulldozed, blacktopped or stuccoed. It hasn't been turned into a crazy-quilt of instant suburbs (go ahead, try to spot a neon sign). Oh, there's been development. Six years and over $100 million worth. But it doesn't stick out like a sore thumb. That's the whole idea.

Rancho California is a place where you can buy land. If you've got extra dollars and a good tax counselor, you know why that's a good idea. Rancho's also a place where you can buy refuge from environmental abuse. If you've got eyes, ears, and a nose, you know why *that's* a good idea.

Pick a day to get away from the way you live. Come to Rancho. You'll like what you see. You'll like what you hear. Its sounds are the sounds of a new life being born: tractors in grape vineyards and citrus farms. Families building new homes out of old dreams. Thoroughbred hoofs on the training center track. Men's boots on wooden walks in the Plaza. Spinning reels on Vail Lake. Children singing in a brand new school. Interstate trucks pulling up to low, modern industrial plants (no pollution-belchers). A constant ocean breeze rustling through oak trees and across vast open fields.

The funny smell is clean air.

If you've ever had the urge to go back in time without giving up a lot of modern conveniences, come down to Rancho California.

See what it was like to own a piece of the West when the West was worth owning.

Rancho California: A Project of Kaiser Aetna

Plate 6. *Real estate advertisement in* San Diego Magazine, *1971.*

Plate 7. *Cover of Wild Animal Park brochure, 1976.*

Plate 8. *White rhino pair on hillside at Wild Animal Park,* Zoonooz, *May 1971. Courtesy of the Zoological Society of San Diego.*

Figure 3.2. Washington Star *photograph of Mohini at the National Zoo, 1961. Reprinted with permission of the D.C. Public Library, Star Collection; copyright* Washington Post.

House (Figure 3.2). A few months later, Mohini made the cover of "This Week in the Nation's Capital." The guidebook for tourists showed the tiger in the same space and pose.[24] Other zoo promoters used archival photographs of Mohini in India, publishing images of her lounging atop the crate that carried her from Govindgarh to the Federal City.[25] The most striking and well-circulated example of the trope was an illustration commissioned by FONZ in 1966 (Figure 3.3). Created to give "the Friends and the Zoo just the extra touch that's needed," the black-and-white drawing of Mohini became the organization's trademark. Membership cards, stationery, and the masthead for FONZ's newsletter, *Spots and Stripes*, were a few of its venues and a reminder that the white tiger at rest, with an outstretched hindquarter and tail, was Mohini's ideal state.

The recurrent theme of a reclining animal body helped retain the twinned femininity and foreignness that Reed and his colleagues generated through the tiger's acquisition narrative. Mohini's was a body that did not appear in vertical positions customary of occidental masculinity. With the repetition of lateral lines, the tiger's

Figure 3.3. *Kiosk with FONZ-commissioned illustration of Mohini, 1966. Reprinted with permission of the D.C. Public Library, Star Collection; copyright* Washington Post.

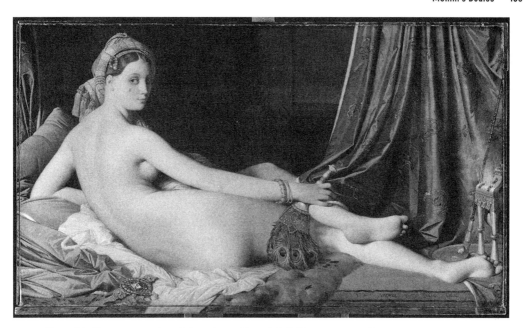

Figure 3.4. *Jean-Auguste-Dominique Ingres,* Grand Odalisque, *1814. Oil on canvas, 91 x 162 cm. Copyright RMN-Grand Palais / Art Resource, New York.*

body became situated within the aesthetic tradition of the odalisque. Recalling Jean-Auguste-Dominique Ingres's *Grand Odalisque* (1814), Mohini's physical form was frequently pictured as horizontality incarnate (Figure 3.4). Like Ingres's use of the "serpentine line" to sensualize the female body, Mohini's stylized body appeared sensual via her extended limbs and serpentine tail.[26] The tiger was an elongated figure that stressed what Reed called "the beautiful line of her back" and what he also identified as a physical quality that distinguished her from her siblings.[27]

Feminist art historians have made a strong case for the image of a nude or seminude female subject, lying in the luxurious confines of an Eastern court, bath, or boudoir, as a symptom and instrument of Orientalism.[28] Both a high art and popular figure in the Western catalog of Eastern visual culture, the odalisque, as such, was produced and consumed as a sexual fantasy with ethnographic trappings. Jo Anna Isaak's analysis of Henri Matisse's odalisques is exemplary in this regard. Isaak locates Matisse's paintings of reclining Moroccan female nudes within the artist's personal creed that art should be the equivalent of a comfortable chair, capable of providing relaxation to the fatigued (male) viewer (Figure 3.5). The women who sat for Matisse, as models for his odalisque works, helped create this comfortable experience—for

Figure 3.5. *Henri Matisse,* Reclining Odalisque (Harmony in Red), *1927. Oil on canvas, 38.4 x 55 cm. Photograph by Malcolm Varon. Image copyright The Metropolitan Museum of Art. Image source: Art Resource, New York. Copyright 2014 Succession H. Matisse / Artists Rights Society (ARS), New York.*

both patron and artist—but not in any sense that could be called empirically accurate. Despite his claims to their ethnographic authenticity, the painter had no access to harems while living in North Africa; Islamic holy law, Moroccan politics, and his own reclusiveness conspired against it. Matisse's odalisques came out of Nice, painted in Riviera hotel rooms staged with French women, props, and souvenirs, and inspired by the harem iconography in earlier French paintings and popular postcards.[29] These Orientalist nudes were thus part of a larger colonial practice of conjuring up a feminine Arab subaltern for and from the contentment of Western male heterosexuality.

The collective construction of Mohini as an odalisque shared some of Matisse's appetites for comfortable exotic subjects and expanded its viewership, echoing Carol Ockman's point that both male and female spectators enjoyed odalisques.[30] Like

Matisse's figures, the often-reclining Mohini was appealing to zoo goers in ways that animals in American zoos had been since the nineteenth century: figures of rest and rejuvenation for a city-weary public. Testifying to the tiger's recuperative powers, visitors in the first year of Mohini's National Zoo residency stood at her cage—painted "tiger orange" to show off her anomalous white fur—for hours at a time.[31] Lucy Mann, zoo publicist and wife of former director William Mann, described them such: "They'd practically bring their lunch with them and just spend the day standing there to watch this beautiful animal."[32] Fan letters to the feline articulated the relaxation she induced in those who watched her, calling attention to how her horizontality was part of the pleasure. Dr. George White of Vienna, Virginia, a long-time Mohini admirer, fondly recalled "a magic queen" of "1001 nights" with "flowing movements and hypnotic eyes."[33] Deirdre W. Magnusson wrote, "I remember the first time I saw you—you were lying in the corner of your confine. Such majesty and serenity."[34] Marcine and Melanie Goodloe of Kensington, Maryland, described the sight of Mohini as "a lovely sunset that you just have to glance at to know it's the most beautiful thing God has created."[35] The tiger had fans within the National Zoo as well. The staff photographer Jessie Cohen took scores of photographs of the feline for various zoo publications, many of which conveyed Mohini's soothing presence on display and the warmth she could generate in her viewers. A typical example showed the cat reclined on the floor of her exterior enclosure in the Lion House (Figure 3.6). Taken at or near ground level, the photograph depicted Mohini leaning against a perforated barrier. Light shines through, casting the animal in a dappled glow of shadow and sun suggestive of a late-day calm and secluded quarters in desert climes.

Thus, like Matisse's odalisques, American views of the white tiger were embroiled in a rich signification system that called attention to Mohini's state of repose. Charles Cooke, for example, was smitten with the big cat. Writing in the *Georgetowner,* he recalled:

> I joined the hypnotized crowd in front of her cage and, for about an hour, gave her my full attention. She upstaged all the other animals, sometimes without moving a muscle. Much of the time she just sat and contemplated us with regal tranquility—a heavenly tigress out of an opium dream—ermine coated, jet-striped, with sapphire eyes.[36]

Cooke's profile piece on "the Enchantress" took rhetorical liberties that captured the densely coded experience of looking at Mohini. Bearing out Pollack's observation that "the Orientalist fantasy usually depended upon the clothes," the journalist draped the tiger's body in furs, gave her jewels for eyes, and topped her off with an aura of tranquillity fit for royalty and/or drug-induced phantasms.[37] Not

Figure 3.6. *Mohini reclining at the National Zoo, circa 1966. Courtesy of the Smithsonian National Zoological Park.*

surprisingly, the article piqued the interest of the National Zoo's management, who forwarded copies to Ralph Scott, Phil Cowar of Metromedia, and the maharaja of Rewa himself. In Cooke's version of the Lion House, Mohini became the reclining subject of a zoological scopophilia whose very captivity recalled the sexual enslavement of other Eastern beauties. But like many of Western culture's most coveted odalisques, this slave girl was also exceptional in pedigree, less a servant to her sexual captors than a kind of captor herself, capable of holding her own spectators hostage to her visual splendor. Captivity was at its most intense when Mohini, "to the delight of her audience . . . deigned to roll over on her back and play with an imaginary ball of tigernip."[38] The sight of the white tiger's body belly-up in full sprawl was the apex of onlookers' raptness and the height of her appearance as an odalisque.

Mohini did not always perform her role as hoped. Occasionally the tiger failed to succumb to her public's expectations of seeing a foreign body. These failures were also recorded by her viewers and complicated their uniform readings of Mohini as a quiescent object of Orientalist desire. On December 1, 1960, the *Washington Post* ran a wire photograph that was also picked up by the *New York Times* and the *Dallas Times Herald*. Taken at New York's Idlewild Airport en route to Washington, the image was a head shot of the tiger in a glass-enclosed, steel-barred cage. With eyes wide open and mouth agape, Mohini looked neither relaxed nor relaxing. The *Post* captioned her a "Disenchanted 'Enchantress'" and explained her expression as displeasure over her arrival in New York. The Dallas newspaper described it as a snarl, while the *New York Times,* eager perhaps to portray the tiger as content in their city, insisted it was a yawn.[39] Mohini's ceremonial presentation to President Eisenhower on the White House lawn was another instance of odalisque imagery troubled by its animal signifier. Upon seeing the tiger pacing, growling, and leaping about in her cage, the president verbally declined to get in, prompting the *Chicago Tribune* to report that "neither the President nor the tiger was particularly enchanted by their meeting."[40] Moreover, the president was, as Reed remembered it, struck by Mohini's dirty coat: "Eisenhower came out, looked at it. 'Well, it's not quite as white as the one I saw in India.'"[41] A similar disappointment registered in the *New York Herald Tribune*'s head-lined reassurance that "White India Tiger Flies In; to be Whiter after a Bath."[42]

In her study of the exoticized female body, Piya Pal-Lipinksi posits the oda-lisque as a figure that has historically accommodated these sorts of disruptions. In its French variants, the odalisque announced both the force and the limitations of a male Orientalist gaze, whose scopic excesses were ultimately returned to the viewer through a foreign female body in possession of her own form and its grotesque po-tential. On Ingres's *Grand Odalisque,* Pal-Lipinksi writes:

> The odalisque's languid and coolly indifferent gaze, as she looks over her shoulders at the viewer, establishes her self-sufficiency and her control of the exotic space as well, anticipating Manet's shockingly self-contained prostitute Olympia. At the same time, Ingres's famous distortion of her body, his "serpentine line," undermines the Praxitelean ideals of proportion and symmetry that were to become so crucial to the construction of the perfect Victorian beauty . . . The Grand Odalisque is sexually desirable and beautiful—but also monstrous, disproportionate, indiffer-ent, and inaccessible. She is disconcerting in her *grande*-ness, her strangely imposing monumentality.[43]

Accounts of Mohini on display conveyed this contradictory quality of the odalisque with some regularity. When zookeepers placed the tiger in the Lion House with the other big cats they reported her to be one of the most aloof animals the zoo had ever exhibited, while the director testified that she "seems to be quite disdainful of other tigers and her human caretakers."[44] Cooke's profile piece concurred. Echoing the

Figure 3.7. *Mohini snarling, National Zoo, 1960. Photograph by Arthur Ellis,* Washington Post, *Getty Images.*

eerie monumentality of Ingres's painted woman, the journalist noted Mohini's extreme composure amid her rowdy animal neighbors: "Such is Mohini's cathedral calm . . . that her only reaction to the zany world of the Lion House is a slight widening of those incredible eyes."[45] Anticipated in the descriptions of the tiger's apparent discomfort while traveling, Mohini's composure occasionally gave way to brute rage. A photograph taken by the *Post*'s Arthur Ellis provides a case in point (Figure 3.7). What would otherwise have appeared as a standard image of the cat's beautiful body in repose was disturbed by a snarl of exceptional ferocity. Squinted eyes and bare fangs defined much of her expression, while prominent markings on her two front paws alluded to (retracted) claws and added to the sense of sheer wildness. Ellis's photograph placed these elements in the foreground, letting the rest of Mohini's frame recede into the background. The effect was an optical distortion of the body that could confuse viewers' sense of her physical proportions. The tiger's back half looked limp and lifeless, the front half looked tense and frighteningly animated, a contrast that challenged Mohini's status as a feminine harem dweller available for complete visual possession. This tiger was not altogether lovable.

The question of whether Mohini's sightings as a self-possessed odalisque signaled a form of agency for the animal is a difficult one to take up, but reasonable given her predecessors. Part of the feminist project in deconstructing this aesthetic tradition is to reassign some power to the living subjects who were painted by Eugène Delacroix, Henri Regnault, Jean-Léon Gérôme, Ingres, and others. Feminist art historians also offer something affirmative to the lives of women who have been affected by these paintings, specifically in considerations that the odalisque may have served as a point of female identification, pleasure, and political promise in the midst of its exploitations. But whether these painted women shared something in common with the National Zoo's white tigress is by no means clear. What is more certain is that Mohini's image as a passive odalisque was not stable and, so, not entirely safe for a seduction between zoo lovers and, at two years of age, a 225-pound cat. Recorded traces of the tiger's discomfort, remoteness, and unruliness punctured her public's enchantment and posed something of a risk to the zoo's plans to breed the animal. Who could sufficiently romance such an unpredictable lady? The identity of Mohini as an odalisque was never fully conducive to a courtship whose endgame was making babies. As Pal-Lapinski notes, the body of the languid harem dweller was historically seductive but not especially *pro*ductive. Her ambiguous racial heritage coupled with an inability (or possible refusal) to get up and do something other than lounge entailed a sexual desirability that was ultimately inappropriate for biological reproduction.[46] New zoo makers in and around Washington responded to these shortcomings by developing a second, parallel line of representation, one that seemed, at least superficially, more conducive to the National Zoo's renewal and its racialized rhetorics of breeding endangered species. As Mohini the odalisque flourished and floundered, so too did Mohini the expectant white mother.

THE DOMESTIC BODY: MOHINI AS WHITE MOTHER

Representations surrounding Mohini's captive reproduction traded the erotic aesthetics of Oriental odalisques for a wholesome aesthetics of reproductive fitness. These representations were no less preoccupied with the superiority of white Americans over other racial and ethnic groups native to non-Western and decolonizing nations. But they gave the preoccupation a different outlet and, moreover, enlarged the roster of others to include U.S. citizens not recognized as white. Idealized as a white mother, Mohini allowed for cross-species intimacies and identifications that revolved not around the imagined differences between Bengal tigers and National Zoo goers but around their similarities. The big cat's white pregnant body, maternal body, and extended body (in the form of her cubs) were fertile points of racial recognition and desire for the revitalizing zoo's collective gaze. As such, Mohini's public life in Washington came to resemble other productions of eugenic ideology not witnessed since the interwar period, even while her offspring's physical health was compromised. Indeed, the paradox of Mohini's symbolic role as a white mother was that its production was partly realized through the planned inbreeding of genetically related animals, resulting in a host of disorders in the ensuing cubs. At the National Zoo, the discursive construction of reproductive fitness had a biological cost, laced with the stigma associated with sexually interactive kin and the inbred. As the *Washington Post* phrased it in 1974, the National Zoo's white tiger breeding program was "a geneaological mess."[47]

Cultural historians have detailed, with an unflinching eye, the popularity and versatility of the "race betterment" movement in American life. These studies retrace how eugenics began in the United States at the opening of the twentieth century as a scientific program for the improvement of the American gene pool and permeated mainstream consciousness through a range of media: eugenic exhibitions at the American Museum of Natural History, "fitter family" contests and information booths in rural state fairs, motion pictures that linked white physical beauty to hereditary health.[48] As the country experienced increased urbanization and immigration, middle-class progressives spearheaded these kinds of educational programs with an eye toward family health and social reform. Their efforts aimed to influence the reproductive choices and outcomes of men and women to maximize the "quality" and demographic count of white American bodies of northern European descent. Concomitant with campaigns for "positive" eugenics were negative eugenic practices that included the forced sterilization of immigrants, African Americans, and the disabled, accompanied by visual and textual propaganda that discouraged these populations from making babies. The popularization of eugenics was thus a nakedly oppressive moment in U.S. history that, by the close of World War II, was also avidly condemned by the American scientific establishment and its nonspecialist arms. In the wake of Nazi Germany's similar practices, the concept of preserving or improving the genetic heritage of Anglo and Nordic American families became seen as a form of scientific wickedness, widely considered a strong cultural taboo, but not an entirely absent possibility. Robert Rydell speculates that "eugenicist sentiment in American popular culture between the world wars was so deep that it formed a reservoir of thought and feeling that lasted well beyond the Second World War."[49]

By showcasing the breeding of its female white tiger as an attractive example of racial whiteness, the National Zoo became one instance of eugenics' continuity in a period of others. Scholars and activists point to the latter half of the twentieth century as a time of eugenic revival wherein the once public crusades that promoted genetically desirable citizens transformed into a marketplace of reproductive technologies that recast genetic health as a private consumer choice. The historian Alexandra Minna Stern, for example, charts the emergence of the genetic counselor as one manifestation of this shift from public to private eugenics, a profession that has advised people in the United States and in the developing world about their modern reproductive options while explicitly avoiding any discussions of a national collectivity.[50] At the postwar National Zoo in the midst of revitalization, eugenics was arguably more conventional. It retained its civic flavor by rooting Mohini's reproductivity in the sagging public space of the Rock Creek Park grounds, the location of all her conceptions and births. As Reed recalled years later, "This animal brought a lot of attention to the zoo when we needed it. It's been very helpful, and we owe the white tiger a lot."[51]

The tiger-mother was made additionally "public" by her abstraction into a scientific teaching tool. In the early 1970s, for example, zoo officials grew interested in various cat films for possible screening at the new Mann Lion–Tiger Exhibit. These films centered on the power of white tiger bodies to educate visitors about the evolutionary history of tigers more broadly. *The Gene Story* was conceived as a film that used white tigers in contrast to normal tigers to explore the concept of heredity.[52] Another film, titled *The Big Cats and How They Came to Be,* began with the black-and-white animated image of a colorless tiger as an example of evolutionary excellence. The tiger awakens from sleep, yawns, and proceeds to move its body through empty black space over the voice of the narrator who begins: "There are certain things in nature in which beauty and utility, artistic and technical perfection combine in some incomprehensible way, and one is the movements of a cat."[53] The establishment of FONZ's Mohini Award cemented the association between Mohini and public science education. The honor was given "to the person who has made the most significant contribution to the educational progress of the Zoo."[54]

Slippage between nonhuman and human breeders was not particularly novel either. Early eugenicists like Dr. Florence Sherborn and Mary Watts, organizers of the state fair contests that gave out awards for good heredity, routinely traversed species boundaries in their promotion of the better breeding cause. Sensitive to a disparity between the care provided to livestock in rural communities and the care provided to young American children, the women approached the evaluation of "human stock" in the rural tradition of judging other agricultural products.[55] Wrote Watts on the subject:

> The horticulturalist brings his best fruit and flowers to the fair, the agriculturalist his best grain and the stockman his finest specimens of livestock; then why not give parents the opportunity to show their fine families of boys and girls and stimulate others to improve the quality of their offspring?[56]

With a similar pride, lovers of the white tiger also drew equivalencies between those bodies deemed representative of their species. More specifically, Mohini's public crafted the cat as a living symbolic measure of their own racial identities, a yardstick by which to evaluate the status and quality of their whiteness, or lack thereof. Wrote one curator on the educational promise of *The Gene Story*: "The Gene Story could be really unique in that the visitor enters a tiger house at the zoo and learns something about himself."[57] More telling was Reed's verbal sketch of Mohini during an interview with the Smithsonian historian Pamela Henson. Reed described Mohini as "a tiger. I mean, a white background with not jet-black stripes, kind of gray stripes, blue eyes. The lips were pink instead of black. The paws were a little pinker. So it's a partial albino, *even as you and I are partial albinos*" (emphasis added).[58] Reed's vision of the cat corresponded to a vision of himself. While physical features signaled Mohini's partial albinism, they likewise served as a zoomorphic reference point to the inherited traits of the director and present company. In an earlier interview, racialized identifications were even more pronounced when Reed explained how he made the concept of partially albino animals understandable to those who were curious and knew little about the genetic science involved. His strategy was to point out that "northern Europe was full of them"—leaving the species identity of "them" undefined—and that he himself was a partial albino, thereby collapsing any distinction between white tigers and human bodies with Anglo and Nordic pedigrees.[59]

In forging a racialized similitude, Reed's explanations also helped normalize the cultural stigma attached to a competing representation of white tigers, as freaks.[60] In the 1980s William Conway, director of the New York Zoological Society, was explicit on the matter: "White tigers are freaks. It's not the role of a zoo to show two-headed calves and white tigers."[61] Reed's informal descriptions countered these timely concerns, which were informed by renewed institutional pledges to scientific integrity over sensationalism. From a phenotypical perspective, Conway's fears were overblown. The partial albino constitutes a milder version of the freakier "true albino," visible in a total lack of epidermal, hair, and iris pigmentation. The pinkish eyes of true albinos are due to blood flow through pigmentless retinas.[62] Writing for the *Journal of the Bombay Natural History Society* in 1959, the Indian biologist E. P. Gee noted that most white tigers do not fall under this category, but still display rare features, from light-colored animals with dark brown stripes to cream-colored ones with dark brown or dark gray stripes, to the Rewa type which had ashy-gray stripes on an almost-white background.[63] Gee cautioned against overbreeding within the same bloodline for a more pronounced expression of these genetic mutations; deterioration of the stock was a risk. At the same time, the biologist was candid about the advantages that a white tiger line could offer his own country. With enough genetic diversity to keep the line robust, a breed of white tigers would give India "a considerable amount of prestige in the zoological world, as well as provide a fillip for tourism and at a later date a possible economically valuable item of export to foreign countries."[64]

Reed's own writing also searched for the brighter side of freakery. An article coauthored with Dr. Paul Leyhausen of Germany's Max Planck Institute and published in the *Smithsonian* included Reed's beloved collection within its purview by asking the question, "Why do 'freaks' like white tigers continue to appear in an otherwise seemingly uniform population, when they are presumably at a disadvantage in competing with their [normal-colored] conspecifics?"[65] The article responded against scientific wisdom. Leyhausen and Reed posited that the oddities worked at an evolutionary advantage, not a liability. Citing another Indian zoologist's observation that "the 'whities' are all particularly impressive specimens," the authors argued that white tigers grew faster and larger than the average tiger. Perhaps, they speculated, genes for white coats also kept a gene that regulates body size within the pool, in case it was needed."[66] Whatever its abnormalities, the genetic freak was still a healthy one, and moreover, it was something worth preserving. The point was made most vividly by contrasting the purportedly universal fascination with white animals with the morally suspect black animals of the world:

> We find it remarkable that some animals are uniformly black or white. The black ones used to be held in awe. The raven was believed to be an emissary of the underworld sent to spy on humans. The black wolf had even more sinister connotations, and even now, well-educated zoo visitors firmly believe that a black leopard is more ferocious than a rosette-patterned leopard, although both color phases can occur in the same litter. Thus, Rudyard Kipling was somewhat out of step with superstitions when he made black Bagheera play a friendly role in *The Jungle Book*. He ought to have chosen a white animal—traditionally held to represent or even incorporate benign gods.[67]

These cultural reflections were in no way challenged by the genetic science that Leyhausen and Reed shared with their readers. Instead they reminded readers that their appetites for whiteness had a long and mystical history that transcended the specific racial anxieties of the mid-twentieth-century United States. In moments of great candor, then, Mohini's visibility as white helped shape zoo goers' profiles of whiteness and defined the universalized parameters of a robust and morally upstanding citizenry.

The *Washington Post* reporter Phil Casey's language in a March 1973 edition of the newspaper lent still more to the comparison, arguing that Mohini and her kind represented "The Great White Hope."[68] The reference came after another round of scheduled tiger matings and the box office success of the racial drama by the same name. Based on the play by Howard Sackler that debuted nationally at the District's Arena Stage in 1967, the 1970 film starring James Earl Jones and Jane Alexander dramatized the life of black prizefighter Jack Johnson, and the boxing establishment's search for a white opponent who could defeat him. The title alluded to this search, but also to Johnson's struggle to have a romantic relationship with a white woman. In the discursive field of the zoo, much of the phrase's political ambiguity was lost. Mating Mohini became more straightforwardly an effort to reproduce phenotypic whiteness and a way to both normalize and sanctify all for which it stood.

The incentives to keep whiteness visible were strong in this period of American public life. With the publication of Betty Friedan's *Feminine Mystique* in 1963, white middle-class women embarked on a new era of skepticism about their prescribed roles as suburban housewives and mothers.[69] Doubts grew with the publication of Shulamith Firestone's utopic *The Dialectic of Sex: The Case for Feminist Revolution* in 1970.[70] Focused on a critique of patriarchy and its social and psychological toll on white women, neither of these incendiary books was critical of the high status of the white mother in U.S. culture. Indeed, they were oblivious to the fact that their arguments were racially specific, as feminist writings thereafter duly noted. But their widespread reception as, what Judith Snitow calls, the "demon texts" of second-wave feminism fed a caricatured image of these writers and their readers as mother-haters.[71] More explicit in their critiques of motherhood, minus again a recognition of its racial dimensions, was Ellen Peck and Judith Senderowitz's edited 1974 volume *Pronatalism: The Myth of Mom and Apple Pie*. Describing pronatalism as "any attitude or policy that is 'pro-birth,' that encourages reproduction, that exalts the role of parenthood," Peck and Senderowitz identified their own historical moment as distinctly pronatalist and helped a generation of white women speak out on the social pressure to bear children.[72] Meanwhile, black women were bearing the brunt of social science literature like the Moynihan report of 1965, which pathologized the black family and laid much of the blame at the feet of African American mothers.[73] In this context, Mohini's public representation as a white maternal body went some way toward fortifying the importance of those human bodies capable of bearing whiteness, even while her own body wavered in that project. The white female tiger became an early example of a eugenical probirth climate that was constitutive of a new National Zoo and that would encourage its white women spectators to do as the animals were doing before their eyes, a sentiment echoed in Deputy Zoo Director Edward Kohn's opening quotation of the zoo's 1976 picture book: "The Zoo's mission is to present the beauty and character of fellow beings in the animal kingdom so that our and future generations of people, enriched by personal discovery, will join in a commitment to cherish and preserve life."[74]

The establishment of the zoo's first pregnancy monitoring program was an early step in this process. When Mohini began to show signs of pregnancy in 1963, local volunteers from the Friends of the National Zoo set up a twenty-four-hour schedule to observe the female cat. Earlier that year, Mohini had been mated to Samson, her orange-colored uncle and half-brother with white genes.[75] By December, zoo staff believed that cubs were on the way, and FONZ prepared accordingly. Mohini was taken off exhibit and relocated to a nest box at the rear of the Lion House. From there began what staff and volunteers called "Preg Watch." The nest box had a boarded-up front and a couple of peepholes, creating necessary privacy for the animal without sacrificing the need to see the avidly awaited event of her delivery. Enhancing the view was a closed-circuit television system that WTTG-TV, a Metromedia station, loaned to the zoo. Predating what would become standard procedure for prominent zoo births, the television system gave Mohini watchers remote visual access to her secluded state from the keeper room.[76] Bright lights were installed in the nest box so that the camera could register activity, with the added benefit of keeping the cat and her cubs, once born, warm.[77] Curators instructed the pregwatchers to look for behavioral and physical changes that could indicate the onset of labor. Restlessness, shown by pacing, by cycles of lying down and getting up, and by circling behavior, was one signal. Others demanded closer inspection, like contractions of the abdominal muscles. Short contractions would signify the onset of labor, longer ones followed by rolling movements would indicate that birthing was imminent. Mohini's labor would also be announced in sounds of her moaning.[78] The list of possible signs encouraged volunteers to stay alert while on watch and created a level of personal attachment to the animal that was likely unprecedented for many participants.

It was certainly the case for Dr. Michael Balbo, who, like many Americans, watched Mohini's delivery on his own television screen from home. On January 12, 1964, six days after the actual delivery, "Birth of a White Tiger" aired on WNEW-TV, broadcasting footage from the closed-circuit surveillance of the event to a nation-wide audience. In a newsletter for the Long Island Ocelot Club, Balbo recounted his memory of the viewing experience:

> It was fascinating to watch the beginning of labor which was characterized by contraction of the muscles on the side of the female's abdomen (the flanks), followed by the appearance of the cub (enclosed in the amniotic sac) and the umbilical cord. While the cub was still attached to the mother by means of the cord, she would stand up and then sit down and seemed to be sitting on the cub. However this was not so but only appeared so due to the angle of the camera. She then severed the cord with her teeth and removed the sac. There were a few anxious moments when after the birth of the third cub, one cub still remained in its sac. If the sac is not removed, the new-born cub would suffocate, but Mohini removed the sac in time. The afterbirth was then expelled and eaten.[79]

Balbo's account emphasized a close viewing range and the intimate sights that it en-abled. Mohini's birthing body was a captivating, if awkward, display that produced other smaller bodies within its televisual frame. A jumbled assemblage of contract-ing muscles, fluid-filled sacs, umbilical cord and teeth, the tiger's form exceeded the bounds of conventional network television, bordering on what Jackie Stacey calls the "monstrous maternal" for its inability to neatly sever ties to its offspring.[80] There were additional worries that Mohini might be monstrous. Pregwatchers closer to the zoo admitted that one concern surrounding the delivery was the possibility that the tiger would behave like other animal mothers in captivity by destroying her first young, either purposely or from neglect.[81] Balbo's description of events offered a bamboozling punch line: Mohini's expulsion and consumption not of her birthed but of her afterbirth.

Nervousness over the tiger's obtuse animality competed with the urgent ques-tion of whether her cubs would be white in coloring. In *Spots and Stripes,* the zoologist Marion McCrane recounted that press and zoo goers' inquiries about the tiger after delivery kept "our nerves as taut as the 'invisible' wire in the new bird house" and offered FONZ members a recap of the event:

> Color was a guess, too. *If* this whiteness in tigers is a true dominant-recessive characteristic, and *if* it follows the Mendelian laws of inheritance, and *if* chance factors happen to be right, and *if* four cubs were born, we *hoped* two would be white. Whew! . . . All we could do was cringe at the "don't-you-know-your-own-business?"

looks and go back to biting our nails. . . . The calmest one of the whole bunch was Mohini.[82]

However uncomfortable, volunteers and other pregwatchers' scrutiny of Mohini's nesting space, with its disorderly bodies, was central to breaking the suspense. McCrane's account noted as much:

Two males, one of them white like Mohini, and a female! Wild horses couldn't have dragged Bert Barker home that night. (Zoo wives get conditioned to this sort of thing.) Ralph Norris, Mike Brown and veterinarian Gray also stayed to keep blood-shot eyes on that TV monitor screen.[83]

Like a maternity ward with expectant fathers, keepers hovering around the tele-vised nest box in the Lion House were thrilled by their statistically good news. McCrane's mention of understanding wives rounded out the familial atmosphere of the night, while her conclusion strengthened the profile of Mohini's respectably white maternity:

Rewa cleaned the first baby until the third baby was born. Then she started clean-ing the second. The third baby didn't get cleaned until about 7.35. At 11.50 the babies started nursing (and the nightwatch started to breathe again). The cubs were estimated to be about 1 to 1½ pounds at birth. At six weeks they weighed in at 10 and 11 pounds and were wobbling around after their mom. A normal birth, a healthy normal litter, and to anyone who has seen the family, an ideal mother.[84]

Different from Balbo's account, McCrane saw Mohini's delivery as remarkable for its unremarkability. The difference was gendered in nature, signaling two distinct models of eugenic spectatorship at the zoo. Balbo's account of this experience constructed Mohini's maternity along a typical dyad of male-viewing subject and female-viewed object, rendering the latter vaguely threatening. McCrane's account gave FONZ members more opportunities for cross-species kinship by emphasizing the event's normalcy and the tiger's status as an ideal mother. For McCrane, there was nothing to fear about Mohini; she was much like any other new mom around the National Zoo.[85] She cleaned her babies, fed them, and guided them through their first attempts to walk. The babies were unremarkable too, whose ordinariness reinforced their mother's credibility as a suitable white role model and caretaker, rather than a potentially monstrous one. Together, they made a family about which the new zoo makers could be relieved, and self-satisfied. The *Washington Post* was one example of the relief, headlining the delivery with a celebration of the whiteness that it revealed: "3 Kittens, One All-White and Rare, Born to Zoo's Exclusive White Tiger." Following the maxim of "so long as my child is healthy," the story reported how zoo officials were unsure of the sex of the white cub, "but they're not upset, just so long as he or she is white."[86]

White women's perspectives continued to characterize representations of the partially albino cubs throughout Mohini's term as a public mother figure. In 1969 Elizabeth Reed, Theodore's wife, took the zoo's second white tiger cub into the Reed home in Montgomery County, Maryland. Born on April 13, this time from Mohini mating with her son Ramana, the female "Rewati" was part of a litter of two whose unnamed orange-colored sibling died days after its birth.[87] This was Mohini's third delivery. Three years earlier, she had given birth to two nonwhite cubs, much to the disappointment of her public. An elderly lady told the press at the cubs' first showing, "it would have been a marvel if it had been white." The same article shared the keepers' retort that Mohini "isn't prejudiced."[88] In terms of species, neither was Elizabeth Reed, who agreed to care for Rewati when Mohini displayed signs of being a stressed mother by carrying the cub around haphazardly and licking her excessively. White tiger fans could read two similar accounts of the cub-rearing experience; first in FONZ's *Spots and Stripes,* followed by a more elaborately photographed essay in the April 1970 issue of *National Geographic.* These articles detailed the day-to-day rhythms of baby animal home care and constructed the white tiger collection as a group of good citizens brought into the fold of new zoo decency.

Early in both pieces, Elizabeth forgave the strange behavior of an otherwise "model mother," explaining in the FONZ piece that "Mohini had become upset over the romantic talk between Romana *[sic],* the cub's father, and another tigress."[89] Given this, the white tiger's actions were understandable. Ramana had violated the monogamy that was central to the internal stability and moral authority of the heterosexual reproductive American family, and Mohini responded much like any jealous wife would.[90] Restoring a much-needed sense of normalcy to family life, Mrs. Reed assumed the role of foster mother with gusto, expanding her identity as a middle-class suburban wife and caretaker to incorporate a "squirming bundle of snowy fur, dark stripes, and pink nose."[91] With middle-of-the-night awakenings, the mysteries of getting baby to feed, and the extra laundry to do, the job recalled her experience of mothering her own children, which made the transition familiar if not easy. "My youngest child is 18," she wrote, "so I had forgotten how exhausting a new baby in the house can be."[92] But it also required Elizabeth to imagine herself in the place of a female tiger, acting as Mohini would toward her own: "A tigress grooms her cubs by licking them. I used a damp washrag on Rewati and she'd roll her ice-blue eyes blissfully during the ceremony."[93] This was not the first time the director's wife had moved across the species barrier. Her previous experiments in interspecies kinship included raising two litters of hybrid bears, a grizzly bear, two leopards, and a ring-tailed lemur. Hers was part of an honored tradition of zoo wives looking after newborn animals to ensure their survival beyond their first weeks of life.[94] But, in the *National Geographic* piece, she singled out Rewati for being the only white tiger cub in the Western Hemisphere, an animal of exceptional popular interest with a ready-made audience awaiting her return to the zoo. For Elizabeth, the pressure to perform her maternal duties to a public standard of competence was unusually high: "What if I blundered in my mother's role? There was so much that I didn't know—that no one knew—about hand-raising a white tiger cub!"[95]

Images in the *National Geographic* article testified to Elizabeth's expertise and ensured that the cub's first weeks unfolded in the cradle of postwar suburban domesticity. Donna Grosvenor, wife of *National Geographic*'s editor Gilbert Grosvenor and a FONZ member, was the enthusiastic photographer who came several times a week to record the cub's growth for the national magazine. Grosvenor's visits produced an intimate and cheerful family album shot with the magazine's signature Ektachrome color film, a Kodak brand that imbued images with high-grade hues. The three-and-a-half-week-old Rewati appeared in her baby blue makeshift crib, snuggling with an orange-colored stuffed tiger toy. The six-week-old Rewati appeared in the arms of yellow-dressed Elizabeth Reed, bottle-feeding the cub in a chair beneath Abercrombie's *National Geographic* portrait of Mohini from May 1961. The rest of the photographs put Rewati and her adopted family on the Reed's suburban lawn in states of play and parent child bonding. Theodore Reed and the eight-week-old Rewati tussled on the grass. The little tiger approached "a plastic ball, her favorite toy." She fed herself like a toddler, recovering from a sickness "that temporarily stole her strength." In the role of friendly neighbor or aunt, Donna Grosvenor herself sat cross-legged and immersed in the wholesomeness. Interestingly, pictures that displayed the tiger at the National Zoo, weeks after Rewati's return, were indistinguishable from the Reed's Montgomery County backyard. All outdoor images situated the cub on a carpet of well-groomed grass that by 1970 had become iconic in the visual representation of suburban family well-being. These lawn shots were arresting in the intensity of their greenness and accentuated Rewati's white coloring. So too did specific photographs of the cub romping with her living orange-colored playmate, Sakhi, a Bengal tiger cub purchased by the zoo to keep Rewati company. The appearance of the two together on their emerald playground reminded readers that the white tiger cub was somewhere between a wild animal and a member of the esteemed Reed clan (see Plate 5).[96] In these ways, Elizabeth Reed's public experience of cross-species mothering became highly compatible with, and prescriptive toward, visions of the new National Zoo as a site for proper childhood development, a place where the continuity of white bourgeois bodies and behaviors could find some teeth.

MOHINI'S DEFECTIVE BODIES

The physical problems with Mohini's white cubs put a sizable wrench in revital-izing representations of the white tiger collection. Reports of fair-coated animals stricken by their inbreeding complicated the overarching narrative of orientalist seduction and eugenical reproduction that Mohini and her cub line inspired, ulti-mately jeopardizing significations of the brood as a happy harbinger of normative whiteness for a new National Zoo. One of the more terse descriptions of the animals' inborn frailty came from the *Post*'s Phil Casey, who speculated that "white tigers, perhaps because of their inbreeding, seem woefully prone to disease, accident and early demise."[97] Meanwhile, the health status of "normals" under the zoo's breeding program was a notable absence in zoo news coverage and the scientific literature, underscoring their peripherality to the birth and longevity of the white cubs.

Nineteen months into his life, Mohini's first white cub, Rajkumar, contracted panleucopenia, a feline form of distemper, from his orange-colored sister, Ramani. Ramani died first, prompting veterinarians to administer an antidistemper serum to Rajkumar. The treatment did not work, and the cub displayed symptoms of in-flammation of the stomach and intestines, and severe depression until his eventual death in July 1965.[98] Mohini's second white cub, Rewati, survived into adulthood, but not without her share of difficulties. At two weeks old, Elizabeth Reed observed an uneven gait, circling behavior, and a head held in a twisted position. She also noticed that the cub could not yet see. In the cub's fourth week, following an in-tense period of circling, Rewati showed signs of listlessness and was unable to use her hind legs. Zoo specialists treated her without knowing the nature of her illness, using penicillin shots, oxygen inhalation, outdoor exercise, and formula fortified with egg and brandy.[99] The treatment seemed to work, but the cub's vision problems persisted, with a noticeable cross-eyed condition. The prospects for Moni, Mohini's only surviving cub of her March 1970 litter, were less bright. When the cub grew to three weeks of age, caretakers became worried. The tiger exhibited aberrant be-havior, described by Reed to Smithsonian secretary Ripley as "a serious spell of violent circling, rolling, and head twisting."[100] May 1970 found the cub returning to the National Zoo from the Reed household, with a press release celebrating his normalcy, omitting any mention of possible disease and comparing his health with Rewati's at the same stage of life: "Moni has been much more precocious—his eyes opened earlier, he was able to crawl sooner and he grew much more rapidly."[101] But problems of balance resurfaced in June. Moni's tendency to tilt his head to the right was a mystery to veterinarians at the zoo and cause for concern. Reed planned for no publicity when he, Elizabeth, and one keeper flew the cub to Cornell University in upstate New York. There, Moni was given a full neurological examination, including X-rays and a cerebral spinal tap, but no diagnosis was forthcoming. The cub's death a year later, attributed to "stress," was particularly disheartening for Washington's new zoo makers, who had planned to tour the animal around India in the spring of 1972.[102] Moni was poised to represent all newly declared endangered tigers in the region and help raise funds for the Smithsonian's 1972 tiger conservation project.[103]

The poor health of Mohini's partial albinos demanded some discursive adjustments to the white tiger breeding program. In the wake of the cubs' deaths, and in the midst of a new commitment to diversify Washington's tiger gene pool through outcross breeding, the National Zoo offered Mohini enthusiasts an altered representation of white tigers.[104] Painted in oil by the wildlife artist Edward J. Bierly, the portrait of a reclining Mohini and a white cub was a new picture of whiteness that circulated throughout the zoo community and stood, in the director's eyes, as "one of the finest animal paintings I have ever seen" (Figure 3.8).[105] As a $100 limited edition print, "Mohini and Cub" raised money for the Smithsonian's new "Save the Tiger Fund." As a framed piece of art, it hung in the reception area of FONZ's office, and in the foyer of the zoo's Mann Lion–Tiger Exhibit when it opened in 1976.

For the new zoo goers, there was much to absorb about the piece. Bierly's painting fixed the collection's discernible flaws, recapturing some of the normalcy of the animals before their reputations had become tainted with genetic misfortune. He painted in a small nip that had been taken out of Mohini's ear by her first prospective, and failed, mate. He also elected to render the white cub as an idealized composite of the three. In a letter to the New Jersey man who eventually acquired the original painting, Reed assured him that everything about this little tiger was normal, healthy, and natural: "The ears may seem to be a little bit large, however, at this stage in their growth and development, this is the way tiger cubs are."[106] Exhibited behavior in the image was also pleasingly ordinary. Bierly's cub "has obviously just become aware of the observer and true to their nature has pushed himself back into the side of his mother. I have seen them do this many times . . . although he still shows the great curiosity of these young kittens."[107] The results of Bierly's artistry would not have come as a surprise to Reed, given that he and Leyhausen had visited Bierly's studio with suggestions on how to make the cats look as normal as possible. This included advice on the angle of the foot and the forepaws of both animals as well as some of the facial characteristics.

Vol. 8, No. 2

Summer 1971

"Mohini and Cub" by Ed Bierly, a limited edition print, copies of which are being sold to save Mohini's species from extinction.

published by FRIENDS OF THE NATIONAL ZOO

NATIONAL ZOOLOGICAL PARK • WASHINGTON, D.C. 20009 • 232-4555

Figure 3.8. Mohini and Cub, *painted by Edward J. Bierly, reproduced in* Spots and Stripes, *Summer 1971. Smithsonian Institution Archives, Image SIA2014–01217.*

But for all these remedial measures, "Mohini and Cub" also displayed signs that the National Zoo's public no longer coveted white tigers as animal articulations of human whiteness. Hints of orange in both animals' coats, veering into light brown, tempered the once-blinding whiteness of the collection, while the darkness outlining the mother-tiger's body framed the pair in a shadow that whispered disgrace. The look of apprehension on the cub's face registered viewers' emergent sense that the purity of the zoo's white tiger line, while genetically true, was culturally suspect and approaching permanent extinction. The next and final breeding of Mohini, to a normal-colored tiger without any white genes from Chicago's Brookfield Zoo, did not result in pregnancy. The same tiger was mated with Ramana's male offspring, Kesari, and produced one of six surviving cubs of orange hue. This loss of whiteness issued a warning to the Federal City's animal breeders. The revitalizing National Zoo would have to find other species whose racial representation could be better synchronized to their biological health—a constitutive part of any viable living symbol of whiteness—or abandon the effort entirely. Washington's new zoo makers had more or less succeeded in enchanting zoo lovers with Mohini's exotic origins, but her status as an animal archetype of white reproductive fitness proved untenable.

On April 16, 1972, Mohini was unofficially retired from her informal job of racializing the National Zoo when the male and female giant pandas, Hsing-Hsing and Ling-Ling, arrived at the zoo from Peking, China, and moved into the specially remodeled Delicate Hoofed Stock building.[108] By most accounts, the pandas stole the crowds, inviting visitors to imagine their own whiteness through the restorative image of an assimilating immigrant couple. A watercolor painting by Rudy Wendelin, noted by the zoo's public affairs office as the "official artist" of the zoo's famous Smokey Bear, was one example (Figure 3.9). The work depicted Smokey standing behind a picket fence with his wife and child, greeting the Chinese newcomers with a bamboo cake. Luggage in hand, the pandas appeared to be walking happily toward the all-American bears, with the smaller (presumably female) panda looking directly at "Little Smokey." In response to such warm welcomes, die-hard Mohini lovers, young and old, penned letters to the white tiger throughout the 1970s to assure her that she still mattered in the face of all the excitement and the eventual switch in trademarks. William Shepard of Potomac, Maryland, for example, admitted that the pandas were interesting, "but they are, of course, pandas, second overgrown cousins to raccoons, who can't seem to figure out the proper way to have a family, at that."[109] Others were more resigned, like Deirdre Magnussen. The same woman who was charmed by Mohini's horizontal majesty and serenity also expressed her gratitude toward the aging animal's reproductive labors, despite all the complications: "Thank you Mohini for the legacy you leave us in your children. I hope we are worthy of your trust."[110]

Figure 3.9. *National Zoo watercolor by Rudy Wendelin, 1972. Smithsonian Institution Archives. Record Unit 365, Oversize, Folder 2: Rudolph Wendelin Painting.*

4

White Open Spaces in San Diego County

In 1971 a business partnership called Kaiser Aetna ran an advertisement in *San Diego Magazine* (see Plate 6). The ad showcased a private land development project in the booming inland region between San Diego and Los Angeles counties. Under the provocative heading "Southern California needs a wildlife refuge. For humans," the developers targeted both seasoned and newly minted suburbanites who were uneasy about the spatial future of their state and longed for its idyllic past. The copy read: "Remember Southern California? The place people used to go to get away from it all? Now, it all is here: Traffic. Factories. Ghettos. Ticky-tacky housing. Unbreathable air. Unpalatable water." Opposite the text, readers could take in the full-page color image of a youthful, denim-clad man, ostensibly of northern European descent, standing steadfast before a rambling landscape. Grassy meadows, receding hillsides, and a demure woman by his side completed the picture. This was, in Kaiser Aetna's imaginary, "The kind of land young men used to go West for," a "95,000 acre chunk of yesterday" that was still available in a place named, appropriately, Rancho California. Here were the sounds of "a new life being born: tractors in grape vineyards and citrus farms. Families building new homes out of old dreams."[1] The orange sun hanging low in the big sky added to the scene's idealism and the feeling that both a new day had begun and that time was running out on the chance to claim a piece of the once vast Southland, free from urban blight.

The irony of the ad was thick, and its racial codings complex. Rancho California, so described, was both a sales pitch for and a critique of development, using a rhetoric that had become familiar to Americans under the rubric of "open space." Prominent in postwar architecture and urban planning, *open space* denotes land that is, or ought to be, protected from urban development and its forms of ecological, aesthetic, and social damage.[2] For the midcentury urbanist William H. Whyte, open space had northeastern accents that included "the meadows, the wooded draws, the stands of pine, the creeks and streams." For the environmental theorist and planner Kevin Lynch, open space was more behavioral, identifying it as "an outdoor area in the metropolitan region which is open to the freely chosen and spontaneous activity, movement, or visual exploration of a significant number of city people."[3] Ideas of open space were especially dear to California critics. With book titles such as *The Destruction of California* (Raymond Dasmann, 1965), *Eden in Jeopardy* (Richard Lillard, 1966), and *How to Kill a Golden State* (William Bronson, 1968), the stakes of continued growth in the nation's already most populous state were becoming clear and indicative of what the rest of the country could expect.[4] Kaiser Aetna's response to the threat was, ironically, more development along with an intricate configuration of racial meanings about development. The ad fed into a larger nationwide campaign by the real estate industry to promote the area to those who, by the 1970s, had come to associate urban space with black poverty, violence, and substandard housing; it reanimated Southern California's turn-of-the-century identity as a post-Mexican agricultural setting for Anglo-American health, vigor, and gentility; and it reserved human status for property owners who longed to participate in this white California fantasy while constructing their endangerment as a distinct species.

The Rancho California development was not the only site offering new life to San Diegans seeking sanctuary from urban life through a version of open space. The renewal undertaken by the Zoological Society of San Diego made a similar proposition, giving explicitly zoological form to the city's postwar growth and its racial anxieties. Examining the renovations of the downtown Balboa Park campus and the brand-new facility constructed in San Pasqual Valley, forty minutes northeast by car, this chapter traces how open space in the society's precincts reflected and responded to San Diego's boom, reiterating preferred residential styles and settings for and by the city's suburbanizing population.

My thesis that zoological open space was expressive of private residential space riffs on the perversion of the concept's postwar proponents by Kaiser Aetna. Open space enthusiasts reserved special vitriol for suburban residential space, since the most acute threat to the countryside was the sprawl incurred by new developments of single-family detached houses. In the decades after World War II, notions of open space were easily entangled with the pastoral ideal at the core of American identity and patterns of residency, an ideal that has constructed suburban homes and their surrounding landscapes as "a preserve of leisure and abundance" for the socially privileged.[5] For a city that rivaled Los Angeles in its culture of home ownership and the municipal works and workers that came to serve it, the popular valences of open space as home space were strong. It is not inconsequential that one of the defining architectural gestures of the postwar suburban dream home—a Southern California invention no less—was the creation of wide open spaces both outdoors and in. Instructive here is what the urbanist Mike Davis identifies as the region's dominant social force: "a middle-class political subjectivity that fitfully constitutes and reconstitutes itself every few years around the defense of household equity and residential privilege."[6] Early zoological incarnations of open space serviced that subjectivity. They composed suburban animal dwellings for the viewing pleasure of San Diegan home owners who were disturbed by contemporary discourses of urban decline, and suburbanized accordingly.

The city's zoo makers were sensitized to these discourses too. Throughout the 1950s and 1960s, the society's management was composed largely of middle-class men with northern European origins. These were first- or second-generation San Diegans, many with ties to eastern and midwestern states, with university degrees, business know-how, or employment history in the U.S. military.[7] While not quite the city's elite, the zoo men of San Diego were the city's bourgeoisie and brought their particular interests to bear on revitalizing animal space. Keeping the zoo and park as blight-free as their own homes and at the literal and figurative frontier of the urban landscape was paramount. Zoo director Charles Schroeder, for instance, made his family residence in North County San Diego near the Wild Animal Park, an occupational convenience but also an opportunity for the veterinarian who was native to New York City to take advantage of the area's "chain reaction" of "Avocados, a new highway, and climate."[8] The ensuing open space displays in San Diego's downtown and edge-of-town zoos offered personal relief from the racialized perils of city living. These displays were nostalgic homesteads with modern touches, rearticulating Anglo-American ideals of the Southern California Good Life: vast, serene, and close to the earth, the way rustic-minded Californians used to occupy the country and could possibly again. Thus, inasmuch as the promise of the society's new exhibits lay in securing the biological survival of endangered species, they also sprang from aspirations to preserve the vitality of the region's historically white sensibility and power. Indeed, the Zoological Society of San Diego made its program of wildlife conservation meaningful through this very impulse, without which the call to save vulnerable animals from extinction would not have found its primary audience.

THE CITY AND THE ZOO: WARTIME AND POSTWAR GROWTH

As Susan Davis has shown in her history of Sea World, the postwar development of San Diego and its recreational centers was mutually constitutive. Davis notes that a "pattern of shared growth and interdependence means that in the strong sense the city and the theme park have shaped each other." Since its opening in 1964, the Anheuser-Busch–owned Sea World helped define California's most southern metropolis as an attractive tourist destination, while the city's expansion helped Sea World become a national chain of marine-themed attractions.[9] In a similar vein, the Zoological Society experienced a growth spurt in the decades after World War II that was attributable to and paralleled by intense urbanization; both it and the city grew together.

San Diego was on its way to becoming a thriving Sun Belt city before 1945. Its love affair with the military created a stable economic base of defense-related manufacturing and services, dating back to its founding as a Spanish colonial presidio on the American frontier.[10] During World War II, the military presence in San Diego mushroomed into a thriving industry, with demographic consequences that were unanticipated by the business leaders, lawyers, and other professionals who made up the city's influential cabal of urban planners. An influx of immigrants from across the nation and around the world boosted San Diego's total population by 67 percent, to around four hundred thousand people. As a multiracial, multi-ethnic, and mixed-gender pool of wartime workers and their families, these new arrivals defied the norms of establishment San Diego. They took jobs in U.S. military installations, aircraft factories, navy ships, and battlefields. They spent their leisure time in the city's lively downtown center and coastline, and they sought homes wherever they could find them cheaply. According to Christine Killory, the impact of this rapid residential increase on the city's character was profound: "A conservative backwater became a cosmopolitan metropolis, frenetic, crowded with strangers, open for three shifts, twenty-four hours a day."[11]

For San Diego's marginalized racial and ethnic communities, the change was especially striking, if short-lived. Some blacks and Latinos took advantage of an unprecedented opportunity to move out of their already established neighborhood enclaves in the southeast section of town and, for new arrivals, to bypass them altogether. A select few took up employment in the labor-strapped war industry and residence in the federally funded housing projects for the city's defense workers.[12] The mobility was an exception to existing residential patterns, given that both communities were, by and large, confined to areas of the city considered less desirable by white residents. By the war's outbreak, San Diego was well practiced in segregating blacks and Latinos from the larger city, in no small part because of the rampant use of restrictive covenants in the first half of the twentieth century that denied property sales to persons recognized as other than white.[13] The demographic shifts of World War II were thus a brief interruption in a longer history of racial discrimination that continued into the postwar period.

The Zoological Society felt the sudden changes. To its dismay, attendance at the zoo dropped in the months after the bombing of Pearl Harbor, as army and navy personnel shipped out and tourist traffic fell to a minimum.[14] But as the city's wartime population grew, and hundreds of military officers brought their charges in for day trips, visitor numbers bounced back and set new records.[15] Seizing this opportunity, the society cultivated its friendship with the city's main employer, ensuring that San Diegans' experience of the grounds in Balboa Park would be pleasurable and patriotic. In the early 1940s designers made physical improvements, including new railings for the elephant enclosures, new concrete in the bird yard, and remodeled feed houses. Builders erected a second gate at the zoo's main entrance to accommodate the Sunday crowds who arrived by a soon-to-be-dismantled trolley system. With foresight, they also established the first of many zoo parking lots for the city's growing population of motorists. At the same time, growth was mitigated by some flag-waving wartime prudence. Some examples of restraint were simply practical: postponing large-scale construction projects because of labor and equipment shortages, or suspending bus tours because of gas rationing. In 1943 the superintendent of the grounds even created several "victory gardens" for animal food requirements, which provided many animals with a local diet of leafy greens and root vegetables. Other examples were more whimsical, such as a chimpanzee's appearance in the national press. Zoo handlers staged a photograph of "Georgie" weighing his own tire toy, to donate it to the scrap rubber drive.[16]

In return for its war effort, the society was rewarded not only with stronger ticket sales but a stronger animal collection. As one zoo historian recalled: "Species began to drift in during World War II from all over the world, wherever the American G.I. found himself, and remembered the Zoo of his home town."[17] Servicemen working in the Asiatic and South Pacific jungles, and to a lesser extent in Africa, captured and shipped their contributions to their local zoo. Thus, while the overall animal inventory declined during the war, thanks to a shrunken economy of food and expertise, the variety and rarity of species on display improved, echoing a city whose human residential population had also become more diverse. The 1944 donation of a Kagu bird was an exemplary addition in this regard. Mauve in color and resembling a small heron, the exotic animal was a gift from a U.S. Navy officer who received it as a token of appreciation for defending New Caledonia. Accompanied by an export permit, the bird was the first of its kind to leave its native Pacific Island territory in several years and enter the United States, where it joined another rare Kagu already on exhibit at the San Diego Zoo.[18]

By the war's end, the city of San Diego and its zoo were close allies in a project of urban development that, once again, radically changed the character of both. Amid lost contracts and worker layoffs, the city's industrial base of military parts and labor was forced to diversify.[19] Tourism, real estate, and research science and technologies assumed a greater role in San Diego's livelihood, generating another swell in residency.[20] New employment opportunities encouraged returning veterans to settle in the area and, more dramatically, lured tens of thousands of city dwellers from the nation's midwestern, northeastern, and mid-Atlantic states. A 1960 report from the city's planning department describes a "population explosion" that increased the number of San Diegans since 1950 by some 75 percent. Current residents were estimated at 300,000 in the immediate metropolitan area and an additional 560,000 within the greater city limits, with more to come. One and a half million people were expected to call San Diego home by 1975.[21]

Newcomers in this period were qualitatively different from their wartime predecessors, opting for the city's edges over its center.[22] By the mid-1960s, San Diego's promise as an exemplar of Sun Belt living was under major construction and had even radiated northward, attracting Los Angeles "refugees," as *San Diego Magazine* referred to them, in flight from their own urban anxiety.[23] Los Angelenos' worst fears were confirmed in August 1965 with the outbreak of the Watts riots and the extensive media coverage, prompting many to leave for San Diego's North County. At the hands of private capital and with the blessing of the municipal government, San Diego's civic energies rapidly moved north of the central city, taking built form as a sea of stucco housing, gleaming shopping malls, office complexes, and freeway routes that were nestled into rustic mesas with hilltop views. In Mike Davis's historical account, the suburban *naissance* followed a particular geography shaped by the investment appetites of land developers.

> In San Diego County, 1950's tract home growth was primarily on the mesas immediately north of Mission Valley and eastward toward the El Cajon Valley. It was well understood, however, that developers of future growth would prefer, first, the mesas of the famed "flower belt" immediately inland from the La Jolla-to-Oceanside coastline and, second, the attractive ranch and citrus corridor running from Miramar to north of Escondido along California 395 (the future I-15). "City North" and "North County" together comprised what 1960's boosters would call San Diego County's "Promised Land."[24]

Suburban San Diego, such as it became, proved more seductive to more people than a downtown that, like downtowns elsewhere, was characterized as blighted in the national press and due for urban renewal.[25] Confined by the Tijuana border on the south and the freshly cemented Mission Valley on the immediate north, the city's original limits deferred to its northern expanses, whose rural landscapes coupled with a new architectural modernism made any urban core feel dismal by comparison.[26] The tragedy of San Diego's own race riot on July 13, 1969, only amplified popular sentiments that North County was the safest and most beautiful environment in which to live—perhaps in the whole country—while downtown was a necessary pit stop for business meetings, airport travel, and the occasional cultural event. Commenting on the night of burning and looting in the city's southeast, an official at the city's human relations agency told reporters, in glaringly pathological terms, "We've been able to prevent an explosion until now because we've worked hard at it, but this area was a festering sore that had to erupt eventually."[27]

Two years later, suburbanizing San Diegans witnessed another challenge to, and validation of, their residential choices. In the downtown neighborhood of Logan Heights, a community of mostly Mexican Americans mobilized to stop the construction of a three-hundred-car parking lot for the California Highway Patrol. Logan Heights residents had already felt the sting of urban renewal, with municipal rezoning for Anglo-owned junkyards, the construction of Interstate 5, and the massive support pylons and on-ramps of the Coronado Bay Bridge. Protest over the parking lot was spontaneous, collective, and heated, calling on city government to authorize the area for a "people's park" amid the concrete, building on a history of resistance to Anglo land-grabbing.[28] Appropriately, demonstrators used cars to form a caravan down Logan Avenue, but they also lay down fertilizer and planted seeds on the contested site, an act that "came to symbolize the renewed sense of community that had sprouted as all segments of the neighborhood joined behind the demand for Chicano Park."[29]

The democratic spirit that created the inner-city park had no place at the San Diego Zoo. When Schroeder assumed the directorship in 1953, he decided that the place was "a mess" and took action.[30] The former zoo veterinarian channeled his long-standing passion for proper animal hygiene toward the zoo at large and began to suburbanize the grounds. A rigorous management style turned the zoo into a beacon of cleanliness and order that appealed directly to its antiurban patrons. As Schroeder's biographer, Douglas Myers, notes, the director's first purchases on the job were a mechanical sweeper and a Dictaphone to use during daily inspections of the property: "The Zoo, he reminded employees, should never look like a trash-strewn carnival."[31] The local press remarked: "Even a casual visitor cannot help but notice that Dr. Schroeder 'runs a tight ship'—a Navy term that is particularly apt in view of the number of retired service personnel who can be found on the staff."[32]

On the eve of his own retirement, the director revealed the extent of his sanitary vision in a memo to his successor that opted out of naval metaphors and presented zoo leadership as a form of skilled housework:

> One has to have a trained eye to see evidence of bad housekeeping, and everyone is not equipped to recognize untidiness. Attention must be paid to the physical equipment in restrooms, paint, broken door latches, broken or nonfunctioning light fixtures, damaged plumbing. Restrooms should always be immaculate. Exhibit signs must be kept clean and must be updated identifying the animal in the enclosures. All exhibit areas should be continuously occupied—never an empty cage. Births and special exhibits should be announced by special signing. Avoid temporary pencil and crayon signs. Attention should be paid to food waste—or inadequate spoiled food—too few stations—unclean water and containers.[33]

For Schroeder, the ideal grounds mirrored the ideal postwar home: unbroken, unpolluted, professional in its domestic expertise, and brimming with healthy new life. While this rule of law was difficult to maintain in practice, it constituted a new standard in the society's public face and internal operations against which all disruptions were measured and controlled. The model was Walt Disney's success with his own grounds in Anaheim, California, a ninety-minute drive from Balboa Park. A personal friend to several zoo executives in the 1960s, Disney shared his advice and staff with the society on more than one occasion. The knowledge and resources were wide ranging, including acquisition of some of Disneyland's rare plantings, lessons on state lobbying, and new family-centered concepts in marketing and commercializing the operation.[34] And much like at Disneyland, vandals at the zoo were turned over to security and employees were admonished for their infractions, from growing beards to littering in public areas.[35] Even potential disruptions were strictly managed. In March 1965, for example, Schroeder and members of the Board of Trustees refused to meet with the Congress of Racial Equality (CORE) to discuss the zoo's working conditions for visible minorities, including hiring and promotion policies. One trustee, former curator of reptiles Laurence Klauber, argued that such a meeting would only generate "the utmost confusion and distortion of their complaints with all kinds of fictitious claims of discrimination." Reinforcing the society's role as an organization by and for a white, and white enough, majority, Klauber's solution was more clear-cut: "Let them picket the zoo and we should get an injunction if they interfere with our customers."[36] The "Disneyland of Zoos," as one reporter called it, would not tolerate these disruptions to its suburbanizing scenes.[37]

HORN AND HOOF MESA AS SUBURBAN HOUSING

The stress on maintaining a tidy zoo landscape, both materially and legally, carried over into a slew of postwar renovations and new structures characterized by up-to-date materials and technologies, clean architectural forms, and family-friendly tableaux of endangered species. Zoo-sponsored profiles of renewal in the early 1960s noted, for example, the outdoor escalator to transport people up and down a sixty-five-foot canyon, the wire-free Flamingo Lagoon, rounded aviaries for Australian bird species, and a "split level" construction for the gorillas housed on the Ape and Bird Mesa. These "changing contours" helped increase attendance by more than a half million visitors every five years and build a membership that would triple in thirty.[38] The revamping of Deer Mesa into Horn and Hoof Mesa provides a case study in the process. Its gradual modernization during the 1950s and 1960s aimed to improve the display of African and Asian mammals and birds along these lines, and in so doing, woo the human residents of a developing North County. A spatial metaphor for the city's expanding fringe, Deer Mesa was the zoo's largest multiunit exhibit, situated at the extreme north of the grounds and most easily reached by tour bus. A two-page photograph of the site in the February 1966 issue of *Zoonooz*, the society's monthly magazine, accentuated its remote location and linked renovations to San Diego's northward boom (Figure 4.1). Alongside the caption, "Meandering on Horn and Hoof Mesa," the photograph represented a recently completed section from an aerial perspective. From this viewpoint, that of city planning, readers could see not only the ample size of the new exhibit and its winding main artery but also a much larger roadway that lay off zoo property and a developing landscape that seemed to reach well beyond the city limits. Growing zoo and city spaces merged into a single image of suburban longing.

Initially, the exhibit displayed a variety of hoofed mammals in separate rectangular paddocks. Each paddock included, in the words of the zoo's 1947 guidebook, "a sturdy stone and concrete house" at the rear, and for species preferring mountains, "concrete pinnacles that the animals climb."[39] To Schroeder, however, the entire exhibit was an eyesore of "cobblestone little buildings and hay racks."[40] Especially intolerable was the pervasive wire fencing that separated the enclosures and, worse, blocked visitor sight lines. A clear view of the animals was crucial to a man who forbade staff photographers from publishing any zoo image with wire in it.[41] During renovations, construction crews ripped out all the wire and replaced it with moats, trenches built into the ground that kept animals physically divided from their viewing public but allowed for unobstructed animal watching. Moating the exhibit produced a more seamless viewing experience. Moreover, it set the physical stage for a

MEANDERING
ON
HORN
AND
HOOF
MESA

Only an aerial view can show an overall of the exhibits completed within recent months, the location of the service areas and retiring quarters, and how the units fit into the contours of the tree-planted mesa. The freeway borders the hillside on the left, and we look north.

Figure 4.1. *Aerial view of Horn and Hoof Mesa at the San Diego Zoo,* Zoonooz, *February 1966. Courtesy of the Zoological Society of San Diego.*

spatial order that echoed the city's burgeoning suburbs and gave North County San Diegans a version of their own ideal habitats.

At Horn and Hoof Mesa, designers adopted the spatial attitude of North County. Generous, uncluttered animal spaces followed a pattern of low density. Large units backed into a tree-planted mesa, which supplied the requisite greenery for a garden suburb. Each faced a single curvilinear asphalt roadway reminiscent of the middle-class neighborhood streets beyond Mission Valley (Figure 4.2).[42] Each appeared architecturally indistinguishable from the next. The ground, outdoor dividing walls, and retiring quarters had little variation in scale or materials, and were further unified by the continuous horizontal lines of roadside ground cover, shrubs, and handrails. Working with a subdued color palate of neutral browns and beiges, designers simulated the desert plains native to many of the exhibited species. In the process, they also created a feeling of homogeneity characteristic of conventional

Figure 4.2. *Horn and Hoof Mesa under construction at the San Diego Zoo,* Zoonooz, *March 1965. Courtesy of the Zoological Society of San Diego.*

suburbia. The effect was a kind of tract housing for animals, an extended stretch of interchangeable abodes that reiterated the monotony of many postwar subdivisions before homeowners personalized their properties according to taste.[43] Years later, Peter Batten, a staunch advocate for American zoo renewal and director of the short-lived San Jose Zoo, underlined the connection in his unfavorable review of the exhibit: "A series of repetitious buff-colored concrete corrals, appropriately dubbed the 'Hoof and Horn Mesa,' house hoofed animals which bear boring similarity to their immediate neighbors."[44] Evidently, the San Diego Zoo's suburban showpiece could produce feelings of sprawl and uniformity as much as a pleasing sense of openness.

Tempering these negative associations was the exhibit's evocation of a signature pattern in U.S. suburban home design, the ranch-style house. For many Americans, the ranch house suggested something considerably attractive about life beyond the city center. Its appeal was far-reaching and became a residential staple in urban outskirts across the United States after World War II, including, most notably, its large-scale realization in Levittown, New Jersey. Architectural historians generally attribute its invention to Cliff May, a self-taught architect and San Diego native.[45] In the 1930s May began to spread the virtues of open-air living to a wider slice of suburban home seekers. Postwar versions of his designs took off. They were inexpensive, mass-produced constructions loosely based on the houses of the Spanish colonial missions in Southern California (Figure 4.3). As Barbara Allen argues, developers and architects imagined open floor plans with basic lines, single stories, and understated materials as the modern invocation of "simple one-room structures with packed dirt floors, a flat roof, and walls of adobe."[46] In addition to harking back to these earlier vernacular forms, ranch house designs sustained a heavily romanticized ideal of mission-era California as a land-centered way of life, slow in tempo and rich in agricultural and dynastic possibility. With its blending of indoors and outdoors, the ranch house was a frontiersman's home, integrated with its natural surroundings, a place where suburbanites could breathe, grow things, raise their children, and their children's children.

A 1970 real estate advertisement for the "Spacemaster I" filled out the dream for North County home buyers. Underneath a pleasant pen and ink drawing of a house with a large ranch-style facade, complete with rustic wooden front door and garage, the developer noted, "What really counts is, the space is there when you need it. No need to move as your family grows." Referencing the style's original inspiration, the Spacemaster I was designated for a tract appropriately called "Encore—on the Mesa." This was the ranch house at its most optimistic, though not necessarily its lived experience. In practice, what Allen calls "ranch-style capitalism" entailed a betrayal of the women and children who spent countless hours in its isolation, and of the men whose quasi-Western fantasies of unbridled agency could never be realized amid the gentle discipline of suburban life. Moreover, it was a betrayal of the natural environment that was violently reshaped into "the zero topography landscape endemic to gridded, featureless, suburban terrain."[47] The damage produced by San Diego's tract housing in particular included stripped ground, cutoff hills and banks, buried natural canyons, wasted water, and smog creation.[48] These social and environmental costs were, of course, entirely absent from the ranch house's aura as

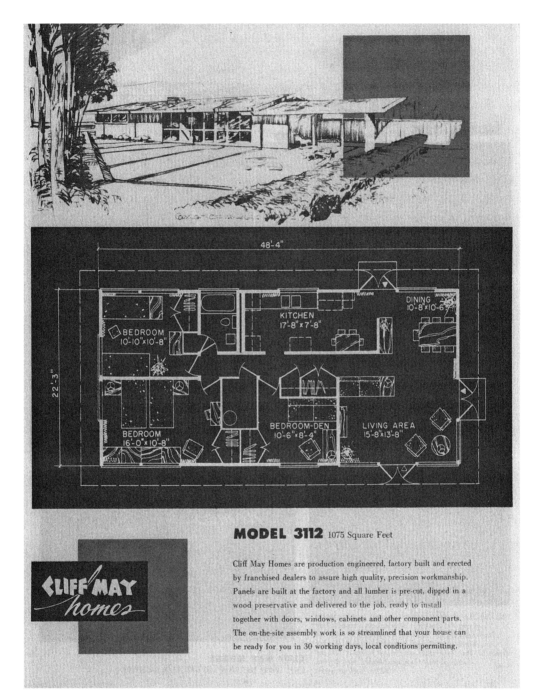

MODEL 3112 1075 Square Feet

Cliff May Homes are production engineered, factory built and erected
by franchised dealers to assure high quality, precision workmanship.
Panels are built at the factory and all lumber is pre-cut, dipped in a
wood preservative and delivered to the job, ready to install
together with doors, windows, cabinets and other component parts.
The on-the-site assembly work is so streamlined that your house can
be ready for you in 30 working days, local conditions permitting.

Figure 4.3. *Cliff May Homes leaflet, 1955. Cliff May papers, Architecture and Design Collection,
Art, Design, and Architecture Museum, University of California, Santa Barbara.*

it circulated in the suburban housing market. Extolling its merits, May stated, "The ranch house was everything a California house should be—it had cross-ventilation, the floor was level with the ground, and with its courtyard and the exterior corridor, it was about sunshine and informal outdoor living."[49]

Horn and Hoof Mesa's new animal spaces were also about sunshine and informal outdoor living. As reported in *Zoonooz,* "The most exciting changes have occurred since the fences were taken away, one by one, on the Horn and Hoof Mesa. Spacious, open, moated enclosures are replacing outmoded chainlink-fenced corrals."[50] The simplicity of forms echoed the fantasy of the California ranch house in its purest Spanish colonial state, enhanced with the principles of architectural modernism. From a visitor's perspective, living areas were largely outside and seemed to emerge from the dirt-covered ground itself. They took organic, sculptural shape in the gently undulating walls that demarcated each paddock, concealed sleeping areas, and articulated the style's rambling asymmetry (Figure 4.4). Surfaced pneumatically with a cement plaster in muted shades of brown, these walls also mimicked the ranch house's original adobe construction. Here was the housing type that May found so compelling, "a house literally molding itself to nature's contours!"[51] And like a ranch house, enclosures never rose beyond the height of a single story. All elements were built long and low, constructing an uninterrupted flow of space that appeared relaxed and uncomplicated.

The mass suburbanism of Horn and Hoof Mesa extended beyond North County's preferred single-family housing type to encompass the region's preferred composition of home owners. What differentiated the exhibit's animals from those housed in older displays were their mixed arrangements. "When we first got this started," recalled Schroeder, "we had zebra, ostriches, impalas, grants gazelle, tommy gazelle and crown cranes, all in one unit. And they all lived together and were doing fine."[52] At a certain angle, the impulse to spatially intermingle different species can be read as continuous with architectural developments within the postwar suburban house itself. The emergence of the family room in particular allowed for the pursuit of "family togetherness" among middle-income homeowners that aimed to cross gender and generational lines.[53] The ample and unpretentious leisure spaces of the new mesa echoed something of this spatial formation and its diversity of users. At another angle, the mixed-species exhibit can be read as an impulse to democratize the zoo's animal suburbia more broadly. Horn and Hoof Mesa was well configured for representing what Robert Fishman calls "the promise of a suburban home for all," a promise fueled by state-sponsored initiatives that gave Americans from various racial, ethnic, and class backgrounds the opportunity to own a home outside the much-feared urban cores.[54] These initiatives included, for example, the Federal

Figure 4.4. *Horn and Hoof Mesa's East Africa sable antelope at the San Diego Zoo,* Zoonooz, *March 1965. Courtesy of the Zoological Society of San Diego.*

Highway Act of 1956, which made suburban areas easier to access, and tax incentives that made suburban real estate easier to purchase.[55] Looking at a range of creatures existing side by side in apparent harmony and material comfort would epitomize the notion of suburbia's suitability for all walks of life. Scenes of animal integration would prove especially powerful for San Diegans grappling with a tenuous period of racial desegregation.

In June 1962 citizens of San Diego saw the prohibition of the city's racial covenants with the passage of California's Rumford Fair Housing Act. Under this act, the real estate industry could no longer legally prohibit the sale of property to people "other than one of the Caucasian race," effectively eliminating racially restrictive clauses in real estate deeds.[56] As Leroy Harris demonstrates, these clauses were responsible for creating a barrier against black residency beyond the southeast area while discouraging Latino relocation to surrounding neighborhoods in a less determined way.[57] Realtor groups, including the San Diego Realty Board, were loath to change their ways, but were forced to do so with the new legislation. They sought to repeal the act on a general election ballot in November 1964, arguing that it violated "the basic American right of freedom of choice placed on property owners" to sell to whomever they wanted, and that real estate sales were not "a racial issue with us."[58] The ballot was successful among California voters but failed when the state's supreme court reinstated the Fair Housing Act a year and a half later. Harris speculates that removal of restrictive clauses in real estate deeds—however unpopular among the majority of Californian home owners—may have motivated black San Diegans in the 1960s to seek housing in neighborhoods that were formerly closed to them.[59] More certain is that local and statewide debate about the directive to diversify neighborhoods stymied the region's habit of discriminatory housing practices and helped California's southernmost city became moderately responsive to its injustices.

The development of Horn and Hoof Mesa was a fitting reminder of San Diego's integration politics, and equally tentative. Preliminary efforts to produce a palatable picture of species multiplicity were conservative, to say the least. In *Zoonooz,* for example, the exhibit's mixed-species scenes appeared firmly controlled. Here, multiplicity became legible only through the spectacle of family unity and sameness. Editors mainly limited photographs of the exhibit's varied residents to same-species formations of male and female, "mother" and "child," and parents and offspring. These images constructed the mesa as a domestic space for heterosexual reproductive pairs and their progeny. They accentuated the visible features of biological kinship, such as the "black leg stripes and white eye rings" of the Uganda kob couple or the intertwined bodies of the new "nilgai twins" huddled close to their parents in a nuclear family portrait (Figure 4.5). Emphasis on morphological similarity suggested that suburban families were similarly bonded by a corporeal likeness, that the suburban family was a natural, and often striking, configuration housed in a pleasingly organic setting of sand, shrub, and curvature. *Zoonooz* editors reduced any heterogeneity in the exhibit to a pan-species assortment of conjugal and filial ties, a *Family of Man* with animal subjects.[60] Different species appeared as agreeable cohabitants so long as they kept to their own kind.

Seven months later, *Zoonooz* revisited the exhibit's theme of mixed-species display in a less repressive mood. An article titled "Togetherness for Mammals and Birds" pictured more than one animal family in the same photographic frame. A mother–daughter duo of addax "share a pen with Demoiselle Cranes"; in another photograph, two Lilford cranes "have been integrated with various Indian antelope

Figure 4.5. *Horn and Hoof Mesa's Nilgai hoofstock at the San Diego Zoo,* Zoonooz, *circa 1966. Courtesy of the Zoological Society of San Diego.*

and deer." The apex of this interspecies integration appeared in the article's first and largest image of a marabou stork, "a huge beautifully absurd bird," which "enjoys freedoms allowed only a few Zoo dwellers" and amounted to the ideal resident of both Horn and Hoof Mesa and North County San Diego (Figure 4.6). Unlike the animals housed in the zoo's older and more congested core, the stork looked strong and proud, standing upright and in the foreground with two African springbok and a white-bellied stork behind it. The everyday routine of the marabou stork was worlds away from those of the monkeys in a mostly wired B Mesa, or the snakes and lizards residing in the pre–World War II Reptile House, none of which had access to the carefree pleasures of a multispecies mosaic. The stork's existence, by contrast, appeared to be more limitless: a self-assured creature able to engage with whatever it seemed to choose. Fueling the larger suburban dream of spatial and social mobility through leisure, the bird "strolls from exhibit to exhibit, spending the day or parts thereof with animals from East Africa or Southern Africa"—or, as it were, socializing with other suburbanites of different ancestry.[61] Such openness made sense for a late-sixties inhabitant of the Sun Belt city's north world, zoologically lived and rendered.

A closer look at the exhibit's renovation suggests that its work as a cautious image of suburban integration ran deeper still. Much of this caution surfaced through the thorny process of building the exhibits moats, a series of trials and errors informed by an au courant concept in zoo design known as "flight distance." In an interview for the Zoological Society of San Diego Oral History Project, the in-house exhibition designer Charles Faust recalled its importance: "When we first did [the hoofstock area] we had pretty severe moats. We tried to figure out the safe distance to which you could work with these animals. Their flight distance and what would spook them and what wouldn't."[62] Flight distance refers to the amount of territory an animal requires between itself and a potential enemy in order to feel comfortable. The term was popularized by the Swiss zoologist Heini Hediger in the widely read 1950 English translation of his book *Wild Animals in Captivity*.[63] In it, Hediger argued that the most significant behavior pattern in a wild animal is a tendency to flee from those organisms that are perceived to endanger its safety, including humans. "In freedom," he wrote, "an animal subordinates everything to flight; that is the prime duty of an individual, for its own preservation, and for that of the race."[64] To accommodate this instinctive response, Hediger advised zoo designers to build enclosures large enough for an animal to gain its necessary and species-specific flight distance. Designing for flight distance meant creating a finite territory in which "the animal could retreat to the centre from a man of enemy significance standing on the perimeter" and could thus "find rest."[65] A technical drawing of the smallest possible enclosure showed a circular space with a diameter that was twice the flight distance of a given animal. Hediger marked its center point with an "H" to designate home (Figure 4.7).

Faust and his colleagues translated Hediger's concept of flight distance to the particularities of moat construction. They were sensitive to the possibility that "home" for the creatures of the new exhibit might be larger than had previously been considered, that distance between humans and animals, and between the various exhibited animals, might need to be increased. From the experiments that fol-

Figure 4.6. *"Togetherness for Mammals and Birds,"* Zoonooz, *September 1966. Courtesy of the Zoological Society of San Diego.*

lowed came a stronger sense of, and commitment to, what constituted biologically sound space for captive animals on display. As it happened, some species, like the giraffes, needed *less* territory and shorter, simpler trenches than initially estimated, a discovery made when observing that giraffes kept a distance of at least four feet from the moated edge. Meanwhile, the crown cranes were disposed to nightly escapes from their allocated home, followed by early morning returns before the

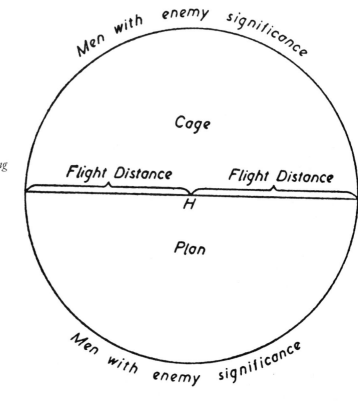

Figure 4.7. *Technical drawing of flight distance in Heini Hediger,* Wild Animals in Captivity *(Dover Publications, Inc., 1950).*

keepers arrived, suggesting that perhaps the birds needed more room.[66] At the same time, the society's investment in the idea of flight distance was fiercely social. In a postwar moment of shifting racial geographies, Hediger's emphasis on interspecies distance as a biological imperative commingled with fears about San Diego's racial communities coming into close contact with each other on the city's northern edges. Designing for "H" articulated and legitimated those fears by giving them architectural shape in revitalized animal display. In this exhibit, the comfort zones of each species were taken seriously, and physical space was modified accordingly. If differences between animals proved too upsetting in their proximity, designers and curators would make the necessary adjustments. If differences were inconsequential, which is to say, tolerable among the residents, the space would hold. Paying heed in this way to the minimum spatial requirements for living in psychic comfort and security, Faust and his colleagues built scenes of suburban harmony that addressed, however indirectly, very contemporary anxieties about who lived next door and who did not. In Horn and Hoof Mesa, most neighbors were "fine," save for the odd "pugnacious" animal that would force other creatures to jump the moat and assert greater flight distances.[67] In those circumstances, animals were simply removed, and patrons were spared the unpleasantness of witnessing any interspecies conflict.

It is no small irony that, on completion, Horn and Hoof Mesa did not immediately attract the expected crowds, on account of it being a "far-flung mesa." When the exhibit was near completion, pedestrian pattern studies showed that its out-of-the-way location was a problem, reporting that "the walking distance and climb is definitely a deterrent."[68] Researchers recommended finding a better way to transport people to and from the area than the traditional tour bus. The solution came in 1969 with the construction of "Skyfari," the zoo's electric cable-car tram system that moved visitors quickly across the grounds in their own suspended traveling cabin. Zoo goers climbed into one of forty-seven brightly painted "cars," each seating a comfortable four.[69] Marking another stage in the suburbanization of the grounds, Skyfari enhanced ordinary zoo transportation with a modern means of family-centered travel. Coasting above and across the zoo core at 490 feet a minute, the technology evoked San Diego's burgeoning freeway system that bypassed many older city neighborhoods, bumping up visitor traffic in the zoo's most remote animal community.

THE WILD ANIMAL PARK AS DESTINED HOMELAND

In the early 1960s Faust drew a blueprint-sized picture of nonnative animals in a rural setting, and titled it *Back Country Conservation Area* (Figure 4.8). The illustration put viewers on the downward slope of a rough and grassy hillside. From this vantage point, they surveyed an immense landscape populated by various mammals and birds in group formations. Some animals, like the zebra, appeared still and relaxed, available for extended contemplation. Others appeared in motion, like the eland leaping behind the giraffes, the ostrich dashing off to the right middle ground, or the three large birds flying high overhead. Still others were notable for their family-like configuration; two groups of hoofstock in the far left of the picture appeared with young animals. Centered in the image was the drawing's only human figure: a light-skinned driver of an all-terrain vehicle steering through a winding dirt path that led down the hillside, deeper into the Arcadian scene brimming with life.

While the Wild Animal Park did not develop exactly according to Faust's vision, his panorama highlights the ambitions of what Sheldon Campbell, a zoo trustee, would (prematurely) call "the last word in open-space zoos."[70] Park planners embraced the idea of open space by expanding exhibit size, retaining and enhancing existing topographic features, combining different animal species from the same geographic zone, and beckoning human visitors to recreate in the midst of it all. In their hands,

Figure 4.8. *Concept drawing for the Wild Animal Park by Charles Faust, 1964. Copyright San Diego History Center.*

some five hundred of the park's full eighteen hundred acres set the stage for 973 animals representing 150 different species, many of which were able to move across its fields without any visible barriers.[71] Visitors, by contrast, were "caged" within a state-of-the-art electric monorail train, which snaked through the facility's outer edges and gave clear sightlines of the roaming herds (Figure 4.9).

Society officials and their allies explained the value of this plan in largely biological terms. More naturalistic animal space, said the experts, would encourage higher reproduction rates, boosting the population of endangered species worldwide and, even more pressingly for zoos, the population of captive animals available for display.[72] A preliminary proposal for the park underscored the urgency: "There is a desperate need to establish local U.S. sources of wild species which are becoming increasingly difficult to obtain abroad and which are actually facing extinction."[73] Open space promised to improve this imminent shortage in supply by encouraging *ex-situ* breeding on a larger, "wilder" scale. In 1971 Ian Player, the prominent white South African conservationist who brought twenty white rhinoceroses into the park, predicted that its exhibition style "will become the chief display concept of the future" largely because "the animals act as they would in the wild state." After tour-

Figure 4.9. *Monorail at the Wild Animal Park, 1972. Copyright San Diego History Center.*

ing the grounds in 1972, Joy Adamson, the British author of the best-selling animal tale *Born Free,* judged them to be "a wonderful improvement in exhibiting wild animals," since "cheetahs need privacy to reproduce—privacy that is not available in San Diego but may be at San Pasqual." *Sunset* magazine elaborated: "Here they have room to run, to stake out territory, to be free of constraints that would keep many of them from reproducing under usual zoo conditions." The *San Diego Union* was more blunt: "Give animal families elbow room, and they will have babies."[74]

But the biology of wildlife conservation was only part of the picture. Vast in acreage and residential in essence, the Wild Animal Park offered San Diegans satisfactions that paralleled those of North County and intensified the whiteness of Horn and Hoof Mesa. Hailed by the popular media as "San Diego's Wild Animal Suburb" and a "Super Home on the Range," the facility strove to meet the appetite for home-based open space in a rustic form that called for some nineteenth-century naturalism amid the region's passion for midcentury modernism. Here, suburbanites were invited to suspend their modernity and acquaint themselves with a Southern

California landscape in the purported pristine glory of its Anglo-American past.[75] The park promised visitors an updated replica of the mythic Southwestern ranch-lands that made western-style yeomen of them all. In doing so, it injected suburban space with renewed vitality, giving shelter from broken downtowns across the country that many communities still called home, or close to home.[76] Commenting on his own downtown in this period, one San Diego urban redevelopment executive reminisced in 1985 from the perspective of a suburbanite: "If ever an urban core cried for change, it was downtown San Diego in the late 1960s and early 1970s. . . . Its tax base was deteriorated, its adult entertainment uses proliferated, most of its residents occupied single rooms in old hotels, its street people abounded, and its overall appearance south of Broadway was one of acute physical decline."[77]

Schroeder, for one, was perceptive about the park's potential to re-create back-country living for a generation of urban exiles.[78] The early days of park planning found the director brainstorming the new zoo's characteristics by conflating open space for nonnative animals with open space for human San Diegans settling north. In a June 1961 memo to the Board of Trustees, he wrote:

> We should identify the area with *San Diego*. We should indicate that it is a refuge. We must infer great size. We must suggest *a preserve for exotic species*. It would be unfortunate to lose the romantic reference to San Pasqual with its historical significance.[79]

The key elements were all there in a suggestive overlap. Planners were to emphasize the physical immensity of the site and the sanctuary it could offer to locals. The character of this sanctuary was double-sided, as both an exotic species preserve and a place to preserve the area's associations with pastoral beauty and well-being. While the mix would be lost on the park's animal population, Schroeder expected visitors would, on some level, appreciate how the new zoo combined the conservation of nonnative animals with the revival of an idealized frontier heritage.

There was plenty of heritage from which to draw. Nestled into the valley were fabled histories of Spanish colonial *ranchos,* American nation building, and agricultural abundance. It was common knowledge that the society's future stomping grounds were close to the site of a crucial battle in the war between California's Mexican settlers and a U.S. federal government in the process of westward expansion. Well-cited in the state's official history, and referenced in the society's promotional apparatus, the 1846 Battle of San Pasqual was a determined *Californio* defense against an American territorial invasion run by Anglo officers with the help of Delaware Indians and African American slaves. Led by Captain Andrés Pico, locals engaged in lanced and hand-to-hand combat with U.S. forces to protect their ranchos and the mission system at large. Their resulting victory, while jubilant, could only be temporary in the face of America's sense of and commitment to its own manifest destiny.[80] The *San Diego Union* reporter Marguerite Sullivan phrased it so on the eve of the park's opening: "The San Pasqual Valley made history nearly 126 years ago as the site of one of the fiercest battles in the winning of California to the United States. This week, that pastoral valley 30 miles north of downtown San Diego is making history again."[81] Sullivan extended the history lesson by adding that after the conflict, "the valley reverted to its serene character, with rabbits outnumbering people three to one" and, later, "citrus, avocados and vegetables grow[ing] on farmland leased from the city."[82] Notable was how this and other popular accounts of the valley portrayed the area's Spanish colonial reign before the American takeover as an age of innocence and serenity. Reporting in *San Diego Magazine,* for example, Dolly Maw described the area as a "beautiful, fertile valley" of "12,654 acres given to Don Juan Bautista by the governor of Mexico in 1843."[83] These treatments overlooked a harsher picture of life on the secular ranchos that replicated the power structures of the missions proper through abusive labor practices and sexual violence toward indigenous workers.[84]

Imagining San Pasqual as a peaceful agricultural landscape in the wake of war was key to the formation of the park's open-space aesthetic and a centerpiece of its whiteness. It marked out a safe and healthy space for mid-twentieth-century suburbanites beleaguered by their own fears of a black urban "underclass" and the environmental costs of a sprawl of their own making. In San Pasqual, safety and health seemed intrinsic to the soil itself, a sentiment that upheld the nineteenth-century portrait of Southern California as the nation's Garden of Eden, placid and ripe for cultivation at the hands of enterprising gentleman farmers. Garden imagery of this sort was a perennial favorite in the United States, as Henry Nash Smith's classic discussion in *Virgin Land* makes clear: "The master symbol of the garden embraced a cluster of metaphors expressing fecundity, growth, increase, and blissful labor in the earth, all centering about the heroic figure of the idealized frontier farmer armed with that supreme agrarian weapon, the sacred plow."[85] For Smith, figurations of an agricultural paradise in the West were fodder for mythmaking and nation building. They created an American identity and the cultural conditions for its material development. With an explicitly Southern Californian focus, Kevin Starr argues that the garden myth was, in turn, bound to a racial myth of the region as the destined homeland for the nation's Anglo bourgeoisie. Mythmakers such as Charles Fletcher Lummis, editor of the turn-of-the-century magazine *Land of Sunshine* (later known as *Out West*), popularized the notion of Southern California as "the new Eden of the Saxon home-seeker" and took possession of the land on evolutionary grounds.[86] Lummis and his fellow "Arroyans" promoted white Protestant Americans of northern European stock as the area's fittest settlers, biologically and spiritually ordained to build a utopic Sun Belt haven. Liberated from the immigration and environmental pollution that was figuratively and materially darkening cities in the eastern United States, they were zealously optimistic about their coastal and inland futures. A good work ethic and appreciation of the region's natural beauty, they believed, would turn the region into an Anglo homage to the fertile Mediterranean soils overseas or, in Lummis's worldview, an imaginary Spanish past of tranquil missions and Arcadian bliss.[87] Starr points to the racial theories of Joseph Pomeroy Widney as one manifestation of Lummis's strand of boosterism. Author of *Race Life of the Aryan Peoples* from 1907, Widney's ideas about the natural superiority of the "Engle" race and its special connection to Southland was, for Starr, more extreme than Lummis's position but also indicative of "an underlying belief that Southern California somehow offered Protestant America a long-desired place in the sun."[88]

The process of claiming and cultivating the park's expansive acreage was conducted with a similar sense of racial entitlement. The society and its chief spokespersons were fond of recapping the story years later in magazine, interview, and biographical formats. As Schroeder remembers it, the park's planning committee underwent a period of deal making with the municipal government in the 1960s before obtaining their plot of choice. The committee invited city managers to the society's future site to witness members drawing straight lines from the extreme east and west of the property to highway 78, delineating the desired eighteen hundred acres. Administrators in the city's utilities department who had been leasing the land to farmers at a fee promptly turned over the property for society use.[89] Around this time, the site also hosted Schroeder and his allies for regular picnics. As Myers narrates it, "Charlie," a native New Yorker who always favored the Southwest, had big plans for the valley:

It happened every few weeks. Charlie would bring a friend, a dignitary, a colleague, a city official, a group of Zoo patrons, a celebrity, a trustee, and usually a bucket of fried chicken. He would stand on the hill, spread his arms as if to take in the whole surrounding valley that was nothing more than scrub brush, cactus, and rattlesnakes, and he would share his dream. Over there, he'd point, will be the East African Valley. Over here will be the Asian plains. And right there, a watering hole designed exactly like one in the South African wild. The animals will roam free—rhinos, antelope, giraffes. People will see them all from a train winding through the preserve, having an experience they could never have anywhere this side of a transcontinental adventure in the wide-open wild.[90]

Arms outstretched and fingers pointed, Myers's snapshot of Schroeder's early settlement conveyed a singularity of vision that mirrored reformers like Lummis, minus the pretension. The director's beloved project did not quite match the exaggerated gentility of its late nineteenth-century predecessors, such as the hotelier Frank Miller's neo-Franciscan Mission Inn in Riverside County or the novelist Helen Jackson's best-selling epic *Ramona*.[91] In place of a whitewashed colonial Spain—a model that worked well for the downtown zoo's earliest designs as well as Horn and Hoof Mesa—Schroeder reimagined the landscape as a wilderness ideal of southeast Africa and, to a lesser extent, Asia. The concept of displaying wild animals on the exotic open range was better suited to Schroeder's folksy frontierism as well as a newly expanded market for safari-style entertainment. Here was a myth that, like all myths, depicted something outside historical time and familiar geographical space. Still, Schroeder understood the imperative to stay close to home: to discuss African and Asian landscapes while eating fried chicken, to foresee wild spectacles delivered from the security of an electric train comparable with the steam engines passing through the western United States a hundred years prior. Anything too exotic risked being received as a threat. Thus, much like Lummis and his inspired contemporaries, the fascination with temporally and spatially distant lands never strayed far. It circled back to local concerns for individual comfort and white supremacy, conjuring up an "adventure" that was domesticated by the safety of a postwar suburbanite's inherited place in the world.

Accompanying the dream work of building an agrarian paradise with African–Asian intonations was the physical work of colonizing the land. According to Schroeder, laborers first sectioned off the property with posts, concrete, and a six-foot-high fence, which arrived by helicopter because of the rugged ground and absence of roads. Next came the construction of separate fenced areas for the animal exhibits. These exhibits did not initially follow a formal plan; their development was as boundless as the park's new acquisition: "Would we dig for moats? Would we put up stone walls? Would we put up fencing? How about in-riggers? How would you do this?"[92] Still more boundless was the director's bravado in laying out the park's monorail line with his righthand men:

And those early days [Construction Manager] Hal Barr, Charles Faust and I, walked the site of the railroad. And my job was to drive in the stakes. And Hal Barr told me where to put them with his hand transit, this hand-held thing you know. He'd say up a little, oh a little, back a little. And you'd get there and he'd say that's it. I'd put the stake down and whack it in, and Charlie Faust would tie the red ribbon on it. And it's surprising, it didn't take us very long to walk the five miles and stick it.[93]

Published photographs in *Zoonooz* and the director's biography emphasized the extent of his performance as a youthful pioneer intuitively marking society territory in the veldt (Figure 4.10). The set of four images depicted a sixty-nine-year-old Schroeder amid the chaparral dressed in work pants and a plaid shirt rolled at the sleeves. The figure was solitary, vertical, and engrossed in the task at hand. In the first, he hammered a wooden post into the dirt. In the second, he appeared striding across the land with post and hammer in hand. The third showed Schroeder in profile against a big sky, looking out over the area with bundled posts under one arm and hammer in the other hand. The final shot pictured him pointing beyond the photographic plane, as if indicating the next spot for rail line construction. That each of these photographs was taken close to the ground augmented the director's physical size in relation to the land and his visual mastery over it. In them, Schroeder appeared as a strapping outdoorsman, inhabiting the future park's wilderness space with a self-confidence that approached Jane Tompkins's interpretation of the star in a western film:

For the setting by its hardiness and austerity seems to have selected its heroes from among strong men in the prime of life, people who have a certain build, complexion, facial type, carriage, gesture, and demeanor; who dress a certain way, carry certain accoutrements, have few or no social ties, are expert at certain skills (riding, tracking, roping, fistfighting, shooting) and terrible at others (dancing, talking to ladies). And because the people who exhibit these traits in Westerns are invariably white, male, and Anglo-Saxon, the Western naturalizes a certain racial, gender, and ethnic type as hero. There is no need to say that men are superior to women, Anglos to Mexicans, white men to black; the scene has already said it.[94]

Indeed, the larger discourse around the park's earliest construction said as much. Reminiscent of the western genre, it glorified the seemingly spontaneous labor of park staff, and the director in particular, while making it seem as if the land itself were endorsing the racial authority of its leading men simply by virtue of it appearing so vacant. Here was a blankness that invited the straightforward occupation traditionally known as white American settlement: clear, energetic, inevitable.

Figure 4.10. *Charles Schroeder laying out the proposed monorail line for the Wild Animal Park, circa 1970. Courtesy of the Zoological Society of San Diego.*

Representations of zoo officials at work in the San Pasqual Valley did not convey the park's history of multiracial, multiethnic workers on-site, they did not profile the role of women volunteers in raising park funds, nor did they speak to its labor disputes. Missing from the preserve's foundational myth were, for instance, the picket lines that formed outside the park during its construction in protest over work restrictions for members of the union Local 89. These more complicated scenarios were all but invisible to public eyes while the society rehearsed a favorite motif in the western's repertoire: just a group of honest, capable guys giving shape to a landscape of equal veracity.[95]

Images of a (re)claimed Southland continued to circulate as park planners introduced nonnative animals into the area and showcased their unhampered movement. The sight of animals dashing about, acting wild, became a primary way to construct the Wild Animal Park as Southern California's preeminent piece of open space real estate: a couple of Boehm's zebra trotting through waist-high shrubbery, a galloping Uganda giraffe testing its pace on a spacious hillside, Kenya impalas making a quick turn.[96] These lively scenes could not be guaranteed to visitors riding on the park's monorail—animals would sometimes move slowly or stay still, particularly in the midday heat—but publicity materials served as a reliable display medium.

Moreover, images like these upstaged quiet anecdotes of animals gone *too* wild: zebras trampling baby deer to death, rhinos destroying shrubbery, parasites ravaging cheetahs, and local bobcats and coyotes preying on the exhibit population.[97] These stories, and their swift, corrective responses, reminded San Diegans who got wind of them that the possibilities evoked by "open space" were not as limitless as they claimed to be; the preserve was never an actual free-for-all for very long.

The park's depiction in the December 1969 issue of *Zoonooz* was a case in point. Between the material reality of alternately sluggish and unruly animals was one article headlined "Running Room." The article updated readers on the progress of construction by featuring the most recent animals "released" into the park's expanse. One photograph captured the transfer of a white-bearded gnu into its new three-to-five-acre enclosure (Figure 4.11). Captioned as a "taste of wilderness" for the gnu, the image showed a hoofed animal with horns, muscular build, and shaggy mane "kicking up a cloud of dust" as it bolted from its transfer crate.[98] Photographed in the middle of its stride, the gnu appeared full of power and focus, moving itself deeper into an enclosure whose western boundary appropriately exceeded the visible frame. A wire fence in the distance, partially covered by shrubs, divided the animal's assigned space from the foothills behind it, but kept the left side of the picture—the West, as it were—clear. Similarly, a second photograph pictured a fringe-eared oryx moving into the same space, freed from the confines of its crate and the control of park staff (Figure 4.12). While its pace appeared slower, the oryx's flight suggested another push westward, created through the diagonal angles of fencing that seemed to point the way and the presence of the gnu on the left, holding itself steady as if waiting for its sidekick from the east.

"Running Room" featured still another representation of animal movement, which conveyed the idea of free-ranging beasts through the appearance of a Chevrolet station wagon (Figure 4.13). A photograph displayed a "handy Suburban Carry-All" parked somewhere on the grounds, painted to look like a zebra with black-and-white stripes. As *Zoonooz* reported, "The Zebra . . . frequently streaks along the 29 miles of highways between the San Diego Zoo and 1,800 acres in San Pasqual Valley bordering Highway 78."[99] In front of the wagon stood two executives from the Chevrolet Dealers of San Diego County, handing over the keys to park representatives cast in the role of a white suburban family: Harold Barr, the park construction manager, JoAnn Thomas, an attendant at the Children's Zoo, and, in her arms, a small bonobo in a puff-sleeved dress. As if stationed on the family's driveway, with a sprawling hillside homestead lying directly behind and other suburban dwellings visible in the far distance, the zebra wagon and its new owners gave magazine readers a sense of

Figures 4.11, 4.12, and 4.13. *"Running Room,"* Zoonooz, *December 1969. Courtesy of the Zoological Society of San Diego.*

their own ex-urban freedom, reviving the long-standing appeal of ample space for able people. Once again, the "animal" in the photograph faced westward.

The day before the park opened to its public, North County businesses ran advertisements in the *Escondido Times-Advocate* to congratulate the new animal preserve and celebrate its potential. Their well-wishing reinforced the notion that the society's aesthetic of open space was not only environmentally sensitive to its animal charges but also constitutive of its whiteness. A local savings and loan association by the name of Home Federal was one example. Likening the San Pasqual facility to an idyllic residential space for America's chosen ones—those who are "born free. To roam free . . ."—the company labeled the park "Home Federal Country" and displayed two birds in midflight. San Diego Glass & Paint took a different approach in its ad by emphasizing safety amid the freedom. Alluding to the installation of the park's safety glass, the company endorsed the entire conservation concept as "*a safe idea for man and beast*," adding that it could also meet "all your glass requirements—including tempered safety glass, mirrors, bath enclosures, sliding window and patio doors."[100] Most striking of all was the submission by a North County furniture store (Figure 4.14). The Wayside Shop forged links between the park's animals and the store's target customers by suggesting that both park and store were attentive to "the importance of setting."[101] Two illustrations of equal size appeared below this heading: one of a charging buffalo standing in for a more exotic species, and the other of a traditional American storefront sign in wood and antiquated script. The copy between the figures states that the Wild Animal Park is "Chaparral Country—it's ideal for the Gnu and other wild animals," and the Wayside Shop was "Early American Country—it's ideal for people who still cherish some of the very simple yet elegant things in life. Our very best regards go to both!"[102] Beneath the superficial distinction between wildness and civility lay a point of similarity, if not outright equivalence. The buffalo/gnu and its surroundings deserved to be treasured not in contrast to the existence embodied by the home furnishing style called Early American but as a version of it. The Wayside Shop provoked San Diegans who loved the rudimentary benches, tables, and chairs first crafted by the nation's earliest colonists to consider their tastes as a charming extension of the animal's ideal habitat. Best regards went to both ways of life and the native land in which they thrived.

These slices of North County's commercial culture, and the zoo boosterism of which they were a part, crystallized the fears and fantasies that the city's open-space enthusiasts took seriously and would find prominent in the Zoological Society's newest spot. The ads constructed the experience of viewing multiple endangered species amid vast naturalistic terrain in terms of the experience of being shielded

the importance
of the
setting.

The San Diego Wild Animal Park is Chaparral Country — it's ideal for the Gnu and other wild animals.

The Wayside Shop is Early American Country- it's ideal for people who still cherish some of the very simple yet elegant things in life.

Our very best regards go to both!

345 W. Grand Ave., Downtown Escondido
745-1001   Free Parking in Rear
Store Hours: Open Daily 9 am to 5:30 pm, Open Monday and Friday 'Til 9 pm

Figure 4.14. *Furniture store advertisement in the* Escondido Times-Advocate, *1972.*

from three decades of postwar urban growth and supposed degeneration. Indeed, local energy and empathy for the plight of endangered species drew directly from the society's aesthetic power to renew a privileged history of unspoiled living and satisfy a white bourgeois desire for more personal space that was shared among different forms of suburban San Diego life. In this new American zoo, feeling for endangered wildlife, or like endangered wildlife, became tantamount to feeling for or like the residents of San Diego's Promised Land.

5

Looking Endangered

In February 1971 staff from the Zoological Society of San Diego released twenty southern white rhinoceroses from South Africa's Umfolozi Game Reserve into the Wild Animal Park in suburban San Diego. As former director Charles Schroeder recalled twelve years later, "We brought the rhinos in very early. And this built enthusiasm, especially on the part of the local people."[1] There was much cause for enthusiasm. The acquisition was the largest collection of these animals in any U.S. zoo to date, matched only by the same number acquired for London Zoo's facility in Whipsnade a few months prior.[2] At fourteen hundred pounds each and $100,000 total, the rhinos were also the heaviest and most costly acquisition in the society's history.[3] Equally impressive was the group's rapid breeding record. In five short years, twenty-five calves were born on-site, confirming the theory that more naturalistic space for animals meant more reproduction and, by extension, a stronger conservation program. With numbers like these, the southern white rhinoceros became the park's flagship (sub)species.[4] Park officials prominently featured the large-horned animals in the new zoo's promotional machine, all of which shaped the physical experience of visiting the society's second campus and seeing the species in the flesh (see Plate 7). Upon entry to the park, visitors moved through elaborate East African–inspired architecture and six different multiacre field exhibits before taking in the grand finale: a white rhino collection grazing, wallowing, gestating, and rearing its young on a ninety-three-acre representation of the southeast African veldt.[5] Even from a distance, the spectacle struck a responsive chord with zoo lovers. A 1971 letter to Schroeder, for example, found Theodore Reed, director of the National Zoo in Washington, D.C., daydreaming about the scene that was under construction: "In my mind's eye I can see those twenty white rhinoceroses romping around in that valley. It is really going to be a magnificent sight."[6]

This chapter analyzes representations of the southern white rhino, focusing on the regionally specific ways in which the species became legible as endangered. Endangerment was the central and overdetermined message of the acquisition, breeding, and exhibition of the collection. The society framed each of these aspects of white rhino display as conservation work for a species at risk of extinction. Publicizing the birth of the first white rhino born on the grounds, for example, writers at *Zoonooz,* the society's monthly magazine, were unambiguous: "The primary reason for the translocation of the White Rhinoceroses . . . is reproduction of the species—to bolster their numbers which not too many years ago were dwindling to a critical point."[7]

The extent to which the species was currently endangered was less clear. By the 1950s rhino counters were reporting that the southern white rhinoceros had recovered from its near extermination at the turn of the century to the point of overpopulation on the Umfolozi Game Reserve.[8] A greater number of animals were putting pressure on limited food supplies. Poachers and squatters entering from Zulu areas surrounding the reserve added to the crowding. Efforts to address the problem began in 1961, when Ian Player, a white South African warden for the reserve, organized an intensive campaign of rhino relocation to other African reserves and international zoos, including the Wild Animal Park. The subsequent immobilization, crating, and shipment of twenty individual animals to San Pasqual were, at this angle, a function of rhino surplus more than scarcity. From the society's point of view, the surplus continued into the next decade. When the American Association of Zoological Parks and Aquariums approached San Diego's new zoo makers with the idea of nationally coordinating the reproduction of white rhino populations, the society turned the offer down, arguing that white rhinos were in no short supply. Wrote a zoo executive, Charles Bieler, to the association in 1982, "Since we are breeding them prolifically and they are also being bred so well throughout the country, we do not wish to participate in this species survival plan."[9] The association countered that the species was not, according to some conservationists, secure in its numbers, despite the apparent "population explosion," adding that "complacency about the southern white rhino does not seem justified."[10]

Endangerment, then, was a contested empirical fact. But it was also a certain quality that emerged from the representational practices of differently situated human and animal actors, cumulatively figuring twenty individuals and their kind as vulnerable creatures worth saving. What made the park's white rhinos look endangered was a process of shifting animal imagery. Further, and like so much of

American zoo renewal, the process by which white rhinos came to look endangered intersected with the racial politics of their immediate postwar environs. In the press and through the landscape, the park's prized collection articulated a broad desire for whiteness in 1970s Southern California, and the strange instability of that whiteness. As I discussed in chapter 4, postwar San Diegans from a range of backgrounds were taking up home ownership in its suburban outskirts at full throttle and, with it, a notion of the Good Life organized around single-family detached houses and the clean, rustic beauty of unspoiled land. Add to this the exponential growth of tourism, which was converting a shady wartime sailor town into a wholesome, family-centered vacation spot with car-centered attractions.[11] Industry analysts were giddy with the possibilities. In a 1973 speech delivered by Robert Smith, a former zoo trustee and California marketing executive, tourism existed as a panacea for racially coded cultural development. It promoted a "greater 'clean-up, fix-up' attitude" while shifting the tax burden from residents to visitors. The industry had already managed to convert San Francisco's Ghirardelli Square and the Cannery from "slum areas" to "a shopper's and tourist's delight," setting "a high value on attractive environment for their people." "Their people" included Americans who had settled in the West and built an "at-home market": consumers with solid incomes and education, more leisure time, and an increased taste for travel.[12]

White rhinos at the Wild Animal Park and their quality of endangerment were connected to these changes. The contexts through which the species became visible and celebrated were rich in the white racial signification that defined the region in the long postwar period. This signification was not discussed as an effort to make and keep Southern California white; race under zoo renewal was seldom if ever so overt or self-aware. Rather, exhibiting white rhinos in ways that conformed to a specific racial ideal functioned along the lines of a shared impulse between curators, designers, and their suburbanizing public. Striking here was the tendency for animals to teeter on the edge of their own constructed whiteness. Extending a history of racially oblique rhinos, the inability of white rhinos to appear white for very long under the park's discursive apparatus was the crux of their potential as a flagship species. Few other species could have conveyed the paradox of a burgeoning white suburban identity, inherited by a few, promoted to many, desired by still more, and so, as it were, endangered by its own democratization.

Unpacking how that paradox manifested at the park is the goal of this chapter, which follows the film scholar Richard Dyer's conception of white representation and a range of rhino-related materials that orbited San Diego's new suburban zoo. I begin by surveying a longer tradition of visualizing race through rhinos, then historicize the production of African safari in the region to consider how its reinvention at the Wild Animal Park nurtured a white racial identity for rhino watchers and their animal subjects, precariously.

RHINO CORPOREALITY AND THE UNCERTAINTY OF RACE

Racializing any organism is an uneven, contradictory, and inconclusive process partly because biological bodies and natural behaviors, some of the chief signifiers of race, can likewise prove uneven, contradictory, and inconclusive to the eye. This slipperiness is notable in histories of people who have migrated in and out of a given racial category through shifting visual registers of corporeality: the Jew's body as variously white and black in Western art and visual culture; the film star Marlene Dietrich's not-quite-aquiline nose; Irish features that were variously simianized or feminized in Victorian graphic satire.[13] We could push this further still to consider how bodies themselves exert an agency of their own that can make it hard for racial assignations to stick with any degree of certainty. The cultural history of rhinos belongs to this tradition. Inasmuch as their racial identity has been associated with their corporeality, it has also been frustrated by it. On the one hand, artists and naturalists have consulted what rhinos look like, how they move, what they do and do not do, to create parallels (or mirrors) of human racial difference. On the other hand, they have also confronted these visual markers as problems for the construction of race, particularly when rhino bodies and behaviors have fallen short or confounded expectations of what is white, black, Asian, or otherwise racially distinct.

One of the most enduring representations of the horned creatures in the zoological canon illustrates how corporeality both confirms and confounds racialization (Figure 5.1). Drawn and cut in 1515, Albrecht Dürer's woodcut of an Indian "Gomda" was based on sketches and a description of the animal by an unknown Portuguese artist, who had laid eyes on a live specimen bound for Lisbon as a royal gift from the sultan of Guzurat.[14] While the specimen eventually died en route from Lisbon to Rome in 1516 (on its way to Pope Leo X), Dürer's rhinoceros took on a life of its own, circulating and being reinterpreted for nearly 250 years in visual art and zoological illustration as a kind of shorthand for exoticism.[15] Versions of the animal found their way into other drawings, engravings, tapestries, reliefs, door faces, dishware, and clocks, lending each object a touch of the unfamiliar. In accounting for this rhino's cultural longevity, art historians have drawn attention to how it made the material form of the living animal much more fanciful. Both Dürer's drawing and woodcut took the physical features of the Indian rhinoceros as a point of wild departure, constructing a strange, wonderful beast whose form was exaggerated in its oddity. That the artist had never seen this or any other living rhinoceros be-

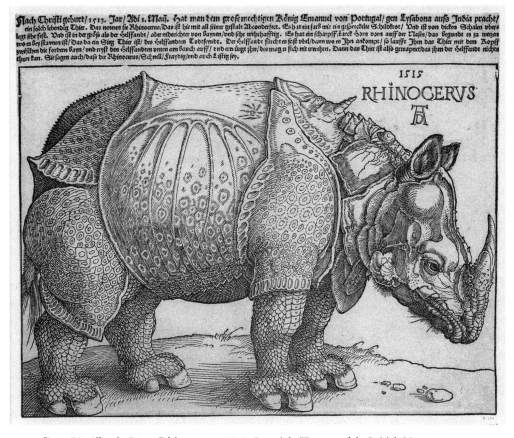

Nach Chrifti geburt/ 1513. Jar/ Adi 1. Maij. Hat man dem grofe mechtigen König Emanuel von Portugal/ gen Lyfabona aufs India pracht/ ein folch lebendig Thier. Das nennen fie Rhinocerus/Das ift hie mit all feiner geftalt Abconberfect. Es ift ein farb wie ein gefprecklete Schildkrot/ Und ift von dicken Schalen uberlegt fehr feft. Und ift in der gröſz als der Helffandt/ aber nidrichter von Baynen/und fehr werhafftig. Es hat ein fcharpff/ftarck Horn vorn auff der Nafen/das begundt es zu wetzen wo es bey ftaynen ift/Das da ein Sieg Thier ift/ des Helffanten Todtfendt. Der Helffandt fürchtet es faft ubel/dann wo es Jhn ankompt/ fo laufft Jhm das Thier mit dem Kopff zwefchen die fordern Bayn/und ryfzt den Helffanten unten am Bauch auff/ und an urgt jhn/des mag er fich nit erwehren. Dann das Thier ift alfo gewapnet/das jhm der Helffandt nichts thun kan. Sie fagen auch/dafz der Rhinocerus/Schnell/Fraydig/und auch Liftig fey.

Figure 5.1. *Albrecht Dürer,* Rhinoceros, *1515. Copyright Trustees of the British Museum.*

fore making his pictures underscores the imaginativeness of his creation: a massive, steadfast creature, encrusted with ornamental detail and barely contained by its frame, an animal larger than its biological life. In addition to a prominent primary horn, Dürer took the liberty of adding a small, spiraling one on the animal's back, a feature that is absent on an actual Indian rhinoceros and possibly referred to the creature's long-held association with the unicorn.[16] More remarkable still, perhaps, was the representation of the rhinoceros's skin. In Dürer's imaginary, folds of thick flesh became a coat of armor, protecting the animal from its ancient foes, like the elephant. Individuated plates covered the animal's torso, upper legs, back, and chest, some elaborated with oval markings, others resembling peculiar flora in some ossified state.

Beyond classical fables of unicorns and elephant rivals, the exuberant exoticism of this rhinoceros expressed Portuguese colonial expansion. Dürer's art used the materiality of *Rhinoceros unicornis,* and other rhino species more generally, to sustain an enduring fantasy of racial otherness evoked by the image of nonindigenous animals. What the body could provide, the artist amplified; what the body could not provide, the artist supplemented, and then some. The degree to which the drawing and woodcut represented the rhino as the zoological embodiment of a colonial human subject is unclear. More certain, however, is that the biological characteristics of a single specimen became a rich source of elaboration to the point where those characteristics, if absent altogether, would appear all the same in Dürer's portrait. These elaborations rendered the creature utterly strange to its European audience, nourishing a persistent and versatile pattern of aesthetically linking nonhuman natural histories to human beings identified as other than white.

In its early sightings by Western eyes, the white rhinoceros underwent a similar process of symbolic exaggeration and disavowal. Explorers, hunters, and artists who saw the species and reproduced it in two-dimensional or textual form, continued to exploit the suggestiveness and struggle with the limitations of the physical animal, particularly as it appeared in comparison to the corporeality of the black rhino.[17] Accounts of how the white rhino acquired its common name are instructive. Many popular explanations have traced the name "white rhino" to the species's wide, square lip. Dutch settlers in the late eighteenth and early nineteenth centuries were thought to have dubbed the animals *weit,* meaning "wide" in Afrikaans. The English misinterpreted *weit* for "white," rendering the species's common name an error of translation. A more controversial theory, however, has linked the name to rhino behaviors as witnessed by the early Boer hunters. The Boers likened one rhino species to the white man and another to the black based on the animals' respective traits of timidity and fierceness.[18] While the story remains unconfirmed (and often unrecognized in popular scientific literature), it is worth noting how certain white rhino behaviors would have likely corroborated the Boers' race-infused fantasy of an animal that was more dignified and noble than its black kin. The species is known to have a calm demeanor toward other species, to spend most of its waking hours grazing, and to take mud baths for cooling off and removing external parasites. White rhinos at their most undisturbed provided a suitable proxy for the white South African settler while allowing the black rhino to symbolize colonial impressions of the region's tribal peoples.

Popular descriptions of the two species repeated these racial connotations well into the twentieth century. Figured "almost as different as black and white," a 1973 issue of the New York Zoological Society's magazine *Animal Kingdom* maintained that "the black rhino has always been characterized as being aggressive, truculent, and unpredictable. The white rhino is docile and mild-tempered, which makes it very vulnerable to poaching."[19] In his popular science book *The White Rhino Saga,* Ian Player offered an understanding of the two subspecies that compounded a racialized sense of rhino difference. His discussions of the black rhino in his narrative describe wanton attacks and deviousness from "one of the most dangerous animals in the bush." Quoting one rhino catcher, Player wrote: "These black rhinos simply melt into the bush and you don't know whether they're waiting for you or not."[20] By contrast, the "poor sighted, gentle white rhino" with a surprisingly "graceful gait" was dangerous only when provoked, and the subject of lengthy passages on its preferences for mud wallowing and constant grazing.[21]

For animal watchers who have inscribed race onto the body proper, the white rhino's whiteness has proved more elusive, a difficulty tied to the Euro-American requirement of a white body to appear—if it is to appear at all—as a beautiful body. Dyer has argued that the white body's condition, its claim to social power, resides in its ability to be alternately invisible, in the sense of occupying the position of the observer who is not seen, and to be highly visible, in the sense of being clearly recognizable and reproducible as an appealing image.[22] In the latter case, when viewers see the white body, its success *as* a white body registers in the degree to which it satisfies certain aesthetic conventions of what is beautiful, which in turn inspire a chain of significations, from feminine sexual purity to enterprising spirit to moral superiority. Foremost among these conventions is the sign of fair, luminescent skin, an epidermis that approximates the color of light itself. Focusing on the illuminative quality of a white woman's skin in Victorian visual culture, for example, Dyer argues that a glow is the ideal, while a shine is to be avoided. As a glow, "the light within or from above appears to suffuse the body. Shine, on the other hand, is light bouncing back off the surface of the skin. It is the mirror effect of sweat, itself connoting physicality, the emissions of the body and unladylike labour." Dyer's list of bodies that are liable to shine within this same nineteenth-century Anglo schema include animals, nonwhites, working-class white women, and even gentlemen.[23] A second convention of white beauty is the appearance of classical Greek or northern European features. Taking up the example of male bodybuilders, Dyer details how the built male body recites "vague notions of the Greek god and the Übermensch."[24] Like a statue, it speaks of hard work, sacrifice, and achievement, "the most literal triumph of mind over matter, imagination over flesh."[25] Crucially, both conventions highlight the contradiction of white beauty being at once spectacularly visible and curiously invisible, tied to a specific body but one that, if honored, would entail the complete absence of said body:

To be seen as white is to have one's corporeality registered, yet true whiteness resides in the non-corporeal. . . . White is both a colour and, at once, not a colour and
the sign of that which is colourless because it cannot be seen: the soul, the mind,
and also emptiness, non-existence and death.[26]

For Dyer, living human bodies cannot fulfill this oppositional criterion, which is
to say, they can never become fully white, lest it result in their total erasure. The
beautiful white body exists as an unattainable ideal.

The impossibility of this whiteness was true for rhino bodies as well. As William
Henry Drummond suggested in his 1875 chronicle of game hunting in south and
southeast Africa, the white rhino does not easily offer up the properties of its name.
Its skin color, for example, is, at best, ambiguous. External factors like the position
of the sun or the kind of mud the animals may have been rolling in last could shape
the extent to which observers could perceive the rhino as white:

I have watched a bull of R. simus trotting past in the full glare of the mid-day sun,
and it has appeared to me almost white, while after following the same animal up,
and finding it feeding with the long shadows of the evening on it, its colour has then
seemed to be, as it really is, a deep brown.[27]

While the effort to see whiteness in the animal is suggestive in its own right, it
did not produce the color under Drummond's gaze. Beyond the light of the South
African sun, the brown hide, shared between all rhino species, was difficult to deny
for the British hunter–naturalist, although he was willing to entertain the possibility
that the black rhino might possess "a tinge of red."[28]

When based on other physical characteristics, the white rhino was just as difficult
to see for markers of whiteness. Indeed, the general profile of the species was less
than flattering. Drummond remarks, "No rhinoceros can fairly be called a handsome
animal" on account of its "long protruding head and neck," its "great uncouth ears, and
small cunning eye," and "the unwieldy size of the great carcase set on such short legs."[29]
He did, however, qualify that "the great white species . . . possesses all of these characteristics in their *least* unpleasing form, and which in size nearly approaches to an elephant, is certainly a noble animal" (emphasis added). These qualities, however, were
apparent only under certain viewing conditions, which are worth quoting at length.
In a passage that Player found "moving," the animal was best appreciated when seen

quietly grazing amid all the beauties of tropical vegetation, lopping up with its
tongue the rank grass in huge mouthfuls, and a whole flock of rhinoceros-birds

perched, half asleep, or lazily picking off an occasional tick, on its broad back, while, it may be, a little hornless calf—a ludicrous miniature of its mother—runs between its legs, and is gently guided forward by the maternal snout. Such scenes often occur towards the evening in the broad bottoms through which the rivers run, or on the edge of some water-hole to which the animal is going to quench its thirst after the long heat of day.[30]

Drummond's description composed the white rhino's whiteness and advised others on how to view it, through a naturalized African safari scene. His pastoral tableau was tranquil and fecund. It infused the awkward-bodied mammal with a certain elegance by allowing for what appeared to be its most natural mode: eating, drinking, and raising offspring in the veldt. At no time did the rhino appear to be too much body; its corporeality exuded a splendor somewhere in the vicinity of a white woman's glow and a muscleman's physique. More precisely, a quiet, naturalistic landscape of "tropical" vegetation, mouthfuls of grass, and wet water holes helped distinguish the white rhino from its unsightly rhino brethren. It placed the animal within an Edenic scene of redemption and rejuvenation, where the white rhino body could rise to its aesthetic potential, however slight. Drummond's scene worked in this way as a form of racial uplift for a species whose historical burden was to appear worlds away from an ideal of white beauty.

FROM DARKNESS TO INNOCENCE: REFINING THE SAFARI FORM IN SOUTHERN CALIFORNIA

A century after Drummond reported his sightings, the Zoological Society of San Diego and its supporters created a similar kind of safari tableau that would likewise imbue the white rhino with whiteness. The production grew meaningful amid a regional craze for the safari form more generally. In the decades after World War II, Southern California became a hotspot for African wildlife tourism. Multiple industries constructed African safaris as holiday adventures overseas, most of which were taken without leaving Los Angeles and San Diego counties. Local audiences, and those passing through, consumed raucous films like *Jungle Drums of Africa* (1953), drive-through safari parks like Lion Country Safari in the Laguna Hills, and exciting newspaper stories about local professionals hunting big game in the naked wilderness. These area-based productions transported Southern Californian residents and tourists into a thrilling heart of Africa while contributing to an expanding leisure industry that was increasingly skilled at manufacturing good spectacle.[31]

Planners for the new zoo sited for San Pasqual sought to capitalize on the popularity of seeing wild African game on California soil. For the enterprising Schroeder, the regional enthusiasm for safaris was difficult to ignore, especially as a potential revenue source. In planning reports drafted throughout the 1960s, the director reminded his board of trustees that financial success for the park was certain with the safari theme.[32] Ideas included having "fold back canvas topped safari trucks to hold perhaps 25 people" and carry them over the entire area. Alternatively, patrons could enter the premises in their own cars and view animals along a predetermined roadway, much like the design for Lion Country Safari, which opened in 1970. Another idea that "would immediately become a source of income" involved installing a standard-gauge railway of six cars with a passenger capacity of 120. Similar to plans for another local safari park venture called Animaland, the railroad would run along the outer edges of field exhibits, giving people a guided tour of the park.[33] By 1967 trustees were on board with the safari concept, particularly considering that the physical topography of San Pasqual already loosely resembled the plains and hillsides of east Africa. As a society press release touted, months of intensive study had confirmed "the possibilities of a highly successful tourist attraction at the Kenya-like site."[34] The *San Diego Union* concurred. Answering their own headline, "An Africa for San Diego?," the article continued, "All aboard—a diesel-powered tractor pulling the canopied passenger cars gives a few low-gear jerks and starts on its six-mile journey through the wilds of Africa. That's the concept of proposed San Diego Zoo's back-country natural habitat zoo."[35]

Although Schroeder and his allies endeavored to exploit the fiscal promise of their theme, they were also focused on upgrading its character. The Wild Animal Park would operate as a refined version of safari, giving visitors an experience of African animal watching that stressed global wildlife conservation as much as wild thrills. Wild thrills were implicit in a market saturated with Africanized entertainments and for a society bent on putting its "foot in the door" of the region's competitive tourist boom.[36] The park's environmentalism, however, was often more overt, delivered in a solemn rhetoric that commanded respect from those who patronized this exceptionally vast zoo. The invitation to visitors upon entry to the grounds, for example, could not have been more dignified:

> Join us here . . . to contemplate the wild animals of the world and nature's wilderness . . . to strengthen a commitment to wild conservation throughout the world . . . and to strive toward Man's own survival through the preservation of nature.[37]

Contemplating, committing, and striving were not typical activities associated with Southern Californian leisure, let alone a typical prerenewal zoo. They summoned a white bourgeois civility and sanctification of nature that social critics of the period argued was alien to the contemporary tourist experience. Tourism, for these critics, had become a debased form of travel, which sacrificed true appreciation of other places for prefabricated spectacles.[38] Park planners were less elitist, recognizing instead a popular form of tourism that, with some adjustments, could be highly compatible with the society's conservation goals.

The refinement of the African safari was faithful to a larger reconstruction of Africa in the popular imaginary of the postwar United States. After World War II, the American idea of Africa changed. A new generation of media makers began producing images of the continent as a tranquil space rather than its classic Western representation as a savage jungle, or a contemporary representation of African nations struggling to assert political independence. Pictures, brochures, stories, and landscapes that cycled through mainstream U.S. markets increasingly depicted a conflict-free continent whose vulnerabilities belonged primarily to animals. In the 1953 film *Below the Sahara,* for example, the filmmaker Armand Denis provided viewers with aerial shots of wild animal life jeopardized only by the presence of black African hunters.[39] In the Academy Award–winning version of Joy Adamson's 1961 popular book *Born Free,* the director James Hill filmed a fair-haired lioness, Elsa, returning to her unspoiled roots on the open plains after being lovingly hand-reared by the blonde and British Adamson and her game warden husband. In these and similar portraits was an Africa of primeval nature teeming with pristine fauna, a set of largely tranquil representations that made up what Gregg Mitman has described as the new image of Africa:

> The "Dark Continent" was rapidly transformed into a place of threatened ecological splendor. Once a land where the great white hunter affirmed both his manliness and the power of empire by subduing savage beasts, the new Africa became a place where a more intimate contact with an innocent serene nature might be had.[40]

Mitman explains the desire for intimate contact in visual terms. Images of the new Africa as a site of human–animal proximity gave audiences some relief from their disturbing wartime experiences. Seeing an African nature up close was an opportunity to escape from the horrors of purported civilization and emotionally reinvest in the more peaceful cause of wildlife conservation. Donna Haraway has called attention to how intimate contact took a physical turn for Americans in this period. Popular scientific media, she argues, conveyed the palliative force of African wildlife in the atomic age through pictures of human–animal touching. The white hands of a Western woman holding the hairy hands of an African nonhuman primate, for instance, became a redemptive nature-meets-culture fantasy, symbolizing cooperation between differentially empowered nations, markets, and cultures.[41] To Renato Rosaldo, these kinds of images have been tinged with an "imperialist nostalgia" that invokes feelings of loss and longing among colonialism's agents precisely for those things that they have themselves destroyed.[42] As such, representations of the new Africa both generated a yearning for intimacy with African wildlife and concealed the circumstances that damaged that same wildlife and gave rise to its very yearning. Any innocence found in this nature was less a product of reunion with a prior "lost" nature than it was a product of historical disavowal: namely, the new Africanists' disassociation from the harmful legacies of colonial power.

For San Diego's resident population, which was transitioning to a life beyond a staple wartime economy of navy goods and services, the representation of a new, more intimate, Africa was particularly appealing. An intimate Africa held the unique promise of helping San Diegans imagine a relationship to natural resources and distant places beyond the military context. Moreover, it allowed them to become travelers in their own city. Local versions of safari could substitute for contact with a wilderness that was beyond the financial reach of many. The escapism was an affordable alternative to Africa proper and, according to the *San Diego Union,* equally striking. Promoting the Wild Animal Park to locals, an enthusiastic Marguerite Sullivan wrote about a posh San Diegan who "has safaried over Africa four times and Asia twice just to see the animals she likes." Now, the La Jolla woman "sees her animals right in her own backyard. Her safari is at the San Diego Wild Animal Park in the San Pasqual Valley."[43] Sullivan's profile gestures toward a safari production that tempered the wholesale adoption of a kinder, gentler Africa. As much as the postwar safari was a departure from the idea of a mysterious and dangerous "Dark Continent," it was also a way to reenact aspects of its sensibility and assume the subjectivity of its primary benefactors within more securely colonized countries: white, wealthy, worldly, and available to commune with animals in an exotic wilderness.

At the turn of the nineteenth century, the continent's wild spaces became "a new playground for the leisure classes."[44] Moneyed sportsmen of high social standing, including former U.S. president and avid conservationist Theodore Roosevelt, journeyed through the bush on extravagant hunting trips that helped generate the cultural value of the African tour. With strict codes about what, when, and how to kill, these gentlemen followed civilizing rules of sportsmanship and, in so doing, experienced something approximating the human–animal intimacy that safari goers in the new Africa would long for years later.[45] Such was the nature of rule-bound amateur hunting, which, according to the anthropologist Garry Marvin, is a practice that constructs closeness where none previously existed. From the hunter's vantage point, "a personal and emotional connectivity is a defining feature of the relation-

ship between the hunter and the hunted. . . . This connectivity is even greater when
the hunter has successfully found, followed, and then killed a particular animal."[46]
In colonial south and east Africa, the connectivity came at the expense of other possible kinships. As the white hunter bonded with his kill, he detached himself from
the people who surrounded him. The safari enabled a certain understanding of the
African animal world and disavowal of the human one, as suggested in the journals
of Edmund Heller, the chronicler of Roosevelt's Smithsonian African Expedition
of 1909. After Roosevelt shot a rhino at a close twelve yards, the job of skinning it
fell to several hungry Kenyan porters, who were, in turn, interrupted by

> a series of hungry Wakamba with large knives who broke in occasionally and cut
> off a chunk of meat. The head man and askaris were in a frenzy driving back with
> whips these Wakamba. The ground about the carcass was ankle deep in blood and
> stomach contents. About one and a half hours of this mob labor, removed the skins
> and then the trunk was taken outside the tent. . . . At once the Wakamba got busy
> and cleaned the meat off to the last shred. The intestines were also eaten by these
> people.[47]

Heller's use of the word *people* betrayed the more consistent depiction of the Wakamba
as something other than human and less than its singular dead rhino. From Heller's
perspective, the skilled porters were frenzied and moblike, while the Wakamba,
likely referring to a Bantu ethnic group in Kenya, were akin to vultures attempting
to pick off the carcass, indiscriminately. The additional image of the motley group
stewing in blood and guts reinforced the hierarchy between hunters and natives;
Heller observed the distasteful activities at a white remove.

Scenes like Heller's were not resold to postwar Californians verbatim, but their
spirit reverberated in safari images that portrayed a continent where emotional and
physical proximity—connectivity—was still prized in animal interactions and wilderness was best experienced without any signs of other life. Constructing the new
Africa necessitated the removal of people from the landscape, both figuratively and
as environmental policy. This was a continent defined by its natural life and de-
void of a human past, present, or future, especially so if the human presence was
black African. Tour companies, filmmakers, television programmers, and journalists
strove to depict the land free of the bodies and architecture that would overly com-
plicate the scenery, and possibly diminish it. Meanwhile, U.S. environmentalists and
their African allies worked to stop poachers from killing wildlife for lucrative parts,
a rampant and necessary practice in a decolonizing continent that produced more
poverty. They also discouraged pastoral tribes, like the Maasai, from traditional

farming practices, which were thought to compromise the well-being of government park lands.⁴⁸ In place of the actual practice came the staged ones, as tour operators hired Maasai to perform their "primitive" way of life as part of the naturalistic tableau, selling goods, posing for pictures by white tourists, and blending into the new Africa.⁴⁹ These efforts to empty the landscape of its history appealed directly to white American tastes for unspoiled wilderness spaces and helped connect the bourgeois aesthetics of traditional U.S. environmentalism to an international conservation effort from the 1950s onward.⁵⁰ An unpeopled African nature—or more precisely, an African nature whose human inhabitants were not quite recognized as such—would attract the tourist's eye and the conservationist's heart, ideally in the same trip.

The new Africa also required the pacification of the wild animals that lived within the landscape. By the 1960s producers of the safari form, as a tourist experience, were exchanging the gun for the camera, producing, in turn, a new expectation that encounters with wildlife could be not only intimate but also safe. A decade later, the cultural critic Susan Sontag recognized the change as symptomatic of a different kind of nature from which people no longer needed to be protected but instead became nostalgic for: "When we are afraid we shoot. But when we are nostalgic, we take pictures."⁵¹ One journalist's account of a "camera expedition" to Kenya both reflected this new possibility of postwar game watching in the east African veldt and created it for her reading public. Published in the *Los Angeles Times* in 1968, Lynn Lilliston's narration began by mentioning her group's guide, who was associated with a prestigious hunting firm operating in Kenya. For this particular job, however, he "laid aside his 12-bore in favor of conservation and shoots only with a camera." Following, Lilliston recounted the group's first wildlife sighting:

> Coming into the lodge at Keekorok, our African driver spotted three lions lying under a tree some distance from the road. To our surprise, he wheeled the bus over a ditch and took off across the plains. We careened to a stop only a few feet from the lions: five tourists in a bus with the top rolled back fully expecting the lions to leap through the roof and devour us all (including W. Jeff Arnett, a broker, and his wife Isabel, and Joseph R. Jones, financial consultant, and his wife Carol). We stared at the lions but they only glanced at us. Lazy. Bored. Disdainful. One rolled over and went back to sleep. Bedlam broke out in the bus as we realized we could take photographs without being rended. I broke three fingernails trying to get to a window and Isabel said, "Look at me, I'm shaking so hard I can't work the camera." We did and she was.⁵²

If not quite an earthy, fragile paradise, the seemingly spontaneous off-road meeting between the docile lions and Southern Californian professionals and their spouses was exhilarating all the same. What read as the lions' indifference, underlined by the fact that "they only glanced," also came across as the animals' unprecedented availability to the tourist gaze and its photographic extensions. However unimpressed, the lions were calm enough to be viewed, and photographed, at close range. This pattern was repeated in Lilliston's story. Finding herself off-road again and again, she was "astonished" to learn that animals would often stand still for photography, including a pair of baby foxes who "stood on top of their den and stared at us in innocent wonder."[53] Animals in free and full motion were also an appealing sight, conveying another dimension to this peaceable kingdom. At the Amboseli Game Reserve, for example, the group witnessed a cheetah's "successful dash across the open plains" to catch a gazelle for her cub. Tsavo National Park gave tourists the spectacle of grazing giraffes. Elephants and Cape buffalo were also common grazers during Lilliston's trip. The only disruption to the safari were reports of poaching and, as it happened, rumors of a Chicago tour group's encounter with a charging rhinoceros.

Building the new Africa in San Pasqual continued in the same vein. Longings for a peaceful, naturalistic nature were well reflected in the park's design process and product, beginning with resident exhibition designer Charles Faust's own trip to Africa. In September 1969 Faust and his wife joined the Zoological Society of San Diego's Second Annual Autumn Safari. They toured Uganda and Kenya to "feel the fascination and see the beauty that is Africa."[54] Faust returned with drawings and watercolors, many of which were published in *Zoonooz*. Described as Faust's "Sketchbook of East Africa," some images represented the region in grand panorama. In one, large cliffs towered in the background against a big sky, dwarfing two giraffes with their prehistoric presence. An African elephant appeared in the foreground of the scene, passing the "fabulous baobab trees laden with legends and superstitions that may be as old as time itself." Other images exchanged the gaze of the nineteenth-century landscape painter for the gaze of the nineteenth-century ethnographer. A two-page watercolor depicted a Maasai village in striking detail. Faust reported making arrangements for a "close examination" of the village structures—and, as the published product demonstrated, the villagers themselves. Adorned in native dress and standing still before the viewer, the human figures occupied the picture plane as exotic objects on display, fully available for tourists eager to see Africa's bounty. Still other images bolstered the park designer's artistic identity, like the sketches of indigenous housing forms. Deviating from new preferences for a landscape free of buildings, Faust embraced them in his small series of quick architectural studies. The collection of various thatched-roof huts cultivated the profile of an artist inspired by surroundings more natural than Southern Californian eyes had known. Collectively, these images helped set the genteel tone of the park's safari concept. By reproducing the experience of a consummate observer on his African tour, they prepared future patrons for a bourgeois spectatorship rich in cultural capital and environmental empathy.

In addition to shaping park viewing practices, the Second Annual Autumn Safari also affected the park's built environment, beginning with its interpretation of African architecture (Figure 5.2). Faust's research on indigenous construction techniques and building styles in east Africa led him to conclude that "African architecture, such as it is . . . is pretty small" in sharp contrast to the classical structures he visited in European cities.[55] While east African structures appeared "primitive," Roman ones, for example, showed evidence of "great creative human imagination."[56] Faust's perception of an architectural primitivism heavily informed the creation of Nairobi Village, envisioned as a "port of entry" to the park as a whole.[57] With the expertise of the San Diego architect Frederick Liebhardt, the designer crafted the village as a sixteen-acre central building complex that housed a conservation information area, the Thorn Tree Terrace, the Mombasa Cooker, retail shops, general services, and Simba Station, from which visitors would depart on their monorail tour of the open plains. Close to two dozen structures were laid out in clusters to give the appearance of "an average scene" in Kenya's capital city at the turn of the nineteenth century.[58] As reported in the *Evening Tribune,* the goal was to create a village environment, "which will allow visitors to forget, for a few hours, at least, the hustle and bustle of the space age." Ideally, Faust and Liebhardt would take people "out of the modern world and into the wilds of Africa."[59] Concept drawings, however, showed the strong influence of a still-popular California modernism. In "Observation & Refreshment Area," for example, Africa's wilds, signified by a baobab tree and two inquisitive giraffes, were made current by the presence a podlike structure not unlike a spaceship (Figure 5.3). As if aware of this, Faust vertically staggered roughly marked posts around and through the building, breaking into the architecture's sleek contemporaneity and luring visitors back in time and place. Speaking to the *Escondido Times-Advocate,* the construction manager Harold Barr divulged the overall objective: "By the time they're in the village, they should have shed their frustrations and become a completely relaxed part of another world."[60]

To encourage this feeling of temporal and spatial relocation, Faust and Liebhardt constructed Nairobi Village with an emphasis on organic materials. After driving over a plank-like bridge, and parking their cars in a secluded area, visitors walked

Figure 5.2. *Concept drawing for Wild Animal Park by Charles Faust, 1970. Copyright San Diego History Center.*

through the ticket and information booths housed in a replica of an African burial hut that resembled an overturned tightly woven basket. Beyond that was the village proper defined by paths roped with uneven eucalyptus branches that formed the majority of walkways, fences, and supports. Reluctant to use any concrete in village buildings, construction crews compromised by mixing concrete with rock to give it a rougher look. The first choice for all roofing was savannah grass, though fire codes required that builders resort to shingle roofs in curved thatched patterns for primary buildings, a technique improvised by the local contractor Louetto Construction, which soaked wood shingles and reshaped them in a press. Secondary structures, however, which visitors could see but not enter, received the "African touch." These included the park's smaller animal enclosures, which were built from palm, reed, timber, and branches, and the village's showpiece, the Congo River fishing village

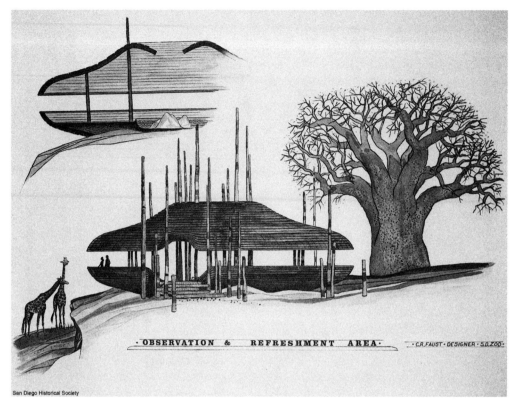

San Diego Historical Society

Figure 5.3. *Concept drawing for the Wild Animal Park by Charles Faust, 1970. Copyright San Diego History Center.*

(Figure 5.4). Located down from Nairobi's main building clusters, at the far end of one of two artificial lagoons, Faust and Liebhardt elevated the fishing village above waterfall rapids. A dense arrangement of wooden scaffolding propped up the open-sided huts while fish traps hung in the water below. Future plans to heighten the material authenticity of Nairobi village included more foot trails in wilder sections of the complex and wild honeysuckle vines to cover existing walkways.[61]

While Nairobi Village was an attempt to immerse visitors in what reporters would describe as a city of "sticks and stones," designers choreographed the experience of seeing the park's largest animals as a picture-perfect image of nature itself.[62] Boarding the Wgasa Bush Line, zoo goers climbed into a state-of-the-art electric monorail train that took them on a fifty-minute tour through exhibits of nonnative species. The ride was quiet. Sixteen double rubber tires under each car turning at a maximum of twelve miles an hour delivered a relatively smooth, pollution-free trip,

San Pasquel

Photo by James Blank

Figure 5.4. *Postcard of Congo River Fishing Village at the Wild Animal Park, circa 1972. John and Jane Adams Postcard Collection. Courtesy of Special Collections and University Archives, San Diego State University Library and Information Access.*

in which the air compressor and the guide's narration were the only audible noise. The train also kept its distance from the animals on exhibit, running along five miles of tracks, each custom-made to fit the curves and dips of the landscape.[63] These innovations in rail technology enabled the park's animals to appear as undisturbed as possible while giving visitors as clean and seamless a view as possible. Local reporters underscored the easy naturalism of the tour. Open cars offered riders "effortless sightseeing," and the route exposed wildlife to their gaze without difficulty; there was "no searching out of animals in the bush as in Africa."[64] A running commentary enhanced the ease and immediacy of the scene. Guides helped spectators "identify the world's vanishing wildlife" and drew attention to the conservation that was happening right before their eyes with each pregnant and nursing animal on exhibit.[65]

In these ways planners orchestrated the park's safari as a refined journey to a more natural space and time, enabling visitors to connect with the new Africa. In San Pasqual, animal watching became newly respectable, reviving a twinned history of touristic pleasure and environmental concern. This pairing made the park's prized white rhino collection appear similarly dignified, availing the animals to California dreams of cross-species connection and white racial surrogacy.

NEW AFRICA, NEW RHINO: THE WHITENESS OF THE SPECIES

There was much to refine in the rhino image repertoire. After World War II, Southern Californian references to the southern white rhinoceros often disagreed with the new Africa and the rhetoric of a placid, conservable wilderness. When regional media sources brought audiences into visible range of the species, the encounters frequently conflated the animals with other species of rhino, reducing them all to a single image of beastly savagery that was utterly unavailable for intimate contact. The 1954 story of the wildlife photographers Alfred and Elma Milotte saving an "ungrateful rhino" is a typical submission to this archive of rhino brutishness. In the pages of the *Los Angeles Times,* readers could absorb a harrowing tale of man versus beast, and a five-part photographic account of the rescue. On location in Kenya to shoot for Disney's "True Life Adventure" series, the American couple stumbled on a bull rhino stuck in a drying mud hole. After hitching a rope "around two tons of bone and muscle" that was "grunting in savage protest," they pulled the creature out with their camera truck, only to notice it standing "groggy, confused, shaking his head and glaring toward us with bloodshot little eyes." What followed was a high-speed chase that found Alfred taking shelter in his vehicle. The animal proceeded to charge, hitting the truck's front "in sharp deadly jabs." Both Milottes escaped the episode unharmed, but not without relearning the lesson that saving rhinos is perilous business.[66] Notable in this story is how the rhino evaded any species moniker, represented instead as irrational violence incarnate. In the charging of its one-thousand-pound-plus body toward a staple marker and apparatus of California living, the automobile, the animal also surpassed any associations to specific racial or ethnic groups by a wide margin. No human subject, in image or practice, could approximate this level of hostility without also approximating a cartoon. The charging rhino constituted a degree of otherness that was largely inaccessible to plausible categories of human difference.[67]

The rhinoceros, as a general type, appeared equally fierce in the safari film *Hatari!* (1961), a Swahili word meaning "danger." The opening scene pictures western film star John Wayne as Sean Mercer, a seasoned animal wrangler on the lookout for rhinos to capture and relocate to European and American zoos. Sean spots his first rhino of the day, and the first of the film, when surveying the east African plains through binoculars. With a crew of African, American, and European men in open trucks, the chase between truck and heaving rhino is intense and zigzagged. In a bid to control the chaos, semantically at least, one man shouts out, "This one must be a female. She can't decide which way to go!" Gendering the beast, however, accomplishes little by way of controlling its irrepressible physicality. Breathing heavily and snorting, the rhino gores the truck several times before finally goring an older white hunter in the leg and escaping from the scene. Later in the film, the crew vindicates the injured coworker by successfully capturing another rhino for transport overseas, but not before an extended sequence that depicts the men roping the animal, bringing it down to the ground, and periodically losing their grip.

When rhinos appeared in the safari park format, image makers continued to define them through a penchant for violence. In 1962, for example, the animal trainers Ralph and Toni Helfer created Africa, U.S.A., located in Soledad Canyon near Los Angeles. On a three-hundred-acre compound that was closed to visitors but open to the press, the Helfers trained elephants, lions, and other nonindigenous species for work in California's film and television industry. The safari comedy *Clarence the Cross-Eyed Lion* (1965) was one forum for the animals' acquired skills, as well as its spin-off network television series *Daktari* (1966–69), parts of which were shot on the premises.[68] Upon acquiring two young white rhinos, one male and one female, in 1966 for the series, Ralph Helfer boasted of his ability to break them, explaining to the *Los Angeles Times* that white rhinos were "considered extremely mean and dangerous, capable of attacking and wrecking a truck." But by putting them in close and constant contact with handlers and other species, Helfer expected to pacify the fifteen-hundred-pound male rhino well enough to allow *Daktari*'s star, Marshall Thompson, to ride on its back.[69]

Five years later, Lion Country Safari Inc. launched their public venue in the Laguna Hills of Orange County, adding to their already successful parks in South Africa and Florida.[70] Initially featuring four hundred animals on five hundred acres, Orange County's Lion Country Safari portrayed the rhino and other species of African wildlife as creatures to be respected, but also feared. Following a three-lane paved trail, families took their own cars into the compound and gazed out over a simulated African landscape of rhinos, giraffes, gazelles, and, of course, lions.[71] With windows closed, visitors could experience the excitement of trading places with the objects of their gaze. Local reporters emphasized the concept of "freeing" wild animals in outdoor fields and confining humans to their automotive enclosures. Writers at the *Los Angeles Times* wrote that the park president Harry Shuster had "bagged good earnings on the theme that humans, not animals, should be 'caged' in an amusement park," and that "any coexistence you have in mind is on [the animals'] terms, not yours."[72] Bradley Smith at *San Diego Magazine* took the thrill a little further, advising visitors to "keep your windows up—in the new Southern California veldt trespassers will be eaten."[73] With animals appearing to enjoy their spatial freedom and visitors encouraged to stay on guard, the novelty factor of Lion Country Safari ran high, engineering the safari experience as a dangerous encounter with untamed beasts.

The Zoological Society of San Diego was not above creating beastly safari images that stymied the production of a peaceable African animal kingdom. The downtown campus had its own record of making rhinos appear exaggerated in their ferocity. In 1967 the agency of Phillips-Ramsey produced a radio advertisement for the society depicting the capture of a rhino in the African wilderness. Part of a series of similar sixty-second spots that aired on local airwaves, "Rhino" sought to take the listener "right there" through generic native drumming, animal sound effects, and the voice of a British white hunter narrating the drama.[74]

NARRATOR (over drumming): Forty miles from Raga on the Central African Sudanese border is Rhino Country. This is where we take the big fellows, the African rhinoceros. Five thousand pounds of dust and temper, powerful as an army tank.

(grunting, heavy breathing, galloping)

NARRATOR: We take them live, usually from a Land Rover by running alongside and slipping a noose over the horn and head.

(Truck engine. A man shouts "All right . . . now!")

NARRATOR: One of the boys slips a rope around one hind leg, and the rhinoceros is all but ready for shipping.

(drumming and singing)

NARRATOR: This is the same type of African Rhinoceros that lives in its simulated natural habitat at the San Diego Zoo. He's still short tempered, dusty, and wild.

(drumming fades out, replaced with grunting from animals and exclamations from zoo goers)

NARRATOR: The San Diego Zoo has the world's largest collection of wild animals—indeed, the wildest show on earth. Visit the San Diego Zoo and have a wild time.

(roar followed by a low growl)[75]

The rhino in this African drama took shape as a jumble of gruff animal sounds, temperament, and body parts, a "big fellow" whose power was analogous to "an army tank" and whose living body, once restrained, could be shipped like cargo. Insisting that the rhino housed at the San Diego Zoo's downtown campus had not changed from its African origins, the advertisement's additional sound effect of startled zoo goers confirmed the expectation that the animal could still put on a good show, giving people "a wild time."

The development of the Wild Animal Park tamed these instances of rhino beastliness. As part of their commitment to converting the San Pasqual site into a version of the new Africa, curators and designers created images of wildlife that were more defenseless than aggressive. This shift epitomized the distinguished, environmentalist turn of the park and challenged a public accustomed to raging rhinos. By the park's opening, the society was producing softer rhino representations. For every image of an animal that was short-tempered, dusty, and wild, many more depicted the rhino as a gentle, sociable behemoth with a penchant for open space.

A 1971 issue of *Zoonooz,* for example, featured as its center spread the picture of ten peace-loving whites, wallowing in mud and the wide-angle company of ostriches, gnus, and zebras (Figure 5.5). At almost one hundred acres, actual paddock sizes for white rhinos at the park were substantially larger than other North American zoos, while the herd was organized into a single male/multiple female configuration to ensure maximum peace.[76] When a rhino did appear charging, its savagery paled in comparison with its rhino contemporaries in other mediums. Another *Zoonooz* photograph, published in 1972, rendered the species strangely innocuous despite the intimation of an animal in midcharge (Figure 5.6). The image showed a large, bovine-like creature guarding its turf against the curious onlooker, as evoked in the caption: "The photographer intrudes on the White Rhino's territory." But with its lowered head, beady eyes, and bony nuchal hump (the same hump that prevents the species from being able to swim), a vulnerability occupied the figure despite its antagonistic posture and some kicked-up earth. At the Wild Animal Park, few rhinos appeared menacing.

By refiguring the species as nonthreatening, park planners simultaneously rejuvenated the white rhino's whiteness. A roster of placid imagery recalled a history of representing the white rhino as a muted version of its rhino kin while updating and upscaling the species for white middle-class fantasies of an innocent nature that was camera-ready for postwar safari goers. A 1971 *Zoonooz* article illustrates the process in more detail. The written text gave future park visitors a sedate history of the species's near extinction and eventual recuperation on African game reserves. Photographs, however, told a more gripping story of the San Diego herd's translocation from South Africa, images that also worked to stage the visual perspective of a

Figure 5.5. *Wallowing white rhinos at the Wild Animal Park,* Zoonooz, *1972. Courtesy of the Zoological Society of San Diego.*

tourist on safari for magazine readers and future park patrons (Figure 5.7). The first full-color image put readers in the backseat of a Land Rover looking on at a small grouping of adult white rhinos. Readers were seated just behind the beret-wearing Ian Player and zoo president Anderson Borthwick. As the caption informed, the photograph was taken on a society-led safari to South Africa in 1970, in which the tour group helped capture these very rhinos for the Wild Animal Park. The landscape before their gaze appeared as dry, pastoral terrain, a timeless wilderness space in which all figures—animal and human—looked their most natural. The group's calm deportment mirrored the serenity of the rhinos, as expressed in Player's rested arm against the vehicle and a performance of rhino watching so experienced that

Figure 5.6. *"Charging" white rhino at the Wild Animal Park,* Zoonooz, *1972. Courtesy of the Zoological Society of San Diego.*

Figure 5.7. *Anderson Borthwick on safari,* Zoonooz, *May 1971. Courtesy of the Zoological Society of San Diego.*

it appeared without effort. Though less reclined, Borthwick appeared composed, suggesting a stillness that good wildlife photographers maintain so as not to alarm their subjects. In this way, four white rhinos and two white men (plus the magazine photographer) collaborated to create the image of a tranquil meeting between archetypal rhinos and archetypal human beings, made so through a photographic sense of getting down to natural essences.

The casual realism of the scene was the pivotal whitener, moving between species, knitting rhinos and spectators together in a pose of authenticity that is often foundational to whiteness. Loose and unpostured, the rhinos appeared as "just rhinos" in much the same way that Dyer maintains that white people signify as "just human." More than luminescent skin or the perfect aquiline nose, the whiteness of human beings is present in the feeling that they are *without* race, that their whiteness is nothing special—that is, nothing extra to the elemental quality of being human. While other racial identities have specific physical and behavioral markers that signify blackness, brownness, and so on, white identity is by and large an effect of representations that seem unsignified, unstylized, unraced.[77] These representations also carry inflections of innocence and virtue, since the pose of being without the "additive" of race is also visible as the pose of having nothing to hide, of being more genuine. The animals in the *Zoonooz* photograph conveyed this racialized sense of easy living. By variously reclining, grazing, and standing flush against the horizon, they appeared without pretension, without excess, the steady, pure baseline of *rhinoness,* what rhinos simply are. Likewise, the safari guides appeared to be doing what came naturally.

In the subsequent image, however, the photographer recast the easygoing rhino as stubborn, disrupting the bond with white spectators and the straightforward naturalism of the safari scene (Figure 5.8). The picture showed a rope tied around the head of a rhino that appeared more as a difficult object than an easy subject, an intractable-looking beast, standing semisquarely in place, apparently reluctant to budge. Dressed in khakis, John Fairfield, the Wild Animal Park's senior keeper, was shown pulling the rope with the help of an unidentified black assistant, while Player and another black man pushed the rhino from behind. The picture was made additionally awkward by the appearance of two white photographers in the background. A man in a sports jacket was pictured holding his own camera and leisurely walking toward the foreground while a woman in a blue dress appeared standing still, absorbed by her own camera. Consummate safari goers in the new Africa, the appearance of these two was, at one angle, an intrusion of sorts, figures who did not quite fit within the scene. At another angle, the safari goers would have made a likely point of reader reference and aspiration for the next-best experience of seeing rhinos on park grounds. In both cases, the tourists' presence, together with all the visible labor exerted by and around the animal's body, was a meddlesome force. It frustrated chances of a cross-species identification between white rhinos and their public by interrupting the requisite effortlessness of being "just rhino."

The interruptions continued in the next series of images, which displayed more fully the difficulties of translocation. A two-page black-and-white photomontage detailed the herd's travels in ways that drained the species of any lingering virtue.

Figure 5.8. *White rhino wrangling,* Zoonooz, *May 1971. Courtesy of the Zoological Society of San Diego.*

In one image Player was shown loading his gun with an immobilization drug; in another, two black horsemen were pictured in the landscape wearing crash helmets and aprons, ready for capture. The sequence of images thereafter showed a robust, presumably male, rhino with its mate and calf, followed by its immobilization and transfer into a wooden crate. Human figures appeared gathering around its massive form, prodding, pushing, and finally relocating. Subsequent images of wooden pens, flatbed trucks, shipyards, and railways cars redefined the species as fleshy, valuable cargo (Figures 5.9–5.11). This intensive denaturalization of the species—its material and aesthetic dislocation from the African savannah—constructed for the white rhino, however momentarily, a loss of its whiteness.

The racial status of the white rhino, or lack thereof, shifted once more in the final series of images, which displayed the soon-to-be-opened Wild Animal Park now populated with African animals. By picturing an enclosure that was indistinguishable from the rhinos' South African home, and a tranquillity on par with their disposition in the initial easygoing photograph, the society in effect restored whiteness to the species. Freed from their crates, pictured in near silhouette by a watering hole, shown in the peaceful company of neighboring antelope, the rhinos assimilated into a gentle wilderness picture that reaffirmed their status as "just rhinos." The accompanying article's news of two pregnancies among the herd heightened their natural splendor—this promised to be a thriving group—while a concluding image of two rhinos on a rocky hillside gave readers more cause for hope (see Plate 8). The full-page color photograph represented an extreme version of the park's safari naturalism, in which the animals appeared virtually undifferentiated from their rustic surroundings. In coloring and texture, the rhino pair blended into their backdrop, loosely heterosexualized as a reproductive unit of diffident female (left) and steadfast male (right). Like two boulders on a steep hill, they appeared enduring in their thickness, prehistoric in longevity, and somewhere near the figurative apex of being "just rhino." But if the couple could ascend, they could also fall, underscoring a lingering and unsettling sense that these rhino rocks were at risk of tumbling down.

Instability of this sort was a perennial theme of the white rhino collection at San Diego's newest zoo. Representations of rhinos simply enjoying life in a renaturalized Africa were frequently matched by indications of rhino lives whose naturalism seemed temporary at best, and strenuous at worst. Some of those indications appeared through other zoo photography, where denotative and connotative meanings jostled with "obtuse meanings," in Roland Barthes's phrasing.[78] Other indications came from mortality records with speculative causes such as stress, drug toxicity, trauma, and gastric ulcers.[79] The recurrent unreliability of rhino whiteness demonstrates once again that rhino bodies, like some human bodies, have had a historically difficult time of sustaining representations of race. In this instance, however, the difficulty was less a sign of failure in racial representation than a feature of the collection's symbolic promise. The capacity of white rhinos to waver in their whiteness was well positioned to touch on the insecurity of San Diegans' white racial identity in the midst of its diffusion and dilution. For the city's white establishment, white rhinos on the park's safari could read as an expression of how endangered

Figures 5.9, 5.10, and 5.11. *Image sequence of white rhino translocation, Zoonooz, May 1971. Courtesy of the Zoological Society of San Diego.*

their own racial privilege had become. For communities invested in acquiring those privileges, the animals could resonate with the pleasures and disappointments of the experience. The construction of endangered white rhinos spoke powerfully to these different uncertainties of being, becoming, and staying white in the region.

Twelve years after the species was first introduced to the park, Schroeder was asked about the future of the facility overall. His response affirmed the continuing value of white rhinos under the pressures of a diversifying population, zoological and otherwise.

> Rhinos: we should have a big area where we can propagate rhinos, where they can have some freedom. And it doesn't mean you can't have two units. You can have white rhinos here, and white rhinos someplace else. And hopefully some blacks. And I guess they're building something right now for the Indians, and that's fine. They've got pretty good reproduction. . . . The prospect is a long way from hopeless, it's very good. But I don't think we can accommodate them all with what we've got.[80]

For this zoo man, white rhinos maintained a special place in Southern California's animal suburb and all of which it epitomized and partook.

AFTERWORD

Good Feelings in Seattle

In August 2007 Seattle's Woodland Park Zoo mounted the Maasai Journey, an educational program whose adaptations continue as of this writing and echo something of the San Diego Zoo's production of African tourism in Southern California. The program expanded Woodland Park Zoo's permanent African Savanna exhibit that opened in 1980 as a large, naturalistic display of multiple animal species native to east Africa. The exhibit was augmented in 2001 with the construction of an African village featuring a classroom based on traditional Kikuyu architecture.[1] The Maasai Journey involved the addition of two giraffes, some ostriches, and most prominently, four Maasai men employed as guides or, in the zoo's terminology, "cultural interpreters." To date, the guides have conducted safari tours of the exhibit, performed as storytellers, and lectured on conservation activities in their native southern Kenya and Tanzania. In 2008 the American Association of Zoos and Aquariums recognized the Maasai Journey with its highest award for educational programming.

The inclusion of black Africans as a highly visible component of a contemporary zoo exhibit triggered a heated public conversation that raises question about the affective state and racial meanings of American zoos today. Pointed criticism came from members of the University of Washington community, which made it to the pages of the *Seattle Times*. These academic critics argued that the zoo's curatorial choice was "insensitive and hearkens back to the days when zoos across the nation used people of color as accessories to exhibits." They also raised the possibility that the Maasai Journey could lead visitors to "associate African people with animals, and African Americans with animalism," and was thus "blurring a dangerous line." "Human culture does not belong in a zoo," said one history professor to the newspaper.[2] The article gave reactions from the Woodland Park Zoo as well. Officials there recognized that human displays were "a repulsive concept." They distanced themselves from the practice by stressing the professional nature of the guides, who dress in Western clothing and have college degrees from U.S. institutions. Kakuta Hamisi, one guide, expressed similar objections over using Maasai history as "a vehicle to raise race issues" and maintained that the zoo's program was different: "We're not out there holding monkeys."[3]

Charges and fears of representing historically marginalized people as exotic animals were well founded. Since their beginnings, public zoos and their intersecting cultural formations, such as the ethnological museum and the international exposition, have served as scientifically oriented forums for exploiting racial difference through explicit depictions of extreme physical difference—or, what Pascal Blanchard et al. aptly term, "Human Zoos."[4] Contemporary zoo exhibits are no stranger to the practice either, though their conflations operate through traces of the body more than its full presence. At the turn of the twenty-first century, the Bronx Zoo opened its Congo Gorilla Forest exhibit with a reprise of its own history, featuring not only nonhuman primates but also a representation of Mbuti Pygmy culture in the form of an abandoned hunting camp.[5] San Diego Zoo debuted its Ituri Forest exhibit, an interpretation of Congolese fauna, with another replica of unoccupied "forest people" dwellings. Providence Rhode Island's Roger Williams Park Zoo erected an interior exhibit space that combined indigenous contemporary art and ceremonial masks from New Guinea, the Philippines, Indonesia, and Australia with biological diversity representative of the region. For its Amazon Rising exhibit, the Shedd Aquarium in Chicago joined the ranks with an eight-foot-high stilt-leg house, complete with utensils, dried fish, and plantains.[6] The aquarium's Karen Furnweger dates the emergence of these and other "cultural resonance" exhibits to the 1980s, with the maturation of a wildlife conservation ethic: "To instruct a largely urban audience that people are a part of nature, not apart from it, exhibit developers are integrating the story of local cultures that live in or near the habitat portrayed, and depend on the health of that ecosystem for their livelihoods."[7] The integration also signals a maturation of zoo naturalism, whereby signs—architectural, artistic, or artifactual—of human life alongside animal life are framed by zoo designers as an important aspect of visitors' immersion experience.[8] It is against this backdrop that the academic and institutional responses to the Maasai Journey were formulated.

Within twenty-four hours of the story's publication, the *Times* website received 112 comments from readers in overwhelming support of the exhibit and condemnation of its critics. Commentary came from an array of voices located in the greater Seattle area, with some respondents self-identifying as, for example, African,

Mexican American, zoo members, former safari goers, UW alumni, high school graduates, parents of young children, and so forth. Amid this heterogeneity, readers consistently applauded the high educational value of the Maasai Journey and its pleasures. A handful of readers did not join the chorus, objecting to insinuations that the Maasai men are representative of all African cultures or are closer to nature than Euro-Americans.[9] But for most, the program represented a "wonderful and unique chance to talk with people with experiences most of us can only imagine!" Respondents appreciated being able to interact with the men, who were considered "conservation professionals" and were "respected for their ability to connect the human experience to the animal kingdom." Their "intimate knowledge" added "another dimension to the Zoo experience," which was occasionally illustrated by noting the men's rapport with inquisitive children. As one reader elaborated, "It is one thing to go from sign to sign learning about the various depleting rainforests and desert colonizations which threaten the flora and fauna of the world, but to hear it from the mouths of the people who live there is completely different." For these readers, the guides thus improved on the zoo's representation of east Africa and its environmental challenges. As spokespersons for a Maasai way of "life," broadly conceived, the men made those problems more engaging, immediate, and holistic to their audience than naturalistic mixed-animal displays could alone. On these terms, Seattlites judged the program to be a resounding success, pedagogically and ethically. "The zoo," wrote one reader, "is doing the right thing and let them continue their great work of educating the people in this community about endangered animals and cultures."[10]

With a similar degree of unanimity and enthusiasm, letter writers, like zoo management, rejected the possibility that the Maasai Journey was racialized. "This has nothing to do with race," "Does it always have to come down to race?" and "Why does the Seattle times give space to these race baiters?" were typical remarks. Others suggested that the controversy detracted from "the more important truly racial issues in existence," while some suggested that there was reverse racism in concerns that the guides were black Africans: "Ask the UW professors if they would still be objecting if the visiting guides were white." Less inflammatory responses included a personal reflection that "I would have NEVER thought of being educated at the zoo by a proud African tribesmen as demeaning or equating people to animals," and another person's observation that "the racist problems of the U.S. do not apply to Africa."[11] Indeed, some commentators believed that the Maasai Journey had transcended conventional concepts of race altogether, through a universal perspective that could see across national as well as species differences. For one man, the exhibit mirrored his own ability to envision this bigger picture: "I do associate African people with African animals. I associate European people with European animals. I associate North American people with North American animals." For another man, the concept of race was trumped by a more comprehensive notion of "Life": "There are Russians, Chinese, and Mexicans. Here the race is about understanding has [sic] humans relate to animals. Let's look for the reality in Life."[12] What is striking about the exhibit's reception is the recurrent failure or refusal to recognize the guides' blackness in favor of a totalizing worldview characterized by a continuum of living organisms. It would appear from the *Times* feedback that race has no place on zoo grounds; that zoos now designate a freedom from the particularities of racial identification; and that feeling optimistic, thankful, and proud at the zoo is a by-product of these seemingly positive changes.[13]

But four decades of new zoo making tell a different story. In the Maasai Journey, management, curators, designers, and guides have not overcome race as much as they have reaped the rewards of its reconfiguration in the wake of American zoo renewal. That the Maasai guides in Seattle have been largely received as "conservation professionals," as "just people," or as an integral part of "Life" is thanks to the converging projects of conserving wildlife and reproducing an urbanized white civility that reemerged in the 1960s. The legacy of this convergence is such that animals and their guides no longer look exotic or unfortunate, but instead like contented subjects that zoo goers can understand, admire, emulate, and otherwise connect with as para-white professionals. Seattle's celebrated zoo exhibit and the good feelings it generates is a benefactor of zoo renewal's racial reinventions. In particular, it upstages an older set of representations of black Africans that have, as an initial exercise of colonial power, portrayed them as savage, bestial, and excessively embodied, and as a latter exercise, portrayed them as self-colonizers still somewhere in the vicinity of beasts.[14] Animality of this ilk, however nuanced, is hard to find in the Maasai Journey, and with good reason. Zoos and their publics began shedding their associations with savages and beasts the moment that their charges got more lavish spaces in which to live and the encouragement to reproduce, and the moment nature lovers of all stripes rehabilitated into environmental stewards who were more fully in command of their urban milieux. On a good day after renewal—that is, a day when the euphoric discourse *about* a new zoo matched the lived experience of going to the zoo, there were fewer "exhibits" per se, fewer displays that could objectify their participants through one-sided encounters and the austere architectures of confinement: no cause for shame at all. Bodies appeared to be more natural *and* more human, underscored by one commentator's remarks that the Maasai Journey "is a far cry from the zoo/fair/circus 'freak shows' of the early 20th Century." Others also seemed aware of a historical change. "I have seen the Zoo transform itself from a collection of cramped cages and pens to the magnificent simulated environments," wrote one zoo goer, while another drew attention to the current absurdity of the idea of exhibiting black people:

> Are these guides behind barriers? Are they being fed on a schedule by other humans? Are they being gawked at but not interacted with? Of course not . . . they are enhancing the exhibit and enriching our knowledge about the culture of East Africa.

However tenuous, however subject to local variation and animal intransigence, this is the new American zoo forty years on, one that has been absorbed into quotidian zoo-going experiences and celebrated in the allied civic space of a city newspaper. Not entirely unlike the animals about which they speak, or the audience to which they speak, the guides of the Maasai Journey have proved indecipherable as anything other than "good people, who enjoy teaching and learning," respectable gentlemen who are close to nature in the way that good people ought to be.[15]

As it happens, postrenewal zoos still need their "others," and their cages. While the men of the Maasai Journey have been neutralized, their skeptics have been construed as something more unhealthy, stilted, and fiendish. The scholarly critique against the exhibit prompted accusations that the UW academics in question were presumptuous "do-gooders" who were "out of touch with real people" and did not know their social place. "The creation of the controversy is an example of 'PC' gone too far," wrote one reader. Others described the critics as "pointy eared intellectual eggheads," engaged in "just another level of super societal, intellectual masturbation." Their activities "project[ed] their personal biases and insecurities on others" and represented "intellectualism gone haywire!," leading one reader to wish that the critics were more like his children: "If only we could all be 5 and see things purely as they were intended, and not read so much into things." Others respondents prescribed the treatment of fresh air. "These 'academics' need to leave their desk and go enjoy the zoo once in awhile" and "why don't you get up from your desk and go and enjoy life" were two such recommendations. The pinnacle of the backlash came from a UW alumnus, who offered this suggestion:

> The UW should build a new exhibit on campus to display PC graduate students and professors in their native habitat. People from the real world could pay to come and watch these magnificent creatures, who are generally docile, but can become extremely dangerous when provoked. There would need to be proper security to protect visitors from harm, and plenty of brick and ivory habitat so the PC creatures feel secure with each other, safely isolated from the real world outside.[16]

Figure A.1. *Banner at the National Zoo, 2009. Photograph by the author.*

Suitable for an outmoded style of animal display and prone to lashing out, the UW scholars became the most antiquated part of a reformed zoo, if any part of it at all. Their segregation from a putatively all-inclusive community reinforces this book's thesis that American zoos have not been innocuous in their representation of a natural and urban world under strain. On the contrary, zoos have choreographed built and imagined environments of normative whiteness, crisscrossing species lines with startling agility. What ideas and practices of nature might become visible if zoo critics and other threatening elements were let out of their cages? What natures follow from attempts to more fully grasp zoos as urban sites of multispecies cultural production? How might these natures manifest as socially just, historically sensitive, and biologically true? The promise of these better natures, which is also the promise of better cities, is subject to our reckoning with a current one that reads as racially white as it does politically green.

Traveling along the Olmsted Walk at the National Zoo in July 2009, I saw a temporary banner that rehearsed the promise and made me smile (Figure A.1). The sign pictured an elephant that was helping build its future exhibit by raising a log into the air with its trunk. The elephant appeared neither exotic nor domesticated, holding its own alongside a man-powered backhoe familiar to construction sites. "We're clearing the way for Elephant Trails!" the text read, keeping the "we" open-ended and the work ahead upbeat. While the zoo's living elephants may not have been laboring bodies in this exact sense, the banners did furnish their public with a spirited picture of the collaborations that make zoo redevelopment possible. Building the zoo's new exhibit could be widely accessed, at least for a time, as some alternate feel-good urbanism marked not by the creation of an elsewhere but by the nurturing of residency, not by the purging of difference but by its flourishing through other-than-human concerns and capacities. It was a glimpse of the radicalism at once constitutive and deferred in American zoos.

NOTES

Introduction

1. John Berger, *About Looking* (New York: Vintage Books, 1980), 28.

2. For a detailed discussion of some of those reasons, see Jonathan Burt, "John Berger's 'Why Look at Animals?' A Close Reading," *Worldviews* 2, no. 2 (2005): 203–18.

3. See, for example, Derek Jensen, *Thought to Exist in the Wild: Awakening from the Nightmare of Zoos* (Santa Cruz, Calif.: No Voice Unheard, 2007); Dale Jamieson, "Zoos Revisited," in *Morality's Progress: Essays on Humans, Other Animals, and the Rest of Nature* (Oxford: Clarendon, 2002), 176–89; Ken Kawata, "Of Circus Wagons and Imagined Nature: A Review of American Zoo Exhibits, Part II," *Zoological Garten N.F.* 80 (2011): 352–65; Randy Malamud, *Reading Zoos: Representations of Animals in Captivity* (New York: New York University Press, 1998); Ralph Acampora, "Zoos and Eyes: Contesting Captivity and Seeking Successor Practices," *Society and Animals* 13, no. 1 (2005): 69–88; *Penned: Zoo Poems,* ed. Stephanie Bolster, Katia Grubisic, and Simon Reader (Montreal: Véhicle, 2010); Frank Noelker, *Captive Beauty: Zoo Portraits by Frank Noelker* (Chicago: University of Illinois Press, 2004); and Banksy, *Wall and Piece* (London: Random House, 2007).

4. For an incisive analysis of biopolitics in zoos, see Matthew Churlew, "Managing Love and Death and the Zoo: The Biopolitics of Endangered Species Preservation," *Australian Humanities Review* 50 (May 2011): 137–57.

5. The paradox pivoted around an idea of nature that, as Raymond Williams tells us, is historically specific to (if not exhausted by) Western Europe and North America, and has constructed the natural world in singular and sovereign terms. This idea of nature makes clear divisions between Nature and Man, is available for study as a scientific object, and can be alternately exploited or rescued. It is also something that speaks with great authority, as in the case of phrases like "Nature shows . . ." or "Nature teaches us . . ." Nature in this abstracted state has worked as humanity's mirror, reflecting human society back to itself in the image of organic life. The mirror, moreover, has obscured the multiplicity of actual living things and processes, and the social relations that are bound to them. Raymond Williams, "Ideas of Nature," *Problems in Materialism and Culture* (London: Verso, 1980).

6. *Zoo Design: Proceedings of the First International Symposium on Zoo Design and Construction, May 13–15th, 1975,* ed. A. P. G. Michelmore, Smithsonian Institution Office of Architectural History and

Historic Preservation Building Files, circa 1850–2006, AC 06–225, box 50, Smithsonian Institution Archives (hereafter cited as SIA). For critical treatments of zoo modernization in Adelaide, Australia, see Kay Anderson, "Culture and Nature at the Adelaide Zoo: At the Frontiers of 'Human' Geography," in *Transactions of the Institute of British Geographers,* n.s., 20, no. 3 (1995): 275–94; in Winnipeg, Canada, see Bonnie C. Hallman and Mary Benbow, "Canadian Human Landscape Examples: Naturally Cultural: The Zoo as Cultural Landscape," *Canadian Geographer* 50, no. 2 (2006): 256–64; in Tokyo, Japan, see Ian Jared Miller, *The Nature of the Beasts: Empire and Exhibition at the Tokyo Imperial Zoo* (Berkeley: University of California Press, 2013).

7. For a sampling of this literature, see Fairfield Osborn, "A New Opportunity—Zoos Help Wildlife," *International Zoo Yearbook* 4 (1962): 65–66; "The Obsolete Zoo vs Future Animal Parks," *Landscape Architecture* 57 (January 1967); Emily Hahn, *Animal Gardens* (Garden City, N.Y.: Doubleday, 1967); "It's a Sad, Sad, Sad, Sad Zoo," *Washingtonian,* December 1970, 49–51, 74–76; "The New Zoos," *Newsweek,* June 1, 1970, 58; Eugene J. Walter Jr., "Zoo People Give a Damn," *Venture* 8 (July–August 1971): 32–35; Robert Sommer, "What Do We Learn at the Zoo?," *Natural History* 81 (August–September 1972): 26–29, 84–85; "'All Is Here' at Microcosmic Zoo-Park for Tehran," *Landscape Architecture* 64 (January 1974): 58, 60; Emily Hahn, "Why Zoos," *New York Times Magazine,* February 23, 1975; Gerald Durrell, *The Stationary Ark* (London: Collins, 1976); Melissa Green, "No Rms, Jungle Vu," *Atlantic Monthly,* December 1987, 62–73; Nancy Gibbs, "The New Zoo: A Modern Ark," *Time,* August 21, 1989, 50–53; Cliff Tarpy, "New Zoos: Taking Down the Bars," *National Geographic,* July 1993, 2–37; Michael Nichols, *Keepers of the Kingdom: The New American Zoo* (New York: Lickle, 1996); and Vicki Croke, *The Modern Ark: The Story of Zoos: Past, Present, and Future* (New York: Scribners, 1997).

8. Caroline Jarvis, "Zoos and Conservation Symposium," *International Zoo Yearbook* 5 (1965): 97–100; R. Michael Schneider, "The Zoo's Changing Role," *Parks and Recreation* 4, no. 9 (1969): 95.

9. Ibid.

10. David Hancocks, *Animals and Architecture* (New York: Praeger, 1971), 10.

11. Weaver served as the first U.S. secretary of housing and urban development between 1966 and 1968. Robert C. Weaver, *The Urban Complex: Human Values in Urban Life,* Anchor Books ed. (Garden City, N.Y.: Doubleday/Anchor, 1968), xii. For an introduction to postwar urban renewal, see Eric Avila and Mark H. Rose, "Race, Culture, Politics, and Urban Renewal: An Introduction," *Journal of Urban History* 35, no. 3 (2009): 335–47.

12. For critiques of these official zoo histories, see Nigel Rothfels, *Savages and Beasts: The Birth of the Modern Zoo* (Baltimore, Md.: Johns Hopkins University Press, 2002); Jeffrey Hyson, "Jungles of Eden: The Design of American Zoos," in *Environmentalism in Landscape Architecture,* ed. Michel Conan (Washington, D.C.: Dumbarton Oaks, 2000), 23–44.

13. Vernon N. Kisling Jr., "Zoological Gardens of the United States," in *Zoo and Aquarium History: Ancient Animal Collections to Zoological Gardens,* ed. Vernon N. Kisling Jr. (Boca Raton, Fla.: CRC, 2001), 151; David Hancocks, *A Different Nature: The Paradoxical World of Zoos and Their Uncertain Future* (Berkeley: University of California Press, 2001), 89–90; Elizabeth Hanson, *Animal Attractions: Nature on Display in American Zoos* (Princeton, N.J.: Princeton University Press, 2002), 11–14. Hanson's study does not belong in the evolutionary zoo history camp, but helps fill out the portrait of the Philadelphia Zoo as an American prototype.

14. Roy Rosenzweig and Elizabeth Blackmar, *The Park and the People: A History of Central Park* (New York: Henry Holt, 1992), 341–49.

15. Kisling, "Zoological Gardens," 151.

16. Vernon N. Kisling Jr., "The Origins and Development of American Zoological Parks to 1899," in *New Worlds, New Animals: From Menagerie to Zoological Park in the Nineteenth Century,* ed. R. J. Joage and William A. Deiss (Baltimore, Md.: Johns Hopkins University Press, 1996), 116–17. Not surprisingly, advocates of mid-twentieth-century zoo revitalization marshaled the reputation of the zoo in Central Park as a substandard menagerie toward an argument for American zoo renewal. According to one zoo watcher in 1971, Central Park's zoo was where animals "are condemned to an irrelevant, bankrupt, freak-show existence in buildings that are eye sores and nose sores," such that "ultimately the spectators become the real freaks." Walter, "Zoo People Give a Damn," 32–35, 60–71.

17. Rothfels, *Savages and Beasts,* 18.

18. Ibid.

19. Ibid., 31.

20. For a discussion of Hagenbeck's influence on American zoo design, see Jeffrey Nugent Hyson, "Urban Jungles: Zoos and American Society" (PhD diss., Cornell University, 1999).

21. Letter from president of the New York Zoological Society, *Animal Kingdom,* June 1969, 2; William G. Conway, "A World of Darkness in the Zoo," *Animal Kingdom,* June 1969, 4–11; James Barron, "The Monkey House Ends a 111-Year Run in the Bronx, a Victim of Zoo Evolution," March 1, 2012, *New York Times.com,* http://www.nytimes.com/2012/03/02/nyregion/the-monkey-house-ends-a-111-year-run-in-the-bronx.html.

22. See, for example, Harriet Ritvo, *The Animal Estate: The English and Other Creatures in the Victorian Era* (Cambridge, Mass.: Harvard University Press, 1987); Anderson, "Culture and Nature"; Ian Miller, "Didactic Nature: Exhibiting Nation and Empire at the Ueno Zoological Gardens," in *JAPANimals: History and Culture in Japan's Animal Life,* ed. Gregory M. Pflugfelder and Brett L. Walker (Ann Arbor: University of Michigan Press, 2005), 273–313; Robert W. Jones, "The Sight of Creatures Strange to Our Clime: London Zoo and the Consumption of the Exotic," *Journal of Victorian Culture* 2 (1997): 1–26; Eric Baratay and Elisabeth Hardouin-Fugier, *Zoo: A History of Zoological Gardens in the West* (London: Reaktion Books, 2002); *New Worlds, New Animals: From Menagerie to Zoological Park in the Nineteenth Century,* ed. R. J. Hoage and William A. Deiss (Baltimore, Md.: Johns Hopkins University Press, 1996); R. Jeffrey Stott, "The Historical Origins of the Zoological Park in American Thought," *Environmental Review* 5 (Fall 1981): 52–65; Helen Lefkowitz Horowitz, "Seeing Ourselves through the Bars: A Historical Tour of American Zoos," *Landscape* 25, no. 2 (1981): 12–19; Hanson, *Animal Attractions;* Hyson, "Urban Jungles"; Catherine Russell, *Experimental Ethnography: The Work of Film in the Age of Video* (Durham, N.C.: Duke University Press, 1999); Patrick H. Wirtz, "Zoo City: Bourgeois Values and Scientific Culture in the Industrial Landscape," *Journal of Urban Design* 2, no. 1 (1997): 61–82; Bob Mullen and Garry Marvin, *Zoo Culture* (London: Weidenfeld and Nicolson, 1987); Malamud, *Reading Zoos;* and Iris Braverman, "Looking at Zoos," *Cultural Studies* 25, no. 6 (2011): 809–42.

23. Fredric Jameson, "Reification and Utopia in Mass Culture," *Social Text,* no. 1 (Winter 1979): 130–48.

24. Claude Lévi-Strauss, *Totemism,* trans. Rodney Needham (Boston: Beacon, 1971). For two superlative exegeses on the field of animal studies and the stakes of retheorizing and historicizing animal representation, see Susan McHugh, *Animal Stories* (Minneapolis: University of Minnesota

Press, 2011), 1–23; and Kari Weil, *Thinking Animals: Why Animal Studies Now?* (New York: Columbia University Press, 2012), chap. 1.

25. Jacques Derrida, "The Animal That Therefore I Am (More to Follow)," *Critical Inquiry* 28 (2002): 297–403; Donna Haraway, *When Species Meet* (Minneapolis: University of Minnesota Press, 2008); and Jonathan Burt, "The Illumination of the Animal Kingdom: The Role of Light and Electricity in Animal Representation," *Society and Animals* 9, no. 3 (2001): 203–28.

26. Cary Wolfe, *Animal Rights: American Culture, the Discourse of Species, and Posthumanist Theory* (Chicago: University of Chicago Press, 2003), 173.

27. Ibid., 178–79.

28. Wolfe ultimately argues, however, that Crichton's is a "faux posthumanism" insofar as the disruption of humanism in the novel is not so radical as to threaten two of humanism's privileged forms of knowledge—namely, technoscience and neocolonialism. Ibid., 182.

29. Steve Baker, *The Postmodern Animal* (London: Reaktion Books, 2000).

30. My appeal to social constructionism signals Barbara Herrnstein Smith's distinction between "social constructivism" in fields like philosophy, psychology, and the history and sociology of science, and its incarnation as "social constructionism" in fields that, Smith notes, are more "culturally focused and politically engaged," and that examine "such problematic practices as racial classifications, gender bias or normative heterosexuality." Barbara Herrnstein Smith, *Scandalous Knowledge: Science, Truth, and the Human* (Durham, N.C.: Duke University Press, 2005), 4–5.

31. Kay Anderson, "'The Beast Within': Race, Humanity, and Animality," *Environment and Planning D: Society and Space* 18 (2000): 302.

32. See, for example, Fatimah Tobin Rony, *The Third Eye: Race, Cinema, and Ethnographic Spectacle* (Durham, N.C.: Duke University Press, 1996); Jane C. Desmond, *Staging Tourism: Bodies on Display from Waikiki to Sea World* (Chicago: University of Chicago Press, 1999); Diana Taylor, "A Savage Performance: Guillermo Gómez-Peña and Coco Fusco's 'Couple in the Cage,'" *TDR/The Drama Review* 42, no. 2 (1998): 160–80; Pauline Wakeham, *Taxidermic Signs: Reconstructing Aboriginality* (Minneapolis: University of Minnesota Press, 2008); *Africans on Stage: Studies in Ethnological Show Business,* ed. Bernth Linfors (Bloomington: Indiana University Press, 1999); *Human Zoos: Science and Spectacle in the Age of Colonial Empires,* ed. Pascal Blanchard, Nicolas Bancel, Gilles Boetsch, Eric Deroo, Sandrine Lemaire, and Charles Forsdick, trans. Teresa Bridgeman (Liverpool: Liverpool University Press, 2008); *Freakery: Cultural Spectacles of the Extraordinary Body,* ed. Rosemarie Garland Thompson (New York: New York University Press, 1996); and Cynthia Chris, *Watching Wildlife* (Minneapolis: University of Minnesota Press, 2006).

33. Hyson, "Urban Jungles," 50–51, 231–34.

34. The story and implications of Ota Benga's life at the Bronx Zoo have received much attention in critical zoo history. See, for example, Harvey Blume, "Ota Benga and the Barnum Complex," in Linfors, *Africans on Stage,* 192; Hanson, *Animal Attractions,* 37; Lefkowitz Horowitz, "Seeing Ourselves," 15–16; Malamud, *Reading Zoos,* 90; Hyson, "Urban Jungles," 181–86.

35. Hyson, "Urban Jungles," 181–86.

36. Lawrence Curtis, *Zoological Park Fundamentals* (Washington, D.C.: National Recreation and Park Association, 1968), 34.

37. Donna Haraway, "Ecce Homo, Ain't (Ar'n't) I a Woman, and Inappropriate/d Others: The

Human in a Post-Humanist Landscape," in *Feminists Theorize the Political,* ed. Judith Butler and Joan Scott (New York: Routledge, 1992), 86.

38. "Antelope Building: Preliminary Study and Definite Plans $39,400," folder 3, box 44, RU 326, SIA.

39. "Keeping Up with Our Gorillas," *Zoonooz,* March 1973, 4–11; On the whiteness of the one-way look, see bell hooks, *Black Looks: Race and Representation* (Boston: South End, 1992), 168.

40. John Hartigan, *What Can You Say? America's National Conversation on Race* (Stanford, Calif.: Stanford University Press, 2010).

41. See, for example, Mike Davis, *City of Quartz: Excavating the Future in Los Angeles* (New York: Vintage Books, 1992); Dolores Hayden, *The Power of Place: Urban Landscapes as Public History* (Cambridge, Mass.: MIT Press, 1997); Elizabeth Wilson, *The Sphinx in the City: Urban Life, the Control of Disorder, and Women* (Berkeley: University of California Press, 1991); George Chauncey, *Gay New York: Gender, Urban Culture, and the Making of the Gay Male World, 1890–1940* (New York: Basic Books, 1994); *Making The Invisible Visible: A Multicultural Planning History,* ed. Leonie Sandercock (Berkeley: University of California Press, 1998).

42. Robert A. Beauregard, *Voices of Decline: The Postwar Fate of U.S. Cities,* 2nd ed. (New York: Routledge, 2003); Steven Macek, *Urban Nightmares: The Media, the Right, and the Moral Panic over the City* (Minneapolis: University of Minnesota Press, 2006); Andrew Wiese, *Places of Their Own: African American Suburbanization in the Twentieth Century* (Chicago: University of Chicago Press, 2004); and Eric Avila, *Popular Culture in the Age of White Flight: Fear and Fantasy in Suburban Los Angeles* (Berkeley: University of California Press, 2004).

43. Avila, *Popular Culture,* 15.

44. Ibid., 14.

45. Ibid., 6.

46. Ibid., 8.

47. Macek, *Urban Nightmares,* xvii.

48. The term *charismatic megafauna* emerged in the 1980s among biologists and environmentalists who argued that popular and legislative conservation discourses fixate on certain species. For example, reviewing George B. Schaller et al.'s book *The Giant Pandas of Wolong* (1985), Devra G. Keliman and John Sedensticker wrote in the journal *Science,* "Most people, if ever exposed, remember and are able to name elephants, tigers, bears, rhinoceroses, and gorillas. The giant panda probably tops this list of charismatic megafauna in terms of attractiveness and mass appeal." Three years later, *New York Times* environmental columnist Philip Shabecoff, assessing the Endangered Species Act, wrote: "While the species that Dr. Cutler [then president of Defenders of Wildlife] called 'charismatic megafauna,' such as whales and grizzly bears, get most of the public attention, he said the law is supposed to provide equal protection for 'enigmatic microfauna and flora,' including insects, plants, fish and mollusks." Devra G. Keliman and John Sedensticker, "Pandas in the Wild," *Science* 228, no. 4701 (1985): 875; Philip Shabecoff, "Fifteen Year Scorecard: The Law Saves a Few Species from Oblivion," *New York Times,* November 27, 1988. On the gender and sexual normativity of one species of charismatic megafauna, see Lisa Uddin, "Panda Gardens and Public Sex at the National Zoological Park," *Public: Art, Culture, Ideas* 41 (2010): 80–93.

49. David R. Roediger, *The Wages of Whiteness: Race and the Making of the American Working Class* (London: Verso, 1991), 8.

50. Michael Omi and Howard Winant, *Racial Formation in the United States: From the 1960's to the 1990's,* 2nd ed. (New York: Routledge, 1994), 55–56.

51. The question of whether materially rooted signifiers are arbitrary or mute is of some debate. Select scholarship in the humanities and humanistic social sciences has begun to theorize race away from the race-as-representation paradigm, with its implicit argument about the randomness and inconsequentiality of what counts in racialization. This work suggests a certain ontology of race, and that ideas of race are (or ought to be) open to the same materialist turn as that taken within feminism and critical theory. In other words, the body matters *as matter* in the production of race, less as raw material than as something more energetic. For an excellent performance of the argument and engagement with its theoretical trajectories, see Arun Saldanha, "Reontologising Race: The Machinic Geography of Phenotype," *Environment and Planning D: Society and Space* 24 (2006): 9–24. See also Michael Hames-Garcia, "How Real Is Race?," in *Material Feminisms,* ed. Stacy Alaimo and Susan Hekman (Bloomington: Indiana University Press, 2008), 308–39.

52. hooks, *Black Looks,* 177.

53. See, for example, Toni Morrison, *Playing in the Dark: Whiteness and the Literary Imagination* (New York: Vintage Books, 1993); Richard Dyer, *White* (New York: Routledge, 1997); Maurice Berger, *White: Whiteness and Race in Contemporary Art* (Baltimore, Md.: Center for Art and Visual Culture, 2004); Martin Berger, *Sight Unseen: Whiteness and American Visual Culture* (Berkeley: University of California Press, 2005); *Landscape and Race in the United States,* ed. Richard Schein (London: Routledge, 2006); Elizabeth Abel, *Signs of the Times: The Visual Politics of Jim Crow* (Berkeley: University of California Press, 2010); Dianne Harris, *Little White Houses: How the Postwar Home Constructed Race in America* (Minneapolis: University of Minnesota Press, 2013).

54. George Lipsitz, *The Possessive Investment in Whiteness: How White People Profit from Identity Politics* (Philadelphia: Temple University Press, 1998); *Displacing Whiteness: Essays in Social and Cultural Criticism,* ed. Ruth Frankenberg (Durham, N.C.: Duke University Press, 1997); Roediger, *Wages of Whiteness,* 1991.

55. Lipsitz, *Possessive Investment,* vii–viii.

56. Matthew Frye Jacobson, *Whiteness of a Different Color: European Immigrants and the Alchemy of Race* (Cambridge, Mass.: Harvard University Press, 1998), 5.

57. Charles Abrams, *The City Is the Frontier* (New York: Harper and Row, 1965), 16.

58. *Animal Geographies: Place, Politics, and Identity in the Nature-Culture Borderlands,* ed. Jennifer Wolch and Jody Emel (London: Verso, 1998); *Animal Spaces, Beastly Places: New Geographies of Human-Animal Relations,* ed. Chris Philo and Chris Wilbert (London: Routledge, 2000); Steve Hinchcliffe, Matthew Kearnes, Monica Degen, and Sarah Whatmore, "Urban Wild Things: A Cosmopolitical Experiment," *Environment and Planning D: Society and Space* 23 (Summer 2003): 643–58; and Dawn Day Biehler, *Pests in the City: Flies, Bedbugs, Cockroaches, and Rats* (Seattle: University of Washington Press, 2013).

59. Alaimo and Hekman, *Material Feminisms.*

60. Burt, "Illumination"; Haraway, *When Species Meet.*

61. Michel Foucault, "Of Other Spaces," trans. J. Miskowiec, *diacritics* 6 (1986): 24, 26.

62. Jennifer Wolch, "Zoöpolis," in *Animal Geographies,* 120.

63. Wirtz, "Zoo City," 61.

64. On nonhuman animals as modern neighbors, see Lisa Uddin, "A Gorilla Lover's Discourse," *Parallax* 38 (2006): 11–119.

65. Nicole Shukin, *Animal Capital: Rendering Life in Biopolitical Times* (Minneapolis: University of Minnesota Press, 2009), 130.

66. Erica Fudge, "A Left-Handed Blow: Writing the History of Animals," in *Representing Animals,* ed. Nigel Rothfels (Bloomington: Indiana University Press, 2002), 3–18.

67. Cary Wolfe, *What Is Posthumanism?* (Minneapolis: University of Minnesota Press, 2010), 120; and Donna Haraway, "Situated Knowledges: The Science Question in Feminism and the Privilege of Partial Perspective," *Feminist Studies* 14, no. 3 (1988): 575–99.

68. Haraway, "Ecce Homo," 96.

69. Roland Barthes, "The Third Meaning," in *Image, Music, Text,* trans. Stephen Heath (New York: Hill and Wang, 1977), 54.

70. Ibid., 62, 55, 63.

71. Barthes writes: "Maternal, cordial, virile, 'sympathetic' without any recourse to stereotypes, the Eisensteinian people is essentially loveable. We savour, we love the two round-capped heads in image X, we enter into complicity, into an understanding with them." Ibid., 59.

72. Wolfe, *What Is Posthumanism?*

73. Timothy Scheie, "Performing Degree Zero: Barthes, Body, Theatre," *Theatre Journal* 52 (2000): 165.

74. In an appendix to his 1971 magazine article, "Zoo People Give a Damn," Eugene J. Walter Jr. gave readers a compendium of institutional standouts in the United States that would have found few objections in the zoo world. Arguing that "while it would be impossible to name any zoo the best in America, several deserve the label 'great' and a few more aren't far behind," based on the criteria of being visibly in transition from outmoded forms of animal exhibition and setting records in captive animal reproduction and longevity. The list included the Bronx Zoo, Philadelphia Zoo, Catskill Game Farm, the National Zoo, Detroit Zoological Park, Cincinnati Zoo, Brookfield Zoo, Lincoln Park Zoo, Milwaukee County Zoo, St. Louis Zoo, Oklahoma City Zoo, Dallas Zoo, San Antonio Zoo, Arizona-Sonora Desert Museum, Los Angeles Zoo, and the San Diego Zoo. Eugene J. Walter Jr., "A Zoo Critic's Notebook," *Venture* 8 (July–August 1971): 60–71.

1. Shame and the Naked Cage

1. Dale Osborn, "Dressing the Naked Cage," *Curator* 14, no. 3 (1971): 194–99.

2. For a sense of the eclecticism, see Curtis, *Zoological Park Fundamentals.*

3. George Leposky, "Getting Back to Nature at Brookfield Zoo," *Inland Architect* 16, no. 5 (1972): 22; Nicholas Polites, "The 'Good' Zoo vs. the 'Bad' City," *Design and Environment* 1, no. 4 (1970): 55; "Assignment Four: Zoo," KRON-TV, 1970, San Francisco Bay Area Television Archive, https://diva.sfsu.edu/collections/sfbatv/bundles/191494; Janet Hopson, "Zoos: Changing Their Spots," *Science News* 110, no. 7 (1976): 106–8.

4. Sara Ahmed, *The Cultural Politics of Emotion* (London: Routledge, 2004), 104.

5. Elspeth Probyn, *Blush: Faces of Shame* (Minneapolis: University of Minnesota Press, 2005), 39.

6. Polites, "'Good' Zoo vs. the 'Bad' City," 54; Field, quoted in "The Obsolete Zoo vs. Future Animal Parks," *Landscape Architecture* 57 (January 1967): 111; Joan Bannon, "Today's Zoos: Animal Ghettos," *Washington Post,* August 31, 1971.

7. Christopher Klemek, *The Transatlantic Collapse of Urban Renewal: Postwar Urbanism from New York to Berlin* (Chicago: University of Chicago Press, 2011), 13; Beauregard, *Voices of Decline,* 136; Avila and Rose, "Race, Culture, Politics, and Urban Renewal."

8. Statistics cited in Thomas S. Hines, "The Imperial Mall: The City Beautiful Moment and the Washington Plan of 1901–1902," in *The Mall in Washington, 1791–1991,* ed. Richard Longstreth (Washington, D.C.: National Gallery of Arts, 1991), 81; Paul Boyer, *Urban Masses and Moral Order in America, 1820–1920* (Cambridge, Mass.: Harvard University Press, 1978), 124–25; Beauregard, *Voices of Decline,* 30.

9. Boyer, *Urban Masses,* 127–29.

10. Ibid., 128; Maren Stange, *Symbols of Ideal Life: Social Documentary Photography in America, 1890–1950* (Cambridge: Cambridge University Press, 1989); Martha Rosler, "in, around, and after-thoughts (on documentary photography)," in *The Contest of Meaning: Critical Histories of Photography,* ed. Richard Bolton (Cambridge, Mass.: MIT Press, 1989), 303–33.

11. Richard Hofstadter, *The Age of Reform: From Bryan to F.D.R.* (New York: Knopf, 1974), 195, 205.

12. Lincoln Steffens, *The Shame of the Cities* (1904; repr. New York: Hill and Wang, 1957), 12.

13. Jacob Riis, *How the Other Half Lives* (1890; repr. Lexington, Ky.: Seven Treasures, 2009), 169–70.

14. Hofstadter, *Age of Reform,* 210.

15. Stange, *Symbols of Ideal Life,* xiii.

16. Riis, *How the Other Half Lives,* 19, 23, 29, 28, 55, 66, 31.

17. Hanson, *Animal Attractions,* 28; Wirtz, "Zoo City," 66.

18. For discussions of how performing animals and their trainers, including P. T. Barnum, regularly moved between low-brow entertainment and zoos, see Hanson, *Animal Attractions,* 16, 34–36; and Hyson, "Urban Jungles," chap. 1.

19. Cited in Hanson, *Animal Attractions,* 16.

20. Affluent German immigrants who settled in Cincinnati, for instance, formed their city's zoo in memory of the civic importance of zoos in their homeland. Ibid., 15–16.

21. Kisling, "Origins and Development of American Zoological Parks," 115–16; Hanson, *Animal Attractions,* 15–16.

22. Hyson, "Jungles of Eden."

23. Ritvo, *Animal Estate,* 205–42; Wirtz, "Zoo City," 63–67.

24. Wilfred Blunt, *The Ark in the Park: The Zoo in the Nineteenth Century* (London: Hamish Hamilton, 1976), 35.

25. Tony Bennett, *The Birth of the Museum: History, Theory, Politics* (London: Routledge, 1995), 52.

26. Jones, "Sight of Creatures Strange," 1.

27. Ritvo, *Animal Estate,* 214; Wirtz, "Zoo City," 68.

28. Hanson, *Animal Attractions,* 23–24.

29. Harrow Strehlow, "Zoos and Aquariums of Berlin," in Joage and Deiss, *New Worlds, New Animals,* 66–68.

30. Hanson, *Animal Attractions,* 23–24.

31. Lincoln Park guidebook and Philadelphia Zoo review, cited in Hyson, "Jungles of Eden," 26.

32. Heather Ewing, "The Architecture of the National Zoological Park," in Joage and Deiss, *New Worlds, New Animals,* 155–57.

33. According to Helen Lefkowitz Horowitz, the complete funding structure for many civic zoos in the United States was taken from the New York Zoological Park. The city provided park land and funds for its development; maintenance of the grounds was supported through membership fees, admission receipts, concessions, and a line in the city budget; private philanthropy financed zoo buildings and animal acquisitions ("Seeing Ourselves," 15).

34. Hanson, *Animal Attractions,* 4, 24.

35. Wirtz, "Zoo City," 70.

36. Hanson, *Animal Attractions,* 26.

37. Galen Cranz, *The Politics of Park Design: A History of Urban Parks in America* (Cambridge, Mass.: MIT Press, 1982), 5.

38. Eliot, quoted in Boyer, *Urban Masses,* 239.

39. Ibid., 236–37.

40. Rosenzweig and Blackmar, *Park and the People,* 131; Boyer, *Urban Masses,* 236–37. Olmsted worked on many other landscaped environments, including Yosemite National Park, the landmark of Niagara Falls, the pastoral estate of George Vanderbilt, and the wetlands of Boston's Fens and Riverway. Anne Whiston Spirn, "Constructing Nature: The Legacy of Frederick Law Olmsted," in *Uncommon Ground: Rethinking the Human Place in Nature,* ed. William Cronon (New York: Norton, 1996), 91–113.

41. Cranz, *Politics of Park Design,* 24.

42. Hanson, *Animal Attractions,* 19; Cranz, *Politics of Park Design,* 8, 32–36.

43. Rosenzweig and Blackmar, *Park and the People,* 130–31.

44. Charles E. Beveridge, "Frederick Law Olmsted's Theory of Landscape Design," reprinted in *Nineteenth Century,* folder 9, box 15, RU 365, SIA.

45. Guidebook quotation, quoted in Boyer, *Urban Masses,* 239.

46. Hyson, "Jungles of Eden," 27; see also Hanson, *Animal Attractions,* 22.

47. Ewing, "Architecture of the National Zoological Park," 154.

48. Quoted in "Olmsted's Concept of the National Zoological Park," folder 9, box 15, RU 365, SIA.

49. Ibid.

50. Hanson, *Animal Attractions,* 17.

51. Peter Schmitt, *Back to Nature: The Arcadian Myth in Urban America* (1969; repr. Baltimore, Md.: Johns Hopkins University Press, 1990), 17.

52. William Cronon, "The Trouble with Wilderness; or, Getting Back to the Wrong Nature," in *Uncommon Ground: Rethinking the Human Place in Nature,* ed. William Cronon (New York: Norton, 1996), 69–90.

53. As Carolyn Merchant notes, Native Americans were not passive inhabitants on the "whitening" landscape. Like African Americans under slavery, they fought against their oppression and retained many of their cultural traditions. Carolyn Merchant, "Shades of Darkness: Race and Environmental History," *Environmental History* 3, no. 3 (2003): 382–84.

54. Muir, quoted in Merchant, "Shades of Darkness," 382.

55. Ibid., 385.

56. Ibid., 384.

57. Sandy Alexandre, "Strange Fruits in the Garden: Surveying the Properties of Lynching"

(PhD diss., University of Virginia, 2006), 13. For a broader literary critique of American pastoralism's exclusions, see Lawrence Buell, "American Pastoral Ideology Reappraised," *American Literary History* 1, no. 1 (1989): 1–29.

58. Schmitt, *Back to Nature,* 9.

59. Wirtz, "Zoo City," 69.

60. William T. Hornaday, *Our Vanishing Wild Life: Its Extermination and Preservation* (New York: New York Zoological Society, 1913), 101.

61. For a discussion of how immigrant groups are negatively racialized through their practices with nonhuman animals, see Glen Elder, Jennifer Wolch, and Jody Emel, "Le Pratique Sauvage: Race, Place, and the Human-Animal Divide," in Wolch and Emel, *Animal Geographies,* 72–90.

62. Hornaday, *Our Vanishing Wild Life,* 101.

63. Ibid., 101–2.

64. As the historian James Andrew Dolph clarifies, scientific taxonomy indicates that American bison are not related to the "true" buffalo, which belong to the genus *Bubalus* and are native only to Africa and Asia. James Andrew Dolph, "Bringing Wildlife to the Millions: William Temple Hornaday; the Early Years: 1854–1896" (PhD diss., University of Massachusetts, 1975), 396.

65. Ibid.; Hanson, *Animal Attractions,* 26.

66. Helen Lefkowitz Horowitz, "The National Zoological Park: 'City of Refuge' or Zoo?" in Joage and Deiss, *New Worlds, New Animals,* 130.

67. Hornaday, quoted in Dolph, "Bringing Wildlife," 511, 516.

68. Ibid., 535–38.

69. Hornaday, *Our Vanishing Wild Life,* 372.

70. Ibid., 542.

71. Dolph, "Bringing Wildlife," 424–26, 432.

72. Hanson, *Animal Attractions,* 134.

73. Hornaday, quoted in Dolph, "Bringing Wildlife," 675.

74. Dolph, "Bringing Wildlife," 130.

75. Hornaday, *Our Vanishing Wild Life,* 395.

76. Dolph, "Bringing Wildlife," 135–37.

77. Hadas A. Steiner, "For the Birds," *Grey Room* 13 (Fall 2003): 7; Hyson, "Jungles of Eden," 35.

78. Pyrs Gruffud, "Biological Cultivation: Lubetkin's Modernism at London Zoo in the 1930s," in Philo and Wilbert, *Animal Spaces, Beastly Places,* 229.

79. The film was produced for the Museum of Modern Art, New York, and the Zoological Society of London. *The New Architecture and the London Zoo* (dir. László Moholy-Nagy, 1936) (Ann Arbor, Mich.: Moholy-Nagy Foundation, 2012), DVD.

80. For a detailed discussion of this understanding and its reversal, see Andrew Shapland and David Van Reybrouck, "Competing Natural and Historical Heritage: The Penguin Pool at London Zoo," *International Journal of Heritage Studies* 14, no. 1 (2008): 10–29.

81. Steiner, "For the Birds," 15–16; See also Peder Anker, "Bauhaus at the Zoo," *Nature,* February 23, 2006, 916.

82. Key examples of zoo modernism in the United States include the Philadelphia Zoo's Carnivora House (1951), Monkey House (1958), and Rare Mammal House (1965). As Hyson observes, these structures made ample use of tiled walls, stainless steel berths, running water, and other

"sanitary modernist" features, underscoring the increasingly clinical aspects of postwar zoo display that also included the employment of resident veterinarians and the use of tranquilizer guns. Hyson, "Jungles of Eden," 35–36. See also Hyson, "Urban Jungles," 447.

83. Desmond Morris, "The Shame of the Naked Cage," *Life,* November 8, 1968, 83–86.

84. Edward O. Wilson, *Sociobiology: The New Synthesis* (Cambridge, Mass.: Harvard University Press, 1975), 4, 547; Elizabeth Allen, Barbara Beckwith, Jon Beckwith, Steven Chorover, and David Culver et al., "Against 'Sociobiology,'" *New York Review of Books,* November 13, 1975; Andy Luttrell, "The History of Edward Wilson's Sociobiology," *Psychology,* November 14, 2009; Desmond Morris, *The Naked Ape: A Zoologist's Study of the Human Animal* (New York: McGraw-Hill, 1967), 12.

85. Silvan Tomkins, "Shame—Humiliation and Contempt—Disgust," in *Shame and Its Sisters: A Silvan Tomkins Reader,* ed. Eve Kosofsky Sedgwick and Adam Frank (Durham, N.C.: Duke University Press, 1995), 136.

86. While beyond the scope of my narrative, the question of whether the cover was also depicting a shamed orangutan is an open and important one. There is mounting evidence of the emotional lives of nonhuman animals from myriad sites of human–animal interaction, with a voluminous scholarly and popular literature as reference. The implications for humanistic theories of shame await study.

87. "Letters to the editor re: the naked cage," *Life,* November 29, 1968, 19.

88. Unpublished information about the photograph relays that the baboons were "sitting on shelves because overheated floor burns their feet." "Baboons in starkly bare cage, sitting on," *Getty Images,* http://www.gettyimages.com/detail/news-photo/baboons-in-starkly-bare-cage-sitting-on -shelves-because-news-photo/50656126 (accessed October 12, 2014).

89. Morris, "Shame of the Naked Cage," 81.

90. Ibid.

91. Lawrence J. Vale, *Reclaiming Public Housing: A Half Century of Struggle in Three Public Neighborhoods* (Cambridge, Mass.: Harvard University Press, 2002), 15. Vale also posits an architectural distance between public housing and the dominant cultural ideal of the single-family home. Lawrence J. Vale, *From the Puritans to the Projects: Public Housing and Public Neighbors* (Cambridge, Mass.: Harvard University Press, 2000), 9, 15.

92. Arnold Hirsch, *Making the Second Ghetto: Race and Housing in Chicago, 1940–1960* (Cambridge: Cambridge University Press, 1983), 2–10.

93. As Le Corbusier phrased it, "Here is the CITY with its crowds living in peace and pure air, where noise is smothered under the foliage of green trees. The chaos of New York is overcome. Here, bathed in light, stands the modern city." Le Corbusier, *The City of Tomorrow and Its Planning,* trans. Frederick Etchells ([1929]; repr. New York: Dover Publications, 1987), 177. For a brief discussion of the gap between ideals and reality in high-rise public housing, see Gwendolyn Wright, *USA: Modern Architectures in History* (London: Reaktion Books, 2008), 177–78.

94. Katherine G. Bristol, "The Pruitt-Igoe Myth," in *American Architectural History: A Contemporary Reader,* ed. Keith Eggener (New York: Routledge, 2004), 355; Gwendolyn Wright, *Building the Dream: A Social History of Housing in America* (New York: Pantheon Books, 1981), 236. For a history of decision making for the Robert Taylor Homes, see D. Bradford Hunt, "What Went Wrong with Public Housing in Chicago? A History of the Robert Taylor Homes," *Journal of the Illinois Historical Society* 94, no. 1 (2001): 96–123.

95. James Bailey, "The Case History of a Failure," *Architectural Forum* 125 (December 1965):

22–25; Jack Rosenthal, "Crime in High-Rise Housing," in *Crisis in Urban Housing,* ed. Grant S. McClellan (New York: H. W. Wilson, 1974), 45.

96. Commenting on the larger schedule of demolition, the architecture critic Charles Jencks famously declared, "Modern Architecture died in St. Louis, Missouri on July 15, 1972 at 3:32 p.m. (or thereabouts)." Bristol complicates this pronouncement considerably by identifying maintenance problems, thin occupancy, and unfair rental policies as the more vital causes of Pruitt-Igoe's demise. Charles A. Jencks, *The Language of Post-Modern Architecture* (New York: Rizzoli, 1977), 9; Bristol, "Pruitt-Igoe Myth." For a complication of the singular narrative of damaged lives, see *The Pruitt-Igoe Myth* (dir. Chad Freidrichs; 2011).

97. For discussions of how the urban reformer Jane Jacobs, for example, understood modernist city space as grounds for human degeneracy, see David Kinkela, "The Ecological Landscapes of Jane Jacobs and Rachel Carson," *American Quarterly* 61 (December 2009): 905–29; Gordon Brent Ingram, "'Open' Space as Strategic Queer Sites," in *Queers in Space: Communities, Public Places, Sites of Resistance,* ed. Gordon Brett Ingram, Annie-Marie Bouthillette, and Yolanda Retter (Seattle: Bay Press, 1997), 95–125.

98. For analysis of the metaphor and its racial meanings within noir fiction specifically, see Ralph Willet, *The Naked City: Urban Crime Fiction in the USA* (Manchester: Manchester University Press, 1996), 12–13.

99. Desmond Morris, *The Human Zoo* (New York: McGraw-Hill, 1969), 8.

100. Herbert Gans has situated the now highly generalized term *underclass* in the social scientific literature of the 1960s and 1970s, which described the condition of chronic poverty, but also black and Hispanic racial identities and aberrant behaviors that could flag unworthiness by planners and policy makers. Attempts to identify the size and nature of this population also focused on census tracts or zip codes, effectively assigning the "underclass" to specific neighborhoods and housing forms. Gans argues that the term has since functioned as a racial code word "that fits in with the tolerant public discourse of our time, but . . . also submerges and may further repress racial—and class—antagonisms that continue to exist." Herbert J. Gans, "Deconstructing the Underclass: The Term's Dangers as a Planning Concept," *Journal of the American Planning Association* 56, no. 3 (1990): 273.

101. William H. Whyte Jr., "Are Cities Un-American?," in *The Exploding Metropolis: A Study of the Assault on Urbanism and How Our Cities Can Resist It* (New York: Doubleday, 1958), 21–26; Whyte, "Urban Sprawl," in *Exploding Metropolis,* 115; Jane Jacobs, *The Death and Life of Great American Cities,* Modern Library Edition (1961; repr. New York: Random House, 1993), 6.

102. Morris, *Human Zoo,* 38–40, 96–97, 99, 163.

103. Ibid., 245–46.

104. In the introduction to the six-hundred-page *Report of the National Advisory Commission of Civil Disorders* from 1968, Tom Wicker sketched the profile of the average looter and arsonist: "By and large, the rioters were young Negroes, native of the ghetto (not of the South), hostile to the white society surrounding and repressing them, and equally hostile to the middle-class Negroes who accommodated themselves to that white dominance. The rioters were mistrustful of white politics, they hated the police, they were proud of their race, and acutely conscious of the discrimination they suffered. They were and they are a time-bomb ticking in the heart of the richest nation in the history of the world. But more than that, the rioters are the personification of that nation's shame."

The Kerner Report (1968; repr. New York: Pantheon Books, 1988), xx. For a critique of the report's findings as being limited in scope and unrealistic in solution, see Janet L. Abu-Lughod, *Race, Space, and Riots in Chicago, New York, and Los Angeles* (Oxford: Oxford University Press, 2007), 4–7.

105. Morris's early scientific career overlapped with his interest in primitivist modern art. He maintained an active practice as a surrealist artist of prefigurative forms and spent the second half of the 1950s training, studying, and promoting Congo, a chimpanzee gestural painter, amid post-war European and American cultural appetites for abstract expressionism. In addition to filming Congo painting at the London Zoo, Morris curated an exhibition of the primate's output at the Institute of Contemporary Art that was scheduled as the second half of a program section titled "Primitivism," the first of which was dedicated to work by Australian Aboriginal children. Thierry Lenain, *Monkey Painting* (London: Reaktion Books, 1997), 93. See also Desmond Morris, *The Biology of Art: A Study of Picture-Making of the Great Apes and Its Relationship to Human Art* (London: Methuen, 1962).

106. Morris, *Human Zoo,* 248.

107. A. D. Coleman, "Diane Arbus, Lee Friedlander, and Garry Winogrand at Century's End," in *The Social Scene, The Ralph R. Parsons Foundation, Photography Collection,* ed. Stephanie Emerson (Los Angeles: Museum of Contemporary Art, 2000), 32, 36.

108. Janet Malcolm, "Photography: Certainties and Possibilities," *New Yorker,* August 4, 1975, 59; Pepe Karmel, "Photography: Garry Winogrand, Public Eye," *Art in America,* November 1981, 40; John Szarkowski, *Winogrand: Figments from the Real World* (New York: Museum of Modern Art, 1988), 21; Kate Pickert, "Intelligencer: Animal Liberation," *New York Magazine,* September 13, 2004.

109. "Monkeys Make the Problem More Difficult: A Collective Interview with Garry Winogrand," *Image Magazine* 15, no. 2 (1972): 3.

110. Ibid., 2.

111. Garry Winogrand, interview by Barbaralee Diamondstein, in *Visions and Images: American Photographers on Photography* (New York: Rizzoli, 1982), 181.

112. Carl Chiarenza, "Standing on the Corner: Reflections upon Garry Winogrand's Photographic Gaze: Mirror of Self or World, Pt. 1," *Image Magazine* 34, nos. 3–4 (1991): 21; Karmel, "Photography," 40.

113. This last photograph appears on the cover of the 1980 and 1990 editions of John Berger's essay collection *About Looking,* which begins with his seminal antizoo piece "Why Look at Animals?"

114. Coleman, "Diane Arbus, Lee Friedlander, and Garry Winogrand," 32.

115. Ben Lifson, "Garry Winogrand's Art of the Actual," in *The Man in the Crowd: The Uneasy Streets of Garry Winogrand* (New York: Fraenkel Gallery, 1999), 154.

116. Allan Sekula, "On the Invention of Photographic Meaning," *Artforum* 13, no. 5 (1975): 37, 45.

117. John Szarkowski, "Afterword," in *The Animals* (1969; repr. New York: Museum of Modern Art, 2004); Rosler, "in, around, and afterthoughts," 322; Andy Grundberg, *Crisis of the Real: Writings on Photography since 1974* (New York: Aperture, 1990), 76.

118. Victor Burgin, "Photography, Phantasy, Function," in *Situational Aesthetics: Selected Writings by Victor Burgin* (Leuven: Leuven University Press, 2009), 136.

119. Ibid., 136, 137.

120. Eugene Walter Jr., "Zoo People Give a Damn," *Venture,* July–August 1971, 65; Field, quoted in " Obsolete Zoo vs. Future Animal Parks," 111.

121. Baratay and Hardouin-Fugier, *History of Zoological Gardens,* 221–22. For examples of how legislation affected animal acquisitions, see "Zoos in Race to Save Endangered Species," *Los Angeles Times,* December 7, 1973; John Kifner, "Central Park Zoo Seeks Very Special Seal," *New York Times,* November 17, 1978.

122. Amendments cited in "Public Law 91–579 Animal Welfare Act Amendments of 1970," Animal Welfare Information Center, http://awic.nal.usda.gov/public-law-91–579-animal-welfare-act -amendments-1970 (accessed October 12, 2014). Curiously, the category of newly legislated exhibitors included zoos but exempted retail pet stores, state and county fairs, rodeos, purebred dog and cat shows, and agricultural exhibitions. The amended act also authorized government inspectors to euthanize "in a humane manner" animals found to be suffering because of a facility's failure to comply.

123. "Zoos in Race to Save Endangered Species"; Dennis D'Antonio, "When Night Falls, 'Lion Country's' a Cage," *Miami Herald,* May 21, 1972; Jack Anderson, "U.S. Zoos Often Chambers of Horror," *Washington Post,* July 26, 1971.

124. Peter Batten, *Living Trophies: A Shocking Look at the Conditions in America's Zoos* (New York: Thomas Crowell, 1976), vii–x.

125. Ibid., 7, 17, 97, 98.

126. This point has since been taken up by other zoo critics, who argue that many versions of aesthetic naturalism in zoo design are as problematic as modernist designs, both of which fail to adequately substitute for *ex-situ* habitats. See Ken Kawata, "Romancing the Celluloid Nature: A Review of American Zoo Exhibits, Part I," *Der Zoologische Garten* 80 (2011): 239–53; Kawata, "Of Circus Wagons and Imagined Nature: A Review of American Zoo Exhibits, Part I," *Der Zoologische Garten* 80 (2011): 352–65; Jensen, *Thought to Exist in the Wild;* Hancocks, *Different Nature.*

127. Batten, *Living Trophies,* 25–26.

128. Ibid., 83, 86–87, 90, 95.

129. Hancocks, *Different Nature,* 78. See also Hyson, "Urban Jungles," 445.

130. Heini Hediger, *Wild Animals in Captivity: An Outline of the Biology of Zoological Gardens* (1950; repr. New York: Dover Publications, 1964), 43.

131. Batten, *Living Trophies,* 95, 179–82.

2. Zoo Slum Clearance in Washington, D.C.

1. Chalmers Roberts, "Progress or Decay?," *Washington Post,* January 27, 28, 1952. By 1960, 54 percent of all District residents were counted as black, and white families had made their residential choices in suburban Maryland and Virginia. By 1970, African Americans represented 71 percent of Washington's population. Steven J. Diner, "From Jim Crow to Home Rule," *Wilson Quarterly* 13, no. 1 (1989): 90; Hyson, "Urban Jungles," 438.

2. Thomas J. Sugrue, *The Origins of the Urban Crisis: Race and Inequality in Postwar Detroit* (Princeton, N.J.: Princeton University Press, 1996), 9.

3. National Capital Planning Commission, *Worthy of the Nation: The History of Planning for the National Capital* (Washington, D.C.: Smithsonian Institution, 1977), 259.

4. Charles N. Concini, "Washington Then and Now," *Washingtonian,* October 1975, 61.

5. For an account of that history, see Howard Gillette Jr., *Between Justice and Beauty: Race, Planning, and the Failure of Urban Policy in Washington, D.C.* (Baltimore, Md.: Johns Hopkins University

Press, 1995). For a social history of African American poverty in Washington, D.C., see Constance Green, *The Secret City: A History of Race Relations in the Nation's Capital* (Princeton, N.J.: Princeton University Press, 1967); Diner, "From Jim Crow to Home Rule," 94.

6. *No Time for Ugliness* (American Institute of Architects, 1965) (Coral Springs, Fla.: Historical Archive, 2006), DVD.

7. Gillette, *Between Justice and Beauty*, 163–65; *City of Magnificent Intentions: A History of the District of Columbia* (Washington, D.C.: Intac, 1983), 459–67; National Capital Planning Commission, *Worthy of the Nation*, 313–30.

8. Concini, "Washington Then and Now," 61.

9. Morris, "Shame of the Naked Cage." See also chapter 1.

10. Charles Abrams, *The City Is the Frontier* (New York: Harper and Row, 1965), 19. Among his contributions, Abrams helped create the New York Housing Authority, was president of the National Committee against Discrimination in Housing, and a visiting professor at MIT's Department of City and Regional Planning.

11. Ibid.

12. Alan Mayne, "Tall Tales but True? New York's 'Five Points' Slum," *Journal of Urban History* 33, no. 2 (2007): 321. See also Mayne, "On the Edge of History," *Journal of Urban History* 26, no. 2 (2000): 249–58.

13. Mayne, "Tall Tales but True?," 323.

14. Chalmers Roberts, "Progress of Decay: A Report on the District's Choice . . . ," *Washington Post,* December 29, 1952.

15. Hine's photograph was first published in the 1909 book *Neglected Neighbors: Stories of Life in the Alleys, Tenements, and Shanties of the National Capitol.*

16. Helen B. Stern and Philip M. Stern, *O, Say Can You See: A Bi-Focal Tour of Washington* (Washington, D.C.: Colortone, 1965).

17. In an interview with the *Washington Post,* another revolutionary turned the rhetorical tables, arguing that the city's destruction was justified because the white man "is a beast. If you dig on his history you see he has done beastly things all his time. I mean, he walks different, smells different." Ben W. Gilbert et al., *Ten Blocks from the White House: Anatomy of the Washington Riots of 1968* (New York: Praeger, 1968), 163–65.

18. Theodore H. Reed, Oral History Interview No. 10 with Pamela Henson, transcript, June 16, 1994, p. 2, RU 9568, SIA.

19. Description of audience comes from Theodore Reed, Oral History Interview No. 3 with Pamela Henson, transcript, April 13, 1989, p. 8, RU 9568, SIA. FONZ was officially established in October 1958, with its own constitution and bylaws. "'Friends of the Zoo': A Group of Citizens," *Uptown Citizen,* August 17, 1961, box 51, RU 326, SIA.

20. Reed, Oral History Interview No. 3, p. 11.

21. In another interview, Reed elaborated on the staff composition when he became director: "We had many guys at the zoo that were illiterate. . . . And we're an Equal Opportunity Employer and welcomed keepers. It was interesting that with blacks, throughout the nation, you don't find a black zoologist, head keepers, senior men, administrative staff. They did not raise their children to be educated to work in the zoo. A zoo is labor. That's the way things are. They could say we're

racist but the, I don't know what the answer to it is." Theodore H. Reed, Oral History Interview No. 2 with Pamela Henson, transcript, 1989, p. 35, RU 9568, SIA.

22. "Death of Julie Ann Vogt," police report by Edward Daly, Det. Sgt. Homicide Squad, May 16, 1958, box 1, RU 380, SIA.

23. Theodore H. Reed Interviews, Interview No. 13, August 24, 1992, RU 9568, SIA.

24. Constance Green elaborates: "the city of slums and broken homes, of unemployed fathers, of wretched living conditions, and of drab streets where vice, disease, and hopelessness were ever-present" (*Secret City*, 8).

25. Citizens' group leader Clifford Newell's description of the city as a "haven for Negroes," quoted in Gillette, *Between Justice and Beauty*, 160. "Black removal" was a term publicly deployed by Senator John Dowdy of Texas as an assessment of the Federal City's urban renewal program, and circulated in critical discussions of renewal more broadly. Gillette, *Between Justice and Beauty*, 171.

26. Harry Gabbet, "Safety Survey Begun at Zoo," *Washington Post*, May 18, 1958; Richard O'Lowe, "Two More Danger Spots at Zoo Get Attention," *Evening Star*, May 21, 1958; Theodore H. Reed, videohistory with Pamela Henson, transcript, September 25, 1990, p. 4, RU 9553, SIA.

27. Jerry O'Leary Jr., "Four Zoo Houses Closed to Visitors," *Evening Star*, September 29, 1958; O'Lowe, "Two More Danger Spots."

28. "$100,000 Suit Filed in Zoo Death," *Washington Post*, December 6, 1958; Leonard Carmichael to Russell Chapin, undated letter, box 1, RU 380, SIA.

29. Frances B. (Mrs. Owen) Richards to T. H. Reed, May 30, 1959, folder 1, box 190, RU 74, SIA.

30. T. H. Reed, June 2, 1959, memo, folder 1, box 190, RU 74, SIA.

31. "Margaret Rhinehart Hood, etc. v. United States of America: Civil Action No, 3067–58: Answers to Interrogatories Propounded by Plaintiff," box 1, RU 380, SIA.

32. Ibid.

33. Morris, "Shame of the Naked Cage"; Morris, *Human Zoo*.

34. Reed, Oral History Interview No. 3, p. 29.

35. Elisha Hanson to Leonard Carmichael, May 20, 1958, box 1, RU 380, SIA.

36. "Zoo Seeking Safety Fund of $86,000," *Evening Star*, March 26, 1959.

37. Gabbet, "Safety Survey Begun at Zoo"; Reed, Oral History Interview No. 3, pp. 9–10.

38. In his 1992 interview with Caroline Winslow and Pamela Henson, Reed shared that "a little seven year old colored boy from Richmond Virginia volunteered that he saw the grandfather lift her over. But in those days we didn't believe a fully adult colored man." Tape 1, side 1.

39. "Zoo Seeking Safety Fund . . ."

40. "Zoo Mending Its Fences to Save Beasts from Us," *Washington Post*, September 30, 1958.

41. Theodore Reed to Ridenour, March 30, 1961, folder 2, box 190, RU 74, SIA.

42. Katherine Thompson to Theodore Reed, May 16, 1958, box 1, RU 380, SIA.

43. Cited from a documentary by Simon Epstein and Jacqueline Todt, *Washington in the '60s* (WETA, 2009).

44. Memo to Dr. Leonard Carmichael thru Dr. Keddy and Mr. Graf, April 29, 1957, folder 5, box 191, RU 74, SIA. For an example of press responses to violence, see Alfred E. Lewis and Jack Eisen, "Park Disorders Feared as 'Habit,'" *Washington Post*, April 25, 1957. For another scholarly account of the holiday's racial tensions, see Hyson, "Urban Jungles," 440–41.

45. Nancy Ross, "Like Slum Children, Animals in Our Zoo Are Killed by Lead Poisoning . . . ," *Washington Post,* August 7, 1971.

46. Marian Newman, "Suffering Animals," *Washington Post,* October 17, 1971.

47. Wolf Von Eckardt, "Time to Bring Nature Back to the Zoo," *Washington Post,* April 22, 1972.

48. Ezra F. Howland Jr. to Sirs, August 10, 1960, folder 2, box 190, RU 74, SIA; William Ridenour to Director of Zoo, March 27, 1961, folder 2, box 190, RU 74, SIA; Mrs. Harold N. Marsh to Dr. Leonard Carmichael, June 3, 1961, box 135, RU 50, SIA; Milton R. Chambers to Gentlemen, November 1, 1962, folder 2, box 190, RU 74, SIA.

49. In 1947, for example, the city's Citizens Council for Community Planning organized "Pictures Talk Housing," a photography contest to encourage the documentation of slum conditions. Other examples include the 1949 tour of the alley slums within sight of the Capitol by U.S. Senator Paul Douglas for his colleagues, and an inspection of slum areas by officials in the Bureau of Public Health Engineering and city health departments. These and other tours were documented on photographic film, and pictures were often published in daily newspapers. Examples are drawn from the Washington Historical Image Collection, District of Columbia Public Library, Washingtoniana Division.

50. Capt. Wm. R. James, "Incident of the Broken Limb in Front of Wolves," June 1, 1958, box 130, RU 50, SIA.

51. Phil Casey, "Federal Support Asked for Our Zoo," *Washington Post,* November 13, 1960.

52. Elsewhere, zoo officials reported the building's constructed frame as a site for disease, after experiencing in this particular exhibit "grievous losses in animal life" from tuberculosis and toxoplasmosis. "Antelope Building: Preliminary Study and Definite Plans $39,400," folder 3, box 44, RU 326, SIA.

53. Arthur W. Arundel to Reed and staff, November 3, 1976, folder 2, box 31, RU 326, SIA; "'Friends of the Zoo': A Group of Citizens," *Uptown Citizen,* n.d., folder 11, box 51, RU 326, SIA.

54. Harry Gabbet, "Attorney Leads Battle for Zoo's Revival," *Washington Post,* December 3, 1958.

55. "Members of Board of Directors, Friends of the National Zoo, 1965–1966," folder 1, box 52, RU 326, SIA.

56. FONZ invitation to Reed, folder 11, box 51, RU 326, SIA; Testimony by Friends of the National Zoo before the Subcommittee on District Appropriations of the House Committee on Appropriations, June 3, 1958, folder 11, box 51, RU 326, SIA.

57. Reed to Kellogg, June 10, 1960, folder 11, box 51, RU 326, SIA.

58. In the late 1970s FONZ made overtures for change. One 1977 meeting report stated that "it was of concern to all present that membership does not reflect low to middle income membership, no black, inner-city membership to any appreciable degree." Subsequent efforts to invite a broader base of support included direct mailings to African Americans living near the zoo and special events catering to organizations that served black and other minority groups. FONZ Membership Committee Report, April 26, 1977, folder 2, box 55, RU 326, SIA.

59. "Feminine Focus," *Washington Star,* September 15, 1968.

60. Quoted in Friends of the National Zoo, "The Crises at Our National Zoo," p. 3, folder 22, box 12, RU 365, SIA.

61. Ibid.

62. Beauregard, *Voices of Decline,* 15–16; John Archer, *Architecture and Suburbia: From English Villa to American Dream House, 1690–2000* (Minneapolis: University of Minnesota Press, 2005), 230–38.

63. Friends of the National Zoo, "Crisis at Our National Zoo," 15, 18.

64. Casey, "Federal Support Asked for Our Zoo"; "Whose Zoo?," *Washington Post,* November 16, 1960; Bess Furman, "Master Plan Laid for National Zoo," *New York Times,* December 18, 1960; Phil Casey, "Outstanding Zoo Is Outlined Here in Friends' Plan," *Washington Post,* December 18, 1960.

65. The term was quoted, for example, in one 1961 Smithsonian report on the National Zoo. Box 127, RU 50, SIA.

66. Beauregard, *Voices of Decline,* 79.

67. Sugrue, *Origins of the Urban Crisis,* 9.

68. FONZ received an initial grant of $1,000 from the Old Dominion Foundation and then raised an additional $3,500 to hire the architects. "Chronological History of the Redevelopment and Modernization Program for the National Zoological Park which Started in 1961," box 10, RU 380, SIA.

69. Friends of the National Zoo, "A Master Plan for the National Zoo," p. 1, folder 11, box 51, RU 326, SIA.

70. This area was also assigned to a new administration building, proposed to replace one that was termite infested and near collapse. Friends of the National Zoo, "Master Plan for the National Zoo," p. 3; Casey, "Federal Support Asked for Our Zoo."

71. SRI analyst Richard McElyea, quoted in Hyson, "Urban Jungles," 439.

72. Friends of the National Zoo, "Master Plan for the National Zoo," 8.

73. The idea came to fruition in 1972 with the opening of the National Zoo's Conservation Research Center in Front Royal, Virginia.

74. Tom Cameron, "Firm Creates Wide Variety of Projects," *Los Angeles Times,* July 26, 1964.

75. Agenda of the National Capital Planning Commission Meeting, April 5, 1962, 9:30 a.m., box 127, RU 60, SIA.

76. For a detailed account of Olmsted's work on the National Zoo's initial design, see Heather Ewing, "An Architectural History of the National Zoological Park" (Smithsonian Institution, S.N., 1990), 13–23.

77. Daniel, Mann, Johnson and Mendenhall, "National Zoological Park Master Development Plan," 1961, Oversized, No. 195A, RU 74, SIA.

78. Ibid.

79. (Assistant Secretary) James Bradley to L. F. Roush, July 30, 1971, "Master Plan: Redevelopment, 1969–72," box 49, AC 06–225, SIA.

80. "Smithsonian Year 1965: Annual Report of the Smithsonian Institution for the Year Ended June 30, 1965" (Washington, D.C.: Smithsonian Institution, 1965), 207.

81. Theodore Reed, quoted in "Birds Always in View for Visitor to New Vinyl Wire Washington Flight Cage," *Gilbert and Bennett Newswire,* folder 2, box 35, RU 365, SIA.

82. Ewing, "Architectural History," 52–53.

83. "Smithsonian Year 1965," 202.

84. Theodore H. Reed, "Remodeled Bird House and New Great Flight Cage at the National Zoological Park," *International Zoo Yearbook* 6 (1966): 129; "Strictly for the Birds," *Spots and Stripes* 1, no. 4 (1964), folder 21, box 17, RU 365, SIA.

85. Identifying the weaknesses of this older display style, Reed named the fact that no birds ever bred there as a primary one. Reed, videohistory interview, 23.

86. "Presenting the New Bird House," February 11, 1965, "Bird House Renovations, Great Flight Cage, 1964," box 48, AC 06227, SIA; Reed, "Remodeled Bird House," 130; "Eyeball to Eyeball," quoted from *Spots and Stripes* 1, no. 4 (1964). By 1990 the visitor walkway was eliminated because it was thought to be disturbing the birds. Reed, videohistory interview, 24.

87. Reed, videohistory interview, 21.

88. Reed, "Remodeled Bird House," 129.

89. *Spots and Stripes* 1, no. 4 (1964); Jean J. Darling, "Zoo's Newest Creation Is for the Birds," *Evening Star,* January 23, 1965; "Zoo Birds Move to Grand Hotel," *Smithsonian Torch,* February 1965, folder 2, box 35, RU 365, SIA.

90. Bill Henry, "A Window on Washington," *Los Angeles Times,* October 18, 1963.

91. In 1912 John B. Henderson Jr., an affluent and new member of the Smithsonian Board of Regents, deemed the zoo's current display of parrots and select 218 other bird species to be "shameful" and felt it "essential for their preservation that they be given some fresh air and light, especially during the hot summer months." Henderson's personal donation resulted in the humble twenty-six-foot-high Beatrice Henderson Cage, named after an adopted daughter. The Henderson cage was a typical industrial-age ironwork construction that mirrored the landscaping of the Bird House's interior flight room with a solitary tree as a visual centerpiece and bird perch. The Henderson Cage did not survive into the 1960s. In 1959, when a boy inadvertently poked his mother in the eye with the broken end of a wire, the cage became the site of yet another accident, marking it as part of the zoological slum and establishing its imminent demolishment. J. B. Henderson to Frank Baker, June 27, 1912, folder 5, box 35, RU 365, SIA; Billie Hamlet, "The Beatrice Henderson Mystery," *Zoogoer* 9, no. 5 (1980): 13–14, folder 5, box 35, RU 365, SIA; Memo from Police Department to Dr. T. H. Reed, June 14, 1959, "Accident-Flight Cage, Mrs. Johnny Ayers, 6/14/59," box 1, RU 380, SIA.

92. In a bid to protect the vitality of various inner-city areas, concerned Washingtonians launched campaigns to stop the construction of other freeways in the District, which were planned to cut through established neighborhoods. *City of Magnificent Intentions,* 454–56.

93. Press release, July 15, 1965, folder 2, box 35, RU 365, SIA; Reed, "Remodeled Bird House," 130–31; "Birds Always in View for Visitor to New Vinyl Wire Washington Flight Cage," *Gilbert and Bennett Newswire,* folder 2, box 35, RU 365, SIA; "Free as a Bird," *American City,* December 1965, folder 2, box 35, RU 365, SIA; "Flight Cage for Birds . . . and People," *Bethlehem Review,* April 1965, folder 2, box 35, RU 365, SIA; Daniel, Mann, Johnson and Mendenhall, "Washington National Zoological Park," n.d., folder 2, box 35, RU 365, SIA.

94. Reed, Oral History Interview No. 10, pp. 47–48.

95. Norma Evenson, "Monumental Spaces," in Longstreth, *Mall in Washington,* 29.

96. This report received scathing criticism in *Architectural Forum* for ignoring the needs of a black urban majority. "An Anti-Urban Design for Washington," *Architectural Forum,* November 1965, 24–25.

97. "Monumental statement," quoted from Reed, Oral History Interview No. 10, p. 47; Reed, videohistory interview, p. 22.

98. Jean Darling, "Zoo's Newest Creation Is for the Birds," *Evening Star,* January 23, 1965.

99. Reed, videohistory interview, p. 22.

100. "Free as a Bird"; Advertisement, *Steelways,* March–April 1965, folder 2, box 35, RU 365, SIA; "Flight Cage for Birds," p. 3.

101. "Saarinen," *Architectural Forum,* September 1961, 113.

102. Margaret C. Peck, *Washington Dulles International Airport* (Charleston, S.C.: Arcadia, 2005), 57.

103. "Concrete Bird: Progress at Idlewild," *Architectural Review,* February 1961, 7.

104. "The Concrete Bird Stands Free," *Architectural Forum,* December 1960, 114–15.

105. Daniel, Mann, Johnson and Mendenhall, "Master Development Plan for the National Zoological Park," September 11, 1961, box 127, RU 50, SIA.

106. "Presenting the New Bird House"; "Birds and People to Mingle at Zoo," *Washington Star,* September 2, 1964.

107. Darling, "Zoo's Newest Creation."

108. Judith Martin, "Vanishing Breed," *Washington Post,* June 29, 1973.

109. "Lion House Torn Down at Zoo," *Washington Post,* March 29, 1974.

110. Theodore H. Reed, Oral History Interview No. 11 with Pamela Henson, transcript, June 23, 1994, p. 46, RU 9358, SIA.

111. Ewing, "Architecture of the National Zoological Park," 157–58; Ewing, "Architectural History," 14–15, 22. See also chapter 1.

112. Gilbert et al., *Ten Blocks from the White House,* 82–83; Gillette, *Between Justice and Beauty,* 165.

113. Reed, Oral History Interview No. 11, p. 44.

114. John Perry to Theodore Reed, June 28, 1967, memo, folder 1, box 45, RU 326, SIA.

115. J. McGarry to John Perry, July 13, 1967, memo, folder 1, box 45, RU 326, SIA.

116. T. H. Reed to John Perry, July 5, 1967, memo, folder 1, box 45, RU 326, SIA.

117. John Perry to John Eisenberg, February 19, 1968, folder 1, box 45, RU 326, SIA.

118. James McAllister et al., April 8, 1968, letter of appreciation, folder 5, box 43, RU 326, SIA; James McAllister et al., April 5, 1968, letter, folder 5, box 43, RU 326, SIA.

119. M. J. J. McGarry to Lt. S. L. Middleton (through Capt. A. S. Kadlusbowki), June 5, 1968, folder 1, box 45, RU 326, SIA.

120. Reed, Oral History Interview No. 11, pp. 6–7.

121. Ibid.

122. Quoted in Louise Lague, "The Zoo Presents a Natural Habitat," *Evening Star,* May 22, 1973.

123. Suzanne Fauber, "The Evolution of the National Zoological Park," p. 22, box 49, AC-06-225, SIA.

124. Reed, Oral History Interview No. 11, pp. 9–10. Documents from the zoo's newly established Office of Construction Management reinforced the objective: "Both planning and construction efforts at the Zoo are now being administered directly and successfully by the Smithsonian. The Zoo reconstruction must be controlled closely and directly every step of the way." "Construction Management at the National Zoological Park," n.d., folder 8, box 44, RU 326, SIA.

125. Reed, Oral History Interview No. 11, p. 25.

126. FONZ Board Meeting minutes, October 20, 1971, folder 1, box 51, RU 326, SIA.

127. Daniel, Mann, Johnson and Mendenhall, "National Zoological Park Master Development Plan."

128. Reed, videohistory interview, p. 22.

129. Faulkner Fryer and Vanderpool, "Zoo: Master Plan Report, National Zoological Park, Smithsonian Institution," Part 1, p. 3, c. 1974, box 14, RU 365, SIA.

130. "Master Plan of the National Zoological Park," September 1971, and "Master Plan: Redevelopment 1969–1972," box 49, AC-06-225, SIA.

131. *Worthy of a Nation,* 326.

132. For an overview of the disillusionment, see *City of Magnificent Intentions,* 452–67.

133. Wolf Von Eckardt, "L'Enfant Plaza Is a Triumph," *Washington Post,* June 9, 1968.

134. Wolf Von Eckardt, "In All Its Dead-End Glory," *Washington Post,* May 5, 1973.

135. Wolf Von Eckardt, "Avenue of Choice," *Washington Post,* December 16, 1978.

136. The Great Flight Cage did not make it on Eckardt's list of public eyesores, possibly because of its minimal use of concrete. Wolf Von Eckardt, "Beaux Arts in Washington," *Washington Post,* November 9, 1975; Wolf Von Eckardt, "The Rosslynization of America's Athens," *Washington Post,* April 7, 1973.

137. Wolf Von Eckardt, "New Church Design: Rude, Brutal Military, Uncivilized," *Washington Post,* November 28, 1970.

138. Wolf Von Eckardt, "Humanism in an Age of Megalomania," *Washington Post,* April 3, 1971.

139. Von Eckardt, "Beaux Arts in Washington." For a scholarly history of the City Beautiful movement in Washington, D.C., see Hines, "Imperial Mall," 79–100; and Gillette, *Between Justice and Beauty,* 107.

140. Eckardt, "Humanism."

141. For a fuller discussion of the race and species politics of nineteenth-century urban reform, see chapter 1.

142. Indoor sections of the exhibit were closed to the public and included a concealed Y-shaped central core holding area with maintenance facilities, and eleven offices that ran around the perimeter of the structure beneath the public viewing space.

143. Descriptive information about the Lion–Tiger Exhibit comes from Robert Engle, "Lion and Tiger Exhibit," n.d., folder 7, box 39, RU 396, SIA.

144. Theodore Reed to Mrs. Justin Dart, March 4, 1975, folder 6, box 44, RU 326, SIA.

145. Interestingly, the Louisville exhibit was designed by DMJM, underscoring the extent to which Reed had parted ways with National Zoo's earlier renewal efforts. Eckardt, "Rosslynization of America's Athens."

146. Carter Brown to Theodore Reed, August 26, 1974, folder 5, box 44, RU 326, SIA.

147. "Modern Alchemist Works 'Magic' on 150-Acre Man-Made Lake," *Los Angeles Times,* January 21, 1968; Dan MacMasters, "Lakeside Living," *Los Angeles Times,* August 22, 1971.

148. N. Kendall Marvin, "Cascade Canyon," *Zoonooz,* August 1973, 5.

149. Richard Sweeny, "Cascade Canyon and Its Antelope," *Zoonooz,* October 1973, 13.

150. (Assistant Secretary) James Bradley to L. F. Roush, July 30, 1971, "Master Plan: Redevelopment, 1969–72," box 49, AC-06-225, SIA.

151. "McClean Plans Anew," *Washington Post,* September 22, 1966.

152. Marion Lynn Clark, "The Ten-Point Lester Collins Garden," *Washington Post,* April 11, 1971.

153. Norman C. Melun to David Wm. Hansen, July 20, 1973, folder 4, box 44, RU 326, SIA.

154. "Lion-Tiger Interpretive Exhibit," n.d., folder 6, box 42, RU 326, SIA.

155. T. H. Reed, "Naming the New Feline Exhibit," June 13, 1973, folder 4, box 44, RU 326, SIA.

156. Judith Martin, "Kings of the Jungle Are Pride of the Hill," *Washington Post,* May 26, 1976.

3. Mohini's Bodies

1. Theodore Reed to Dr. Porter M. Keir, August 16, 1977, folder 23, box 25, RU 365, SIA. The museum did accept Mohini's body posthumously, which remains in their collection, off exhibit.

2. Edward J. Maruska, "White Tiger: Phantom or Freak?," in *Tigers of the World: The Biology, Biopolitics, Management, and Conservation of an Endangered Species,* ed. Ronald L. Tilson and Ulysses S. Seal (Park Ridge, N.J.: Noyes, 1987), 373.

3. For a critical history of Toung Taloung in captivity, see Sarah Amato, "The White Elephant in London: An Episode of Trickery, Racism, and Advertising," *Journal of Social History* 23, no. 1 (2009): 31–66. For an early institutional perspective on Snowflake, see Antonio Jonch, "The White Gorilla (Gorilla g. gorilla) at Barcelona Zoo," *International Zoo Yearbook* 13 (1967): 196. A representative discussion of Blizzard is "Top-Secret Mission Brings Rare White Bison to Winnipeg Zoo," *Ottawa Citizen,* June 6, 2006, http://www.canada.com/ottawacitizen/news/story.html?id=81c6edbd -4224–4684–8a08-dc6b2a16023d; on King Louie, see Amy Stallings, "Creature Feature: King Louie the Albino Alligator," *WHAS11.com,* August 9, 2013, http://www.whas11.com/community/ Creature-Feature-King-Louie-the-albino-alligator-219014301.html. While a comprehensive history of white tiger captivity is still unwritten, in 1984 *Geo* reported, "Of the 100 or so white tigers in captivity, more than 50 are in zoos in the United States," with a list that included zoos in Washington, D.C., Knoxville, Miami, Columbus, Cincinnati, Milwaukee, Omaha, and San Francisco. J. Isaac, "Tiger Tale," *Geo* 6 (August 1984): 84. For a glimpse of the world of white tigers in the precincts of the Las Vegas illusionists Siegfried Fischbacher and Roy Horn, see "Sigfried and Roy's Secret Garden and Dolphin Habitat," http://www.miragehabitat.com/pages/index_flash.asp.

4. "Municipal character," quoted in Progress Report, Part One from John Perry to Dr. Reed, January 28, 1966, folder 3, box 4, RU 326, SIA; "Tremendous potential resource," quoted in Memorandum re: Developing a master plan for the National Zoo from John Perry to Friends of the National Zoo, Inc., May 23, 1959, folder 11, box 51, RU 326, SIA.

5. Theodore H. Reed, Oral History Interview No. 5 with Pamela Henson, transcript, August 8, 1989, pp. 14–15, RU 9568, SIA.

6. Ibid.

7. Edward Said, *Orientalism* (New York: Vintage Books, 1978), 1–4.

8. Griselda Pollack, *Differencing the Canon: Feminist Desire and the Writing of Art's Histories* (London: Routledge, 1999), 286.

9. "Tiger Cub Stars at Outing," *Washington Star,* August 11, 1959.

10. Reed, Oral History Interview No. 5, p. 5; Kuldip Singh, "Obituary: Maharaja Martand Singh of Rewa," *Independent,* December 1, 1995, http://www.independent.co.uk/news/obituaries/ obituary-maharaja-martand-singh-of-rewa-1523492.html.

11. Ibid.

12. Said, *Orientalism,* 104.

13. Reed, Oral History Interview No. 5, p. 36.

14. "India Keeping Its White Tigers," *Chicago Tribune*, July 17, 1966; *Kailash Sankhala, Tiger! The Story of the Indian Tiger* (New York: Simon and Schuster, 1977), 157.

15. At least one other source disputes the price paid for Mohini, citing her acquisition at a reported cost of $25,000. Meryle Secrest, "Rare Tigers Born at Zoo," *Washington Post*, March 10, 1970.

16. Reed, Oral History Interview No. 5, pp. 15, 18; Quotation from "Zoo to Have White Tiger from India," *Washington Post*, October 19, 1960.

17. Reed was likely heavily edited, advised, and otherwise guided in writing his piece for *National Geographic*, destabilizing the notion that this travel narrative was a personal account from a single author.

18. Theodore Reed, "Enchantress!," *National Geographic*, May 1961, 628.

19. Malek Alloula, *The Colonial Harem*, trans. Myrna Godzich and Wlad Godzich (1981; repr. Minneapolis: University of Minnesota Press, 1986), 69.

20. Reed, "Enchantress!," 631.

21. Catherine A. Lutz and Jane L. Collins, *Reading National Geographic* (Chicago: University of Chicago Press, 1993), 97.

22. Reed, "Enchantress!," p. 637.

23. Mary Louise Pratt, "Conventions of Representation: Where Discourse and Ideology Meet," in *Contemporary Perceptions of Language: Interdisciplinary Dimensions*, ed. Heidi Byrnes (Washington, D.C.: Georgetown University Press, 1982), 145, 148–50.

24. "This Week in the Nation's Capital," May 28, 1961, Scrapbook 11/1960–9/1961, box 52, RU 365, SIA.

25. One newspaper misidentified Mohini's homeland as Nepal, suggesting that the historical and geographic specificity of the animal's origins was less important than her general aura of exoticism. Steve Trumbull, "Will Motherhood Spoil Mohini, the White Tigress of Nepal?," *Miami Herald Sunday Magazine*, March 3, 1963, Scrapbook 11/1962–5/1963, box 53, RU 365, SIA.

26. Carol Ockman, "A Woman's Pleasure: Ingres's Grande Odalisque," in *Reclaiming Female Agency: Feminist Art History after Postmodernism*, ed. Norma Broude and Mayr D. Garrard (Berkeley: University of California Press, 2005), 187.

27. Reed, quoted in Charles Cook, "The Enchantress," *Georgetowner*, January 26, 1961, folder 25, box 25, RU 365, SIA.

28. One of the earliest feminist formulations of this critique came from Linda Nochlin's application of Said's thesis on Orientalism to French nineteenth-century paintings by Jean-Léon Gérôme. Linda Nochlin, *The Politics of Vision: Essays on Nineteenth-Century Art and Society* (New York: Harper and Row, 1989), 33–59.

29. Jo Anna Isaak, *Feminism and Contemporary Art: The Revolutionary Power of Women's Laughter* (London: Routledge, 1996), 55–59. Nochlin reminds us that some of these earlier French works, namely, Eugène Delacroix's *Death of Sardanapalus* and, later, Jean-Léon Gérôme's *Slave Markets* were, in turn, references to other fantastic descriptions of exoticized debauchery, emphasizing that "the motivations behind the creation of such Orientalist erotica, and the appetite for it, had little to do with pure ethnography." Nochlin, *Politics of Vision*, 44.

30. Ockman's study analyzes the patronage of Ingres's *Grande Odalisque* by Caroline Bonaparte Murat, sister of Napoléon, who commissioned the work and thus complicated assumptions that the figure was exclusively for male heterosexual pleasure. Ockman, "Woman's Pleasure," 187.

31. Robert Young, "Ike, Priceless White Tigress Meet on Lawn," *Chicago Tribune,* December 6, 1960, Scrapbook 3/12—1960, box 52, RU 365, SIA.

32. Lucile Quarry Mann, Oral History Interview with Pamela Henson, transcript, August 11, 1977, p. 211, box 1, RU 9513, SIA.

33. George E. White to Mohini c/o Dr. Theodore H. Reed, August 26, 1977, folder 10, box 27, RU 365, SIA.

34. Deirdre W. Magnussen to Mohini c/o The National Zoo, August 10, 1977, folder 10, box 27, RU 365, SIA.

35. Marcine and Melanie Goodloe to Mohini, August 10, 1977, folder 10, box 27, RU 365, SIA.

36. Cooke, "Enchantress."

37. Pollack, *Differencing the Canon,* 293.

38. Cooke, "Enchantress."

39. "Disenchanted 'Enchantress,'" *Washington Post,* December 1, 1960, Scrapbook 3/12—1960, box 52, RU 365, SIA; "She Doesn't Look So Enchanting," *Dallas Times Herald,* December 5, 1960, Scrapbook 3/12—1960, box 52, RU 365, SIA; "White Tigress Arrives by Air and Just Yawns at All the Fuss," *New York Times,* December 1, 1960, Scrapbook 3/12—1960, box 52, RU 365, SIA.

40. Young, "Ike, Priceless White Tigress"; "Ike Receives Growling Tiger at Safe Distance," *Boston Globe,* December 1960, Scrapbook 3/12—1960, box 52, RU 365, SIA.

41. Reed, Oral History Interview No. 5, p. 51.

42. David Miller, "White India Tiger Flies In; to Be Whiter after a Bath," *New York Herald Tribune,* December 1, 1960, Scrapbook 3/12—1960, box 52, RU 365, SIA.

43. Piya Pal-Lipinksi, *The Exotic Woman in Nineteenth-Century British Fiction and Culture* (Lebanon, N.H.: University of New Hampshire Press, 2005), 7.

44. Theodore Reed, "Mohini, the White Tiger in the National Zoological Park Washington," *Der Zoologische Garten* 27, nos. 1–3 (1963): 126–27.

45. Cooke, "Enchantress."

46. Pal-Lapinski, *Exotic Woman,* 23.

47. Phil Casey, "White Tigers: A Zoo Story," *Washington Post,* August 1, 1974.

48. Robert W. Rydell, *World of Fairs: The Century of Progress Expositions* (Chicago: University of Chicago Press, 1993); Martin Pernick, *The Black Stork: Eugenics and the Death of "Defective" Babies in American Medicine and Motion Pictures* (Oxford: Oxford University Press, 1996); Laura L. Lovett, *Conceiving the Future: Pronatalism, Reproduction, and the Family in the United States, 1890–1930* (Chapel Hill: University of North Carolina Press, 2007).

49. Rydell, *World of Fairs,* 38.

50. To the Critical Art Ensemble writing in 2002, this form of eugenics "pays for itself, thereby killing two birds with one stone by achieving both profits and a better worker/citizen." Alexandra Minna Stern, *Eugenic Nation: Faults and Frontiers of Better Breeding in Modern America* (Berkeley: University of California Press, 2005), 4; Critical Art Ensemble, *Molecular Invasion* (Brooklyn: Autonomedia, 2002), 54.

51. Reed, videohistory interview, p. 9.

52. Warren Iliff to B. Mulcahy, J. Eisenberg, and J. Horsley, October 11, 1974, memorandum, folder 10, box 37, RU 396, SIA.

53. *The Big Cats and How They Came to Be* (dir. Andrezj Kolodynski, 1976).

54. Minutes of the Annual Meeting for Friends of the National Zoo, May 20, 1970, folder 1, box 51, RU 326, SIA.

55. Lovett, *Conceiving the Future,* 132, 136.

56. Watts, quoted in Rydell, *World of Fairs,* 49.

57. Jim Mahoney to Warren Iliff, September 19, 1974, memorandum, folder 10, box 37, RU 396, SIA.

58. Reed, videohistory interview, p. 9.

59. Reed, Oral History Interview No. 5, p. 39.

60. As Rosemarie Garland Thompson and other cultural historians in her edited volume note, freaks are heavy with stigma. Their extraordinary bodies have a rich tradition of disturbing key concepts in Western modernity, such as the physical and psychic integrity of the individual human subject (Garland Thompson, *Freakery*).

61. Conway, quoted in Isaac, "Tiger Tale," 85.

62. Maruska, "White Tiger," 373.

63. E. P. Gee, "Albinism and Partial Albinism in Tigers," *Journal of the Bombay National History Association* 56 (December 1959): 1–7.

64. Ibid.

65. Paul Leyhausen and Theodore H. Reed, "The White Tiger: Care and Breeding of a Genetic Freak," *Smithsonian* 2, no. 1 (1971): 25, folder 25, box 35, RU 365, SIA.

66. Ibid., 27.

67. Ibid., 24.

68. Phil Casey, "The Great White Hope," *Washington Post,* March 19, 1973.

69. Betty Friedan, *The Feminine Mystique* (New York: Norton, 1963).

70. Shulamith Firestone, *The Dialectic of Sex: The Case for Feminist Revolution* (New York: Farrar, Straus and Giroux, 1970).

71. Judith Snitow, "Feminism and Motherhood: An American Reading," *Feminist Review,* no. 40 (Spring 1992): 35–56.

72. *Pronatalism: The Myth of Mom and Apple Pie,* ed. Ellen Peck and Judith Senderowitz (New York: Thomas Y. Crowell, 1974), 1; Lovett, *Conceiving the Future,* 2.

73. Snitow, "Feminism and Motherhood," 37.

74. National Zoological Park, *Zoobook* (Washington, D.C.: Smithsonian Institution Press, 1976).

75. Once again, Ralph Scott was a part of Mohini's fate, having instigated negotiations for a mate and ultimately acquiring Samson for the National Zoo. The acquisition came after an unsuccessful attempt to mate Mohini with Mighty Mo. "For the Press—Mohini," March 21, 1970, folder 25, box 25, RU 365, SIA.

76. Subsequent television monitorings included watching the (false) pregnancy of Princess, the lion, in 1967, and Snowstar, the polar bear, in 1970. In that same year, FONZ reported over one hundred families on the Pregwatch duty. Reed to FONZ members, April 28, 1967, folder 1, box 51, RU 326, SIA; Minutes of the Annual Meeting for Friends of the National Zoo, May 20, 1970.

77. Marion McCrane, "Mohini's Cubs," *Spots and Stripes,* March 1964, folder 21, box 17, RU 365, SIA; Michael P. Balbo, "A Star Is Born," *Long Island Ocelot Club Newsletter,* May 1964, folder 25, box 25, RU 365, SIA.

78. Bill Xanten to Pregwatchers, "Animal Problems, Animal Collection, White Tiger," July 23, 1973, box 6, RU 385, SIA.

79. Balbo, "Star Is Born."

80. Jackie Stacey, *Teratologies: A Cultural Study of Cancer* (London: Routledge, 1997).

81. McCrane, "Mohini's Cubs."

82. Ibid.

83. Ibid.

84. Ibid.

85. Stories in the local press underlined how McCrane, the first female zoologist hired by the National Zoo, was uniquely positioned for giving it "a woman's touch." Jerry O'Leary Jr., "Zoo Gets a Woman's Touch," *Washington Star,* May 20, 1962, Scrapbook?, box 52, RU 365, SIA.

86. Phil Casey, "3 Kittens, One All-White and Rare, Born to Zoo's Exclusive White Tiger," *Washington Post,* January 8, 1964.

87. Press reports of the death cited prenatal brain damage as the cause and related the zoo's distress over the loss, since "it was hoped that it would help propagate the line of white tigers." "Zoo's White Tiger Loses Yellow Cub," *Washington Star,* April 21, 1969.

88. Nancy Morgan, "Zoo's Hopes for a White Tiger Cub Fizzle," *Washington Post,* March 1, 1966.

89. Elizabeth Reed, "A Tiger in the House," *Spots and Stripes,* Summer 1969, box 18, RU 365, SIA.

90. For a historical analysis of heterosexual monogamy at the National Zoo, see Lisa Uddin, "Panda Gardens and Public Sex at the National Zoological Park," *Public: Art/Culture/Ideas,* no. 41 (2010): 80–93.

91. Elizabeth C. Reed, "White Tiger in My House," *National Geographic,* April 1970, 484.

92. Ibid.

93. Ibid., 486.

94. In 1959 the National Zoo held a dinner to thank the volunteer mothers, including Lucile Mann, wife of former director William Mann; Louise E. Gallagher, wife of Bernard Gallagher, supervisory keeper for great apes; and Elizabeth Reed. Guests of honor received a certificate of appreciation for their service. T. H. Reed to Dr. Kellog, March 6, 1959, memo, folder 12, box 11, RU 365, SIA.

95. Reed, "White Tiger in My House," 484.

96. Ibid., 484–88.

97. Casey, "White Tigers."

98. Herman Schaden, "White Tiger Cub Stricken by Distemper, Sister Dies," *Washington Star,* August 24, 1965.

99. Accounts of Rewati's failing health come from Elizabeth Reed's two articles describing her life with the new tiger: "Tiger in the House" and "White Tiger in My House."

100. T. H. Reed to Mr. Ripley, June 19, 1970, folder 26, box 25, RU 365, SIA.

101. "Moni Comes Home," press release, May 11, 1970, folder 22, box 25, RU 365, SIA.

102. Moni's cause of death as described in a letter from Sybil E. Hamlet, Public Information Officer, to Mrs. Hilda W. Federico, February 20, 1974, folder 23, box 25, RU 365, SIA.

103. Leyhausen and Reed, "White Tiger," 30. Tigers were declared endangered in 1968.

104. In 1972 Poona, an orange-colored male without white genes, was sent to the National Zoo from Chicago's Brookfield Zoo to breed with Mohini. Edward Maruska of the Cincinnati Zoo

continued to urge the National Zoo "not to inbreed but rather to outbreed for an infusion of new blood. Then you can begin a long term program of line breeding and weed out any undesirable traits that might be occurring because of severe inbreeding." Edward J. Maruska to Reed, August 2, 1974, folder 23, box 25, RU 365, SIA.

105. Reed to Dr. Irving E. Dardik, December 1, 1972, Doler 23, box 25, RU 365, SIA.

106. Ibid.

107. Ibid.

108. Saul W. Schiffman, "National Zoo Received Gift of Giant Pandas," May 18, 1972, folder 21, box 13, RU 365, SIA.

109. William S. Shepard to Mohini the White Bengal Tiger, undated, folder 10, box 27, RU 365, SIA.

110. Deirdre W. Magnussen to Mohini c/o The National Zoo, August 10, 1977, folder 10, box 27, RU 365, SIA.

4. White Open Spaces in San Diego County

1. Kaiser-Aetna real estate advertisement, *San Diego Magazine,* August 1971.

2. For a history of campaigns to save open space in the years after World War II, see Adam Rome, *The Bulldozer and the Countryside: Suburban Sprawl and the Rise of American Environmentalism* (New York: Cambridge University Press, 2001).

3. William H. Whyte Jr., "A Plan to Save Vanishing U.S. Countryside," *Life,* August 17, 1959, 88; Kevin Lynch, "The Openness of Open Space," in *The Arts of Environment,* ed. Gyorgy Kepes (New York: Braziller, 1972), 108.

4. Charles Abrams, "California: Going, Going . . . ," *Architectural Forum,* September 1963, 105.

5. Archer, *Architecture and Suburbia,* 296.

6. Davis, *City of Quartz,* 159.

7. Biographical information is drawn from interviews of Timothy Aller, Charles Bieler, Sheldon Campbell, Howard Chernoff, Dallas Clark, Chuck Faust, Victor Krulak, Kenton Lint, Charles Schroeder, Robert Sullivan, and Eugene Trepte. Zoological Society of San Diego Oral History Project, San Diego State University Library, Special Collections. Hereafter cited as ZSSD Oral History Project.

8. "A Visit to the Wild Animal Park," *Escondido Realtor,* April 1981, 7; text from photo-essay on Escondido, *San Diego Magazine,* May–June 1953.

9. Susan Davis, *Spectacular Nature: Corporate Culture and the Sea World Experience* (Berkeley: University of California Press, 1997), 40.

10. Christine Killory, "Temporary Suburbs: The Lost Opportunity of San Diego's National Defense Housing Projects," *Journal of San Diego History* 39, nos. 1–2 (1993).

11. Ibid.

12. Ibid.

13. Leroy Harris, "The Other Side of the Freeway: A Study of Settlement Patterns of Negroes and Mexican Americans in San Diego, California" (PhD diss., Carnegie-Mellon University, 1974), iii–iv.

14. Harry Milton Wegeforth and Neil Morgan, *It Began with a Roar: The Story of San Diego's World-Famed Zoo* (1953; repr. San Diego: Zoological Society of San Diego, 1969), 161.

15. In the year ending June 30, 1942, for example, the society reported a record-breaking zoo

admission of 600,000 persons. The record was broken again in 1945 with 652,468 visitors. Ibid., 165, 169, 175.

16. Ibid., 165, 166, 173, 174.

17. Ibid., 167. The acquisitions were not particular to the San Diego Zoo. Other zoos in the United States received animals as a by-product of military activity overseas.

18. Ibid., 171.

19. Bill Becker, "Cloud over Californians," *New York Times,* July 3, 1962; Gladwin Hill, "San Diego Has a Boom Air, with Little Discontent Voiced," *New York Times,* October 31, 1962.

20. See, for example, James Edgeworth, "San Diego Boom," *New York Times,* January 17, 1954. This diversification was not entirely unfamiliar, given that real estate speculation was, like the military, a staple of San Diego's growth in the late nineteenth century. Davis, *Spectacular Nature,* 40.

21. City of San Diego Planning Department, *Urban Open Space Synopsis,* February 1960.

22. San Diego's coastline, however, remained a popular leisure spot for all city residents, despite a growing lack of public access in these postwar years. Donald Appleyard and Kevin Lynch, *Temporary Paradise? A Look at the Special Landscape of the San Diego Region: Report to the City of San Diego* (San Diego: City Planning Department, 1974), 5, 14–16.

23. "Building '66," *San Diego Magazine,* March 1966, 74.

24. Mike Davis, "The Next Little Dollar: The Private Governments of San Diego," in *Under the Perfect Sun: The San Diego Tourists Never See,* ed. Mike Davis, Kelly Mayhew, and Jim Miller (New York: New Press, 2003), 85.

25. Peter Barts, "San Diego Opens Its Civic Theater: Urban Renewal as Well as Cultural Lift Sought," *New York Times,* January 13, 1965, 36; John Herbers, "Nation's Urban Officials Foresee Continuation of Acute Problems," *New York Times,* December 7, 1969, 67. For a description of southeast San Diego as a dilapidated black ghetto, see Larry Ford and Ernst Griffin, "The Ghettoization of Paradise," *Geographical Review* 69, no. 2 (1979): 146–49.

26. On the region's postwar school of modernism, see Michael Stepner, "Opening Remarks," *American Institute of Architects,* http://www.aia.org/cod_lajolla_042404_sandiego_opening (accessed November 30, 2006); "Modern San Diego," http://www.modernsandiego.com (accessed February 13, 2007).

27. Steven V. Roberts, "San Diego at the Age of Two Hundred," *New York Times,* August 4, 1969, 9. For a history of racial injustices experienced and inflicted in San Diego, see Jim Miller, "Just Another Day in Paradise? An Episodic History of Rebellions and Repression in America's Finest City," in Davis, Mayhew, and Miller, *Under the Perfect Sun,* 159–261; and Carlos M. Larralde and Richard Griswold del Castillo, "San Diego's Ku Klux Klan, 1920–1980," *Journal of San Diego History* 46, nos. 2–3 (2000).

28. T. V. Reed, *The Art of Protest: Culture and Activism from the Civil Rights Movement to the Streets of Seattle* (Minneapolis: University of Minnesota Press, 2005), 116.

29. Kevin Delgado, "A Turning Point: The Conception and Realization of Chicano Park," *Journal of San Diego History* 44, no. 1 (1998). After the initial reclamation of the space, the park became a prominent site of Chicano/a murals. Carlos Francisco Jackson, *Chicana and Chicano Art* (Tucson: University of Arizona Press, 2009), 78–80.

30. Charles Schroeder, interview with Stephen Colston, July 17, 1983, ZSSD Oral History Project.

31. Douglas G. Meyers, *Mister Zoo: The Life and Legacy of Dr. Charles Schroeder* (San Diego: Zoological Society of San Diego, 1999), 70. Significantly, Meyers's book is an official biography, written by the former general manager of the Wild Animal Park (1982–85) and, thereafter, the director of the San Diego Zoo.

32. Roberta Ridgely, "The Zoo Story," *San Diego Magazine,* April 1966, 53.

33. Quoted in Meyers, *Mister Zoo,* 72–73.

34. One of the earlier stamps of Disney on the San Diego Zoo was Disney-designed letterhead for the zoo's Office of Public Information in 1954. A row of cheerful cartoon animals in bright colors gave the zoo the Disney touch. Lloyd Mason Smith to W. M. Mann, November 5, 1965, SIA; Eugene Trepte, interview with Tom Jamison, October 29, 1985, transcript edited, ZSSD Oral History Project; Timothy Aller, interview with Steven Wolz, May 14 and July 23, 1984, transcript edited, ZSSD Oral History Project; Sam Fuller, "Disneyland Food Operation Survey for the San Diego Zoo," February 23, 1964, Klauber Zoological Society Collection, San Diego Public Library, California Room (hereafter cited as Klauber).

35. Aller interview, 18–21; Meyers, *Mister Zoo,* 133.

36. Memo from Laurence Klauber, March 1965, Klauber; C. R. Schroeder to David H. Thompson, March 8, 1965, Klauber.

37. Quoted in Richard Joseph, "Sunny San Diego," *New York Post,* September 22, 1966. As CORE San Diego founder Harold Brown recalled in 2003, protests at the zoo were part of other demonstrations against the city's white power structures, including the San Diego Real Estate Association, banks, and the San Diego Gas and Electric Company. Kelly Mayhew, "Life in Vacationland: The 'Other' San Diego," in Davis, Mayhew, and Miller, *Under the Perfect Sun,* 276.

38. Robert E. Jarboe, "Changing Contours," *Zoonooz,* March 1965; Robert E. Jarboe, "Natural Canyon Settings," *Zoonooz,* July 1963. In 1955 attendance was recorded at 1,347,499; 1960, 1,952,879; 1965, 2,252,225. Schroeder estimated 500 zoo members in 1953 and, thirty years later, 150,000 members. Ridgely, "Zoo Story," 53; Schroeder interview, July 17, 1983.

39. *San Diego Zoo Official Guide Book* (San Diego: Zoological Society of San Diego, 1947), 6.

40. Charles Schroeder, interview with Stephen Colston, October 4, 1983, ZSSD Oral History Project, San Diego State University Library, Special Collections.

41. Meyers, *Mister Zoo,* 84. For a firsthand account from one San Diego Zoo photographer on overcoming wire in zoo photography, see Ronald Garrison and Robert Gray, *Secrets of Zoo Photography* (Garden City, N.Y.: Doubleday, 1972).

42. Here, I am drawing on D. J. Waldie's distinction between middle-class "garden suburbs," with curved roads and fulsome greenery, and blue-collar suburbs that followed grid patterns, included sidewalks, and kept vegetation to a minimum. D. J. Waldie, *Holy Land: A Suburban Memoir* (New York: Norton, 1996), 21, 103.

43. Kenneth Jackson, *Crabgrass Frontier: The Suburbanization of the United States* (New York: Oxford University Press, 1985), 239–40. For a discussion of the shortcomings of suburban design according to twentieth-century critics, see John Archer, "The Place We Love to Hate: The Critics Confront Suburbia, 1920–1960," in *Constructions of Home,* ed. Klaus Stierstofer and Franziska Quabeck (New York: AMS, 2010). Whether the uniformity of postwar subdivisions was uniformly unwelcome is an open question, given that many suburbanites chose their housing based on a consistency that was measured against the perceived chaos of inner cities.

44. Batten, *Living Trophies,* 101–2.

45. Mary A. van Balgooy, "Designer of the Dream: Cliff May and the California Ranch House," *Southern California Quarterly* 86 (2004): 127–44.

46. Barbara L. Allen, "The Ranch-Style House in America: A Cultural and Environmental Discourse," *Journal of Architectural Education* 49, no. 3 (1996): 156–65.

47. Ibid., 183.

48. Appleyard and Lynch, *Temporary Paradise?,* 27.

49. Quoted in Joseph Giovannini, "The Man behind the Ranch House," *New York Times,* July 3, 1986.

50. Jarboe, "Changing Contours."

51. Ibid.; May, quoted in Allen, "Ranch-Style House," 180.

52. Schroeder interview, October 4, 1983.

53. James A. Jacobs, "Social and Spatial Change in the Postwar Family Room," *Perspectives in Vernacular Architecture* 13, no. 1 (2006): 70–85.

54. Robert Fishman, *Bourgeois Utopias: The Rise and Fall of Suburbia* (New York: Basic Books, 1987), 15; Macek, *Urban Nightmares,* 7–8.

55. Significantly, other critics argue that the diversification of U.S. suburbs has always been illusory insofar as residential segregation by race persisted. See, for example, William Sharpe and Leonard Wallock, "Bold New City or Built-up 'Burb'? Redefining Contemporary Suburbia," in *The Making of Urban America,* ed. Raymond A. Mohl, 2nd ed. (Wilmington, Del.: Scholarly Resources, 1997), 309–31.

56. Harris, "Other Side of the Freeway," 176.

57. Harris argues that determining the degree to which postwar Latinos faced housing discrimination is difficult, partly because Latino identities were more possible to conceal or blur, which improved their residential mobility. By the 1960s Latinos were more dispersed throughout the city than their black neighbors, but the majority still lived in the southeast. Harris, "Other Side of the Freeway," 92–120, 145–92.

58. San Diego realtor Jim Cotton, quoted in Harris, "Other Side of the Freeway," 187.

59. Harris is cautious in his speculation about the impact of this legislation. The low number of complaints about racial discrimination filed after the act's reinstatement suggests that blacks did not make widespread use of it to fight for their interests, but this may also have been a result of a change in realtors' behaviors under the fear of prosecution. Ibid., 188.

60. Edward Steichen, *The Family of Man: The Photographic Exhibition* (New York: Museum of Modern Art, 1955). For the critique of this exhibition that informs my own, see Roland Barthes, *Mythologies,* trans. Annette Lavers (New York: Hill and Wang, 1972).

61. "Togetherness for Mammals and Birds," *Zoonooz,* September 1966, 11.

62. Faust interview, 8, 12.

63. For another discussion of Hediger's contribution to zoo design, see chapter 1.

64. Hediger, *Wild Animals in Captivity,* 20.

65. Ibid., 32.

66. Faust interview, 8, 12; Meyers, *Mister Zoo,* 84.

67. Schroeder interview, October 4, 1983.

68. Jarboe, "Changing Contours"; memorandum from Marty Bouman to Zoo Transportation Committee, April 4, 1966, Klauber.

69. "High Adventure at the Zoo," *Zoonooz*, February 1969, 6–14.

70. Sheldon Campbell, "The Zoo as Ark," *San Diego Magazine*, September 1970, 110.

71. Figures cited in a San Diego Zoo press release, January 14, 1975, Frances Bevan Ryan Collection, folder 9, box 5, Escondido Public Library, Pioneer Room. Local reporters, however, inflated these numbers to make the park's open space seem more striking, citing, as one example, four hundred different species and fourteen hundred specimens. Marguerite Sullivan, "Animal Park to Open Gates on Wednesday," *San Diego Union*, May 7, 1972.

72. For a sampling of the politics of the international wildlife trade and its animal breeding concerns, see David Van Vleck, "Animal Crowding," *Animal Kingdom* 75, no. 6 (1972): 9–14; Barbara Harrison, "Animal Trade: An International Issue," *International Zoo Yearbook* 14, no. 1 (1974): 13–21; Wayne F. King, "International Trade and Endangered Species," *International Zoo Yearbook* 14, no. 1 (1974): 2–13.

73. Zoological Society of San Diego, "Preliminary Proposal: To Establish a Self-Sustaining Back Country Exotic Animal Farm," circa 1961, Klauber.

74. Tim Watkin, "Expert Hails San Pasqual as Zoo of Future," *San Diego Union*, May 17, 1971; John Burns, "'Born Free' Author Wants to Keep Cheetahs That Way," *San Diego Union*, January 16, 1972; "Africa Comes to San Diego: Innovative New Zoo Puts Animals in Acres of Open Country," *Sunset*, August 1972; Marguerite Sullivan, "Population Explodes at Animal Park," *San Diego Union*, July 29, 1972.

75. The invitation was accepted. Attendance in its first year of public operation was 1,011,817 visitors, exceeding expectations of half a million. "More Popular Than Ever: Annual Meeting Activities," *Zoonooz*, October 1973, 5; Betty Peach, "Attendance Easily Exceeds Forecast," *San Diego Tribune*, April 14, 1973.

76. As Harris makes clear, not all San Diegans were able or willing to suburbanize, or suburbanize along the same spatial trajectory. While Latinos remained concentrated in the southeast into the 1970s (by choice or otherwise), blacks were seeking out their suburban experience toward the city's eastern boundaries and just north of Highway 94. Harris, "Other Side of the Freeway," 117.

77. Gerald M. Trimble, executive vice president of the Center City Development Corporation, cited in Leland Saito, "Reclamation and Preservation: The San Diego Chinese Mission, 1927–1996," *Journal of San Diego History* 49, no. 1 (2003).

78. Some of Schroeder's colleagues were less perceptive, resisting the society's plans to build the park for multiple reasons. For an account of the objections, see Brent Jay, "Animals in a Second Nature Wilderness: San Diego's Wild Animal Park" (MA thesis, San Diego State University, 2001).

79. Memorandum from Charles Schroeder to Board of Directors, June 5, 1961, Klauber.

80. Kevin Starr, *Inventing the Dream: California through the Progressive Era* (New York: Oxford University Press, 1985), 16–17. For another critical account of the battle, see Richard Griswold del Castillo, "The U.S.-Mexican War in San Diego, 1846–1847: Loyalty and Resistance," *Journal of San Diego History* 49, no. 1 (2003).

81. Sullivan, "Animal Park to Open Gates on Wednesday."

82. Ibid.

83. Dolly Maw, "The Escondido Story," *San Diego Magazine*, June 1972, 99.

84. Allen, "Ranch-Style House," 157.

85. Henry Nash Smith, *Virgin Land: The American West as Symbol and Myth* (Cambridge, Mass.: Harvard University Press, 1950), 123. For a more contemporary reading of California as garden, and its social and environmental failures, see Robert Dawson and Gray Brechin, *Farewell, Promised Land: Waking from the California Dream* (Berkeley: University of California Press, 1999).

86. Lummis, quoted in Starr, *Inventing the Dream,* 89.

87. Ibid., 45–46, 75–98.

88. Ibid., 90–91, 98.

89. Property ownership remained with the city of San Diego, who rented the land to the Zoological Society. The extent to which this prompted society officials to aggressively assert their jurisdiction over it, as a compensatory gesture, is an open question. Schroeder interview, July 17, 1983; Schroeder interview, October 7, 1983.

90. Meyers, *Mister Zoo,* 171.

91. Starr, *Inventing the Dream,* 86–87, 59–63.

92. Walls and fencing, however, were soon largely replaced with moating techniques honed at Horn and Hoof Mesa. Rolling fields and wire fences did not mix well. Schroeder interview, October 7, 1983.

93. Ibid.

94. Jane Tompkins, *West of Everything: The Inner Life of Westerns* (New York: Oxford University Press, 1992), 73.

95. "Pickets Halt Animal Park Landscaping," *San Diego Union,* March 9, 1972. In recent years, the archives of the Zoological Society of San Diego have been closed to nonscientific researchers, making challenges to its mythmaking harder to find.

96. "San Diego Wild Animal Park: A Community Effort," *Zoonooz,* May 1972.

97. Schroeder interview, July 17, 1983; "Wild Animal Park: Nibbling in the Garden," *San Diego Union,* December 31, 1972; "Pesty Flies Eliminated from Cheetahs," *San Diego Union,* January 6, 1973; Betty Peach, "San Pasqual Park Officials Defend Removal of Bobcats, Coyotes," *San Diego Tribune,* July 23, 1971.

98. "Running Room," *Zoonooz,* December 1969, 13.

99. Ibid., 12.

100. Home Federal advertisement, *Escondido Times-Advocate,* May 9, 1972; San Diego Glass & Paint advertisement, *Escondido Times-Advocate,* May 9, 1972.

101. Wayside Shop advertisement, *Escondido Times-Advocate,* May 9, 1972.

102. Ibid.

5. Looking Endangered

1. Charles Schroeder, interview with Stephen Colston, October 7, 1983, ZSSD Oral History Project.

2. John Toovey, "African Plains Exhibit at Whipsnade Park," *International Zoo Yearbook* 19 (1970): 270.

3. Bill Seaton, "Twenty White Rhinos for San Diego," *International Zoo News* 18, no. 2 (1971): 51; "Old San Diego Train Has Fat Load—Twenty Rhinos," *Los Angeles Times,* February 19, 1971.

4. The southern white rhinoceros is one of two subspecies of white rhinos, the second being

the northern white rhinoceros. For brevity, I refer to the rhinos in the Wild Animal Park's collection as a species. However, by August 1972, the park also housed four northern white rhinos. "Africa Comes to San Diego," *Sunset*, August 1972.

5. Architects named Nairobi, Kenya, as the specific inspiration for the park's buildings, while the outdoor enclosures were more generalized as southeast African landscapes. San Diego Wild Animal Park at San Pasqual map, *Times-Advocate*, May 9, 1972, 20.

6. Theodore Reed to Charles Schroeder, January 27, 1971, folder 2, box 94, RU 326, SIA.

7. "Intensive Care for Baby Rhinos," *Zoonooz*, February 1973.

8. Ian Player, "Translocation of White Rhinoceros in South Africa," *Oryx* 9, no. 2 (1967): 137–38; J. D. Wallach, "Immobilization and Translocation of the White (Square-Lipped) Rhinoceros," *Journal of the American Veterinary Medical Association* 149, no. 7 (1966): 871.

9. Charles L. Bieler to Thomas J. Foose, August 17, 1982, box 32, AC 96–024, SIA.

10. Thomas J. Foose to Charles L. Bieler, September 10, 1982, box 32, AC 96–024, SIA.

11. Davis, *Spectacular Nature*, 42–43.

12. Robert Smith, "Forces and Values: Western Tourism Decides Its Future," address republished in *Zoonooz*, April 1973, 16–17.

13. Sander Gilman, *Making the Body Beautiful: A Cultural History of Aesthetic Surgery* (Princeton, N.J.: Princeton University Press, 2001), chaps. 3, 6; Dyer, *White*, 42–43; Perry L. Curtis Jr., *Apes and Angels: The Irishman in Victorian Caricature*, rev. ed. (Newton Abbot, UK: David and Charles, 1997), chap. 10.

14. "Gomda" was the Hindu name for rhinoceros, which was adopted by Dürer himself in his first drawing. Francis Joseph Cole, "The History of Albrecht Dürer's Rhinoceros in Zoological Literature," ed. Edgar Ashworth, *Science, Medicine, and History: Essays on the Evolution of Scientific Thought and Medical Practice Written in Honour of Charles Singer* (London: Oxford University Press, 1953), 337; T. H. Clarke, "The Iconography of the Rhinoceros from Dürer to Stubbs," *Connoisseur* 184, no. 739 (1973): 2.

15. Clarke, "Iconography of the Rhinoceros," 5.

16. Ibid., 3.

17. To date, there are five recognized species of rhinos: white, black, Indian, Javan, and Sumatran.

18. Player, "Translocation of White Rhinoceros," 138.

19. Frants Hartmann, "Saving the African Rhino," *Animal Kingdom*, February 1973, 25. See also Ken Stott Jr., "As Different as Black and White," *Zoonooz*, January 1963, 11.

20. Ian Player, *The White Rhino Saga* (New York: Stein and Day, 1972), 186–88.

21. Ibid., 63, 138, 132–40.

22. Dyer, *White*, 44–45.

23. Ibid., 122.

24. Ibid., 151.

25. Ibid., 152–53.

26. Ibid., 45.

27. W. H. Drummond, *The Large Game and Natural History of South and South-East Africa* (Edinburgh: Edmonston and Douglas, 1875), 84–85.

28. Ibid., 83.

29. Ibid., 86.

30. Ibid. Player's paraphrasing of the passage can be found in Player, *White Rhino Saga,* 26.

31. For an analysis of the growing tourism industry, see Susan Davis, "Landscapes of Imagination: Tourism in Southern California," *Pacific Historical Review* 68 (1999): 173–91.

32. For a detailed account of the San Diego Zoo's assessment of the park's revenue potential, see James Lee Milliken, "A Critical Appraisal of Two Stanford Research Institute Studies" (MA thesis, San Diego State University, 1975).

33. Animaland was a concept for a 345-acre private game reserve developed by area realtors, lawyers, and financiers and sited for Orange County. By 1968 it folded after land-leasing disputes, but remained on the planning radar of the Zoological Society of San Diego. Ed Harrison to Lawrence Klauber, September 15, 1967; Jack Boettner, "African Wildlife Will Roam New Orange County Park," *Los Angeles Times,* December 20, 1963. For Schroeder's park plans, see "Preliminary Proposal to Establish a Self-Sustaining Back County-Exotic Animal Farm," circa 1961, Klauber.

34. Board president Eugene Trepte, quoted in press release, June 23, 1967, Klauber.

35. Quoted in Meyers, *Mister Zoo,* 196.

36. By the 1960s the list of competitors included, according to one zoo board member's list, a small zoo in Los Angeles, Sea World, Mission Bay, Disneyland, Knott's Berry Farm, Universal Studios, and television, football, and baseball. Charles Blier, interview with Tom Jamison, October 16, 1985, transcript edited, 8, ZSSD Oral History Project.

37. Quoted in Batten, *Living Trophies,* 9.

38. See, for example, Daniel Boorstin, "From Traveler to Tourist: The Lost Art of Travel," in *The Image: A Guide to Pseudo-events in America* (1961; repr. New York: Harper and Row, 1964). In his 1976 study Dean MacCannell sized up these antitourists and found a reluctant affinity with the targets of their derision. If traditional travel was no longer possible, then any contemporary practice of going abroad was constituted through the logic of tourism, including their own. Everyone was now a tourist. Dean MacCannell, *The Tourist: A New Theory of the Leisure Class* (1976; repr. Berkeley: University of California Press, 1999), 107.

39. Gregg Mitman, *Reel Nature: America's Romance with Wildlife on Film* (Cambridge, Mass.: Harvard University Press, 1999), 188–90.

40. Ibid., 187–90.

41. Donna Haraway, *Primate Visions: Gender, Race, and Nature in the World of Modern Science* (New York: Routledge, 1989), 133–36.

42. Rosaldo takes specific issue with films of the 1980s, such as *A Passage to India* (1984), *Out of Africa* (1985), and *The Gods Must Be Crazy* (1980). Renato Rosaldo, *Culture and Truth: The Remaking of Social Analysis* (Boston: Beacon, 1989), 68–70.

43. Marguerite Sullivan, "Monorail Safari Surveys Wild Animal Scene," *San Diego Union,* April 8, 1973.

44. E. I. Stenhardt, "Hunters, Poachers, and Gamekeepers: Towards a Social History of Hunting in Colonial Kenya," *Journal of African History* 30 (1980): 253.

45. For discussion of Roosevelt's conservationism and hunting practices, see Matthew Brower, "Trophy Shots: Early North American Photographs of Nonhuman Animals and the Display of Masculine Prowess," *Society and Animals* 13, no. 1 (2005): 13–32.

46. Garry Marvin, "Wild Killing: Contesting the Animal in Hunting," in *Killing Animals,* ed. Animal Studies Group (Urbana: University of Illinois Press, 2006), 25.

47. Edmund Heller, "Typewritten copy of Edmund Heller's Journal of the Expedition from 21 April 1909 to 30 March 1910," folder 56, box 4, RU 7179, SIA.

48. Mitman, *Reel Nature,* 194.

49. The role of Maasai in the safari spectacle is disputed. Kenneth Little argues that they came to resemble wildlife themselves, as dehumanized images in the landscape. Edward Bruner and Barbara Kirschenblatt-Gimblett, on the other hand, argue for Maasai agency in these tourist practices, interpreting their presence as a knowing performance in the spectacle. Kenneth Little, "On Safari: The Visual Politics of a Tourist Representation," in *The Varieties of Sensory Experience: A Sourcebook in the Anthropology of the Senses,* ed. David Howes (Toronto: University of Toronto Press, 1991), 148–63; Edward Bruner and Barbara Kirschenblatt-Gimblett, "Maasai on the Lawn: Tourist Realism in East Africa," *Cultural Anthropology* 9, no. 4 (1994): 435–70.

50. Mitman, *Reel Nature,* 196. Catherine Lutz and Jane Collins have observed the same process of unpeopling African landscapes in the pages of *National Geographic* magazine after the 1950s, including the contentious presence of the white Western explorer. Lutz and Collins, *Reading National Geographic,* 133, 159–60.

51. Susan Sontag, *On Photography* (New York: Farrar, Straus and Giroux, 1978), 14.

52. Lynn Lilliston, "Safari Brings 'Em Back Alive on Film," *Los Angeles Times,* November 17, 1968.

53. Ibid.

54. Charles Faust, "Sketchbook of East Africa," *Zoonooz,* February 1970, 4.

55. Faust interview.

56. Faust, "Sketchbook of East Africa," 5.

57. "San Diego Wild Animal Park" brochure, circa 1976.

58. Charles L. Bieler, "On the Grand Tour," *Zoonooz,* May 1972; "Take Wild Animal Safari in San Diego's Back Yard," *San Diego Union,* May 8, 1972; G. L. Schultz, "San Pasqual Park Leaves Space Age Behind," *Evening Tribune,* July 30, 1971.

59. Schultz, "San Pasqual Park Leaves Space Age Behind."

60. "Africa Reshaped in Village Design," *Times-Advocate,* May 9, 1972.

61. Marguerite Sullivan, "Wild Animal Park Nears Completion," *San Diego Union,* April 2, 1972; "Africa Reshaped in Village Design," *Times-Advocate,* May 9, 1972; Schultz, "San Pasqual Park Leaves Space Age Behind."

62. Marguerite Sullivan, "Animal Park to Open Gates on Wednesday," *San Diego Union,* May 7, 1972; Schultz, "San Pasqual Park Leaves Space Age Behind."

63. Schroeder interview.

64. Sullivan, "Wild Animal Park Nears Completion"; Sullivan, "Animal Park to Open Gates on Wednesday."

65. "San Diego Wild Animal Park" brochure.

66. Louis Berg, "The Case of the Ungrateful Rhino," *Los Angeles Times,* September 5, 1954.

67. For a discussion of the charge as an established motif of human–rhino interaction, see Kelly Enright, *Rhinoceros* (London: Reaktion, 2008), 65.

68. Plans to open Africa, U.S.A. to the public were made in conjunction with film and television producer Ivan Tors, but never realized. Gordon Grant, "Wild Animals at Africa, U.S.A. Live in Harmony," *Los Angeles Times,* July, 10, 1966.

69. Ibid.

70. John Gregory, "Caging People, Freeing Beasts Profitable Idea," *Los Angeles Times,* September 26, 1971.

71. Gordon Grant, "Four Hundred Animals, Running Free, Await 'Caged' Spectators," *Los Angeles Times,* June 16, 1970.

72. Gregory, "Caging People"; Maggie Savoy, "Born Free and Still Free at Lion Country Safari," *Los Angeles Times,* June 17, 1970.

73. Bradley Smith, "Wild Animals All around Us," *San Diego Magazine,* August 1971, 101.

74. Mel Hall, interview by author, August 28, 2006, Carlsbad, California.

75. "Rhino," radio advertisement, 1967.

76. Jeff Swift and David Anderson, "Final Report: Species Survival Plan Program Survey on the Husbandry, Reproduction, and Health of the White Rhinoceros," 1986, 4, 7–8; "White Rhinoceros"; both in box 32, AC96–024, SIA.

77. Dyer, *White,* 2.

78. For a discussion of Barthes's concept of obtuse meaning, see the Introduction.

79. Swift and Anderson, "Final Report," 12–13. Another account of rhino pathologies at the Wild Animal Park noted that two of the original herd transported from South Africa died in transport, while another was "harassed by other animals in a 125 acre enclosure" and was euthanized. Lynn A. Griner, *Pathology of Zoo Animals: A Review of Necropsies Conducted over a Fourteen-Year Period at the San Diego Zoo and San Diego Wild Animal Park* (San Diego: Zoological Society of San Diego, 1983), 486.

80. Schroeder interview.

Afterword

1. Kathy Mulady, "Masai Warriors to Teach Zoo Visitors about Life in Africa," *Seattlepi.com,* April 28, 2007, http://seattlepi.nwsource.com/local/313568_maasai28.html; Karen Furnweger, "The Exhibit Triangle: Animals, Habitats, People," *AZA Communiqué,* March 2003.

2. Manuel Valdes, "A Misguided Use of Zoo Guides?," *Seattle Times,* August 8, 2007, http://seattletimes.com/html/localnews/2003826534_maasai08m.html.

3. Ibid.

4. Blanchard et al., *Human Zoos,* 21.

5. For a discussion of the Bronx Zoo's exhibit of a living pygmy, see chapter 1.

6. For industry perspectives on some of these exhibits, see Furnweger, "Exhibit Triangle," 11, 20, 48.

7. Ibid., 11.

8. Collaboration between those same designers and makers who are local to the represented regions lend still more authenticity to the production. For critical discussions of "landscape immersion" as the optimum design for contemporary zoos, see Nigel Rothfels, "Immersed with Animals," in *Representing Animals,* ed. Nigel Rothfels (Bloomington: Indiana University Press, 2002); Hyson, "Jungles of Eden."

9. More criticism, particularly from African studies scholars, surfaced elsewhere in cyberspace, joining a critique of the same development in German zoos. For a well-researched sample of this latter critique, see Nina Glick Schiller, Data Dea, and Markus Höhne, "African Culture and the Zoo in the Twenty-First Century: The 'African Village in the Augsburg Zoo and Its Wider Implications" (Report to the Max Planck Institute for Social Anthropology, July 4, 2005), http://www.eth.mpg.de.

10. Auntie Kel from Kirkland, Catherine from Seattle, Not a Husky from Seattle, Mike from SeaTac, Jason from Seattle, Hank Vyner from Seattle, comments on "A Misguided Use of Zoo Guides?," *Seattle Times,* posted August 8, 2007, http://community.seattletimes.nwsource.com/reader_feedback/public/display.php?id=233.

11. Lourdes from Bellvue, L Brown from Seattle, Len from Woodinville, Eileen from Bellevue, T from Seattle, Tim F from Seatac, KC from Eastside, Del from Big Bear City, comments on "A Misguided Use of Zoo Guides?," *Seattle Times,* posted August 8, 2007, http://community.seattletimes.nwsource.com/reader_feedback/public/display.php?id=233.

12. Mike from Covington, Richard from Kent, comments on "A Misguided Use of Zoo Guides?," *Seattle Times,* posted August 8, 2007, http://community.seattletimes.nwsource.com/reader_feedback/public/display.php?id=233.

13. Surveying contemporary U.S. social life, Michael Omi and Howard Winant elaborate: "This post-racial optimism reflects contemporary 'colorblind' racial ideology: the belief that the goals of the civil rights movement have been substantially achieved, that overt forms of racial discrimination are a thing of the past, and that the United States has successfully transitioned to a 'post-' or even 'nonracist' society." Michael Omi and Howard Winant, "Racial Formation Rules: Continuity, Instability, and Change," in *Racial Formation in the Twenty-First Century,* ed. Daniel Martinez HoSang, Oneka LaBennett, and Laura Pulido (Berkeley: University of California Press, 2012), 309.

14. Historians of human zoos have observed a shift in the display of non-Western Europeans in zoological settings from savage to protohuman. Around the 1930s the living human trophies of colonization in the period of conquest became the trophies of civilization, capable of confirming the rightness of activities in the colonies through their own adherence to its worldview. This is manifested as a more subtle rendering of blackness, "tamed, domesticated and moving towards progress." Blanchard et al., *Human Zoos,* 37–38. See also Robert W. Rydell, "'Darkest Africa': African Shows at America's World's Fairs, 1893–1940," in Linfors, *Africans on Stage,* 135–55.

15. Brian from Renton, RG from Seattle, Lake Lady, Jim from Seattle, comments on "A Misguided Use of Zoo Guides?," *Seattle Times,* posted August 8, 2007, http://community.seattletimes.nwsource.com/reader_feedback/public/display.php?id=233.

16. Old Man from Issaquah, Mac from Seattle, HM from Seattle, Hank Vyner from Seattle, Carlos Ramos from Newcastle, Troy from Seattle, Jane from Chippewa Falls, Rob from Bothell, Jim from Ballard, Jennifer from Gig Harbor, comments on "A Misguided Use of Zoo Guides?," *Seattle Times,* posted August 8, 2007; UW Alum Guy from Snohomish, comment on "A Misguided Use of Zoo Guides?," *Seattle Times,* posted August 9, 2007, http://community.seattletimes.nwsource.com/reader_feedback/public/display.php?id=233.

INDEX

Abercrombie, Thomas J., 130–31
abjection, 133, 134, 135
Abrams, Charles, 18, 74
Adamson, Joy, 178–79, 201
Africa: image of, 201, 203
Africa, U.S.A., 211
African Americans: and nature, 42; poor urban, 30, 51, 54. *See also* blackness
Ahmed, Sarah, 29
albinism, animal, 126, 144–45, 152–53
Alexandre, Sandy, 42
alienation, 2, 42, 49, 55
Allen, Barbara, 168
Alloula, Malek, 130
Amboseli Game Reserve (Kenya), 205
American Association of Zoological Parks and Aquariums, 192
American Institute of Architects, 72
American Museum of Natural History, 142
Anheuser-Busch, 160
animal advocacy, 64–70, 84–88
Animal and safari park (uncompleted), 200
animality, 9, 11, 34, 74–90, 223–24, 226
Animal Kingdom (magazine), 196–97
Animals, The (Winogrand photographs), 55–64
Animal Welfare Act (1968), 64–65
antiurbanism, 14, 23, 55, 73, 91–95, 106, 126
Arbus, Diane, 55–56, 59
Architectural Forum (magazine), 106

Architectural Review (magazine), 106
architecture, modernist, 46–55
Ark Trust, 64
Avila, Eric, 13

Back Country Conservation Area (Faust), 177–78
bad zoo feelings, 1–25
Baker, Steve, 9
Balbo, Michael, 147–48
Balboa Park (San Diego), 158, 161
Barker, Burt, 128
Barnum, P. T., 5
Barr, Harold, 183–84, 186, 206
Barthes, Roland, 20–21, 219
Batten, Peter, 30–31, 64–70, 167–68
Battle of San Pasqual (1846), 180–81
Beauregard, Robert, 91–92
belonging, 8, 72
Below the Sahara (film), 201
Benga, Ota, 10
Bengal tigers, white, 125, 128–29, 147. *See also* Mohini (white Bengal tiger)
Bennett, Tony, 36
Berger, John, 1–2
Berlin Zoo, 26–27
Bethlehem Steel Corporation advertisement, plate 3
Bieler, Charles, 192

Bierly, Edward J., 153–54
Big Cats and How They Came to Be, The (film), 143
"Birth of a White Tiger" (television documentary), 147–48
bison: as threatened species, 43–46
blackness: and animality, 9, 74–90; and fair housing, 171–72; Moynihan report on, 146–47; and segregation, 160; and urban decline, 13–15, 52, 71, 83, 87–89; and urban reform, 13–15, 71–72; zoo labor force, 80–81; in zoo renewal, 11, 15–16, 19, 25, 72–73, 90, 223, 228
Blanchard, Pascal, 224
Boone and Crockett Club, 42
Born Free (Adamson book), 178–79, 201
Born Free (Hill film), 201
Borthwick, Anderson, 214–16
Boyer, Paul, 32
Bronx Zoo, 38, 42–43; African Plains exhibit, 6–7; Beaux-Arts Monkey House, 7; Congo Gorilla Forest, 224; World of Darkness, 7
Brookfield Zoo, 28, 125–26, 155
Brown, Michael, 79
Burgin, Victor, 63
Burt, Jonathan, 18

Camac, William, 35
Campbell, Sheldon, 177
Carmichael, Leonard, 84, 93
Casey, Phil, 146, 152
Central Park Zoo (New York City), 5–6, 35, 39, 65, 233n16
charismatic megafauna: use of term, 15
Clarence the Cross-Eyed Lion (film), 211
class: and race, 13, 16, 242n100; warfare, 32. *See also* middle class
Cleveland Park Citizens Association, 77
Cliff May homes, 168, 170
Cohen, Jessie, 137
Collins, Jane, 131
Collins, Lester, 114, 121
Commission of Fine Arts (Washington, D.C.), 113, 114
concrete jungle: use of term, 52

Congo (Crichton), 9
Congress of Racial Equality (CORE), 164
Conway, William, 144
Cooke, Charles, 137–40
CORE. *See* Congress of Racial Equality
corporeality and race, 16–17, 194–99, 235n51
Cossutta, Araldo, 116, 117
Crichton, Michael, 9
"Crisis at Our National Zoo, The" (FONZ), 91
Curator (periodical), 27

Daktari (television series), 211
Dallas Times (newspaper), 138–39
Daniel, Mann, Johnson and Mendenall (architectural-engineering firm), 96–97, 114
Davis, Mike, 159, 162
Davis, Susan, 159–60
Deleuze, Gilles, 9
Denis, Armand, 201
Design and Environment (periodical), 28
Detroit Zoo, 10
de Vincent, George, 75
Dialectic of Sex, The (Firestone), 146
Dietrich, Marlene, 194
Dimon, Richard, 97–108, 113–14
Disney, Walt, 164
DMJM. *See* Daniel, Mann, Johnson and Mendenall
Dolph, James Andrew, 44
Downing, Andrew Jackson, 35
"Dressing the Naked Cage" (Osborn), 27
Drummond, William Henry, 198–99
Dulles International Airport (Chantilly, Virginia), 106, 107
Dürer, Albrecht, 194–96
Dyer, Richard, 193, 197

Eckardt, Wolf Von, 84, 115, 116, 118
Eisenhower, Dwight, 129, 139
Eisenstein, Sergei, 20
Eliot, Charles, 39
Ellis, Arthur, 140–41
Emerson, William Ralph, 38, 108, 117

"Enchantress!" *(National Geographic)*, 129–30, 137

endangered species, 2–3, 4, 24, 96, 178, 190, 192–93, 219–21. *See also* wildlife conservation

Endangered Species Act (1973), 64

Erie Zoo, 66

Escondido Times-Advocate (newspaper), 188, 206

eugenics, 142–43

Evening Tribune (newspaper), 206

Evenson, Norma, 104

Ewing, Heather, 108

Extermination of the American Bison, The (Dolph), 44

Fairfield, John, 217

Fauber, Suzanne, 114

Faulkner Fryer and Vanderpool (architectural firm), 114–15, 117–18

Faust, Charles, 174, 176, 177, 178, 183–84, 205–8

Federal Highway Act (1956), 4, 170–71

Feminine Mystique (Friedan), 146

feminism, second-wave, 146

Field, Julia Allen, 29, 64

Firestone, Shulamith, 146

First International Symposium on Zoo Design and Construction (1975), 3

Fishman, Robert, 170

Fleishhacker Zoo (San Francisco), 28–29

FONZ. *See* Friends of the National Zoo

Foucault, Michel, 18–19

Friedan, Betty, 146

Friedlander, Lee, 55–56, 59

Friends of the National Zoo (FONZ), 77, 90–96, 114, 125, 127, 133–34, 143, 147, 148–51

Frye, Matthew, 17

Fudge, Erica, 20

Fuller, Buckminster, 106–7

Furnweger, Karen, 224

gaze: animal to human, 2, 12, 57, 129–30, 139, 205; ethnographic, 8, 205; human to animal, 63–64, 81, 118, 205, 209, 211; Orientalist, 139

Gee, E. P., 145

gender, 15–16, 126, 130, 149, 211

Gene Story, The (film), 143

George, Julian, 119–20

Georgetowner (newspaper), 137

Gladys Porter Zoo (Brownsville, Texas), 65

Goodloe, Marcine, 137

Goodloe, Melanie, 137

gorilla mob construct, 9

Grand Odalisque (Ingres painting), 135, 139–40

Great Flight Cage. *See under* National Zoo

Great White Hope, The (play and film), 146

Grimmer, J. Lear, 90

Grosvenor, Donna, 90–91, 151

Gruffud, Pyrs, 46–47

Grundberg, Andy, 62

Guattari, Félix, 9

Hagenbeck, Carl, 6

Hamisi, Kakuta, 224

Hancocks, David, 3–4

Hanes, Larry, 49

Hanson, Elizabeth, 40

Haraway, Donna, 10, 20, 201

Harris, Albert L., 97

Harris, Leroy, 171–72

Hartigan, John, 12

Hatari! (film), 210–11

Hediger, Heini, 67, 174–76

Helfer, Ralph, 211

Helfer, Toni, 211

Heller, Edmund, 203

Henderson, John B., Jr., 249n91

Henderson, Malcolm, 90

Henry, Bill, 102

Henson, Pamela, 144

high rises, 51

Hine, Lewis, 75, 76

Hofstadter, Richard, 33

Home Federal advertisement, 188

hooks, bell, 17

Hornaday, William, 35, 42–46

Horowitz, Helen Lefkowitz, 239n33

Housing Act (1949), 4

Housing Act (1954), 4

housing projects. *See* public housing
How the Other Half Lives (Riis), 33
human–animal intimacy, 97, 129–30, 148,
    150–52, 201–3
Humane Society of the United States, 65
humanistic architecture, 116–17
humanity, 9, 10–11, 34
Human Zoo, The (Morris), 51–54
human zoos: use of term, 224
hunting, amateur, 202–3
Hyson, Jeffrey, 38, 240–41n82

imperialism, 8; imperialist nostalgia, 202
Ingres, Jean-Auguste-Dominque, 135, 139–40
Inland Architect (magazine), 28
integration, 172–74
intelligibility in zoos, 8
International Zoo Yearbook, 3, 30–31
Isaak, Jo Anna, 135
Italians: racism toward, 42–43

Jackson, Helen, 183
Jacobs, Jane, 53
Jameson, Fredric, 8
Jencks, Charles, 242n96
Johnson, Haynes, 108–9
Johnson, Jack, 146
Journal of the Bombay Natural History Society, 145

Kaiser Aetna advertisement, 157–58, plate 6
Kampelman, Max, 90
Keir, Porter, 125
Killory, Christine, 160
King, Martin Luther, Jr., 54, 75
Kisling, Vernon, 5–6
Klauber, Laurence, 164
Klemek, Christopher, 30
Kluge, John, 129
Kohn, Edward, 147

Landscape Architecture (magazine), 29
Langley, Samuel P., 91
Latinos: segregation of, 160

Le Corbusier, 51
L'Enfant Plaza (Washington, D.C.), 115
Lévi-Strauss, Claude, 8
Leyhausen, Paul, 145–46
Liebhardt, Frederick, 206–8
Life (magazine), 27–28, 49–50, plate 1
Lifson, Ben, 61
Lilliston, Lynn, 204–5
Lincoln Park Zoo (Chicago), 5, 38, 65
Lion Country Safari (West Palm Beach), 65,
    199, 211–12
Lion House accident (National Zoo), 78–83,
    110–11
Lipsitz, George, 17
Living Trophies (Batten), 31, 64–70
Logan Heights community (San Diego), 163
London Zoo (Regent's Park), 35–36, 37;
    Penguin Pool, 46–47
Los Angeles Times (newspaper), 102, 204, 210, 211
Louetto Construction, 207
Louisville Zoological Gardens, 118–20
Lubetkin, Berthold, 46
Lummis, Charles Fletcher, 181–82, 183
Lutz, Catherine, 131
Lynch, Kevin, 158

Maasai tribe, 203–4, 205
Macek, Steve, 14
Magnusson, Deirdre W., 137
Mann, Lucy, 137
Mann, William, 121–22
Mann Lion–Tiger Exhibit. *See under* National
    Zoo
Marine Mammal Protection Act (1972), 64
Martin, Judith, 122
Marvin, Garry, 202–3
Marxism, 16
mass culture, 8
"Master Plan for the National Zoo, A" (Palmer
    and Trotter), 93–96
Matisse, Henri, 135–36
Maw, Dolly, 181
May, Cliff, 168, 170

Mayne, Alan, 74
Mbuti Pygmy culture, 224
McCrane, Marion, 148–49
McMillan Plan, 104
Melun, Norman, 114, 121
Merchant, Carolyn, 41, 239n53
Miami Herald (newspaper), 65
middle class: shame, 22, 29, 33, 70; urbanism,
    13–14, 71–72, 91–92; values, 31, 34–35,
    51–52; whiteness, 4, 16, 24, 33, 102, 142, 159
Mighty Mo (Bengal tiger), 127–28
Miller, Frank, 183
Milotte, Alfred, 210
Milotte, Elma, 210
Mitman, Gregg, 201
modernization of zoos. *See* zoo renewal
Mohini (white Bengal tiger), 24–25; breeding
    of, 142, 147–49; defective cubs of, 152–56;
    as domestic body, 126–27, 141–52; as foreign
    body, 126–41; illustration for FONZ,
    133–34; as odalisque, 133–37, 139–41; Ori-
    entalism of, 129–30, 135; portraits, 133, 138,
    140–41, 153–55, plate 4; Reed on, 125; as
    tiger-woman, 130–31; zoo goers' descrip-
    tions, 137
"Mohini and Cub" (Bierly portrait), 153–55
Mohini Award (FONZ), 143
Moholy-Nagy, László, 47
"Monkey House at the Zoological Gardens,
    Regent's Park" (Scharf lithograph), 35–36,
    37
monumentalist architecture, 104, 111, 113, 122
Morris, Desmond, 22, 27–28, 30, 81; design
    criticism of, 48–55
Moynihan report, 146–47
Muir, John, 41
Museum of Modern Art, 55–56, 62
Myers, Douglas, 163, 182–83

Naked Ape, The (Morris), 48
naked cage discourse, 22, 27–31, 48–52, 54, 65
National Capital Planning Commission, 96,
    104, 113–14

National Geographic (magazine), 129, 130–31,
    150, plate 4, plate 5
nationalism, 8
National Zoo (Washington, D.C.), 22–23;
    Antelope House, 80, 87; Bird House, 73–74,
    80, 97–99; bison exhibit, 44–46; Central
    Flight Room, 98–102; Elephant House,
    80; founding of, 43–44; giant pandas, 155;
    Great Flight Cage, 7, 73–74, 97, 102–8,
    113, 114, plate 3; hoofstock quarters, 88;
    Lion House, 73–74, 78–83, 110–11; Mann
    Lion–Tiger Exhibit, 73–74, 110–11, 115,
    117–19, 121–23, 143, 153; master plan, 11, 12,
    93–96, 110; Monkey House, 80; naturalis-
    tic environment, 38, 40, 108, 114, 116–23;
    Olmsted Walk, 228–29; and urban renewal,
    72–74, 122; as zoological slum, 76–90, 91,
    126. *See also* Friends of the National Zoo
Native Americans, 41, 44, 239n53
native species: treatment of, 66–67
naturalistic environments, 38–41, 46, 66, 108,
    114, 116–23, 178, 224
nature: concept of, 231n5
Nearing, Scott, 75
New Architecture and the London Zoo, The
    (Moholy-Nagy film), 47
"New Documents" (art exhibition), 55–56
Newman, Marian, 84
"New Photography USA" (art exhibition), 62
New York Magazine, 56
New York Times (newspaper), 138–39
New York Zoological Society, 38, 42–43,
    196–97, 239n33. *See also* Bronx Zoo
new zoo: concept of, 3, 8, 226. *See also* zoo
    renewal

Ockman, Carol, 136
odalisques, 135–36, 139
Olmsted, Frederick Law, 22–23, 39–40, 46, 96
Omi, Michael, 16, 267n13
open space aesthetic, 157–58, 177–78, 181, 186,
    188, 190
Oregon Zoo (Portland): Steller Cove exhibit, 1

Orientalism, 127–30, 135, 137
O, Say Can You See? A Bifocal Tour of Washington, 75
Osborn, Dale, 27–28, 66
otherness, 129–30, 196
Our Vanishing Wild Life (Hornaday), 42

Pal-Lipinski, Piya, 139, 141
Palmer, Meade, 93–95
pandas, giant, 155
Peck, Ellen, 146
Peck, Margaret, 106
Pei, I. M., 115
People for the Ethical Treatment of Animals (PETA), 64
Perry, John, 113
PETA. *See* People for the Ethical Treatment of Animals
Philadelphia Zoo, 5, 6, 38, 240n82
Phillips-Ramsey (ad agency), 212
Pittsburgh Zoo, 65
Player, Ian, 178, 192, 197, 214–18
Pollack, Griselda, 128
Poverty and Riches, 76
Pratt, Mary Louise, 131
Pressman, Susan, 29
Probyn, Elspeth, 29
"Progress or Decay?" (Roberts), 71, 75
Pronatalism (Peck and Senderowitz, eds.), 146
Pruitt-Igoe housing project (St. Louis), 51, 52
public housing, 51, 54, 74, 109
public parks: zoos within, 38–39, 41

race: and class, 13; and corporeality, 16–17, 194–99, 235n51; and entitlement, 182; and modernism, 116; politics, 9; as racial formation 16–17; and rhinoceroses, 194–99, 219–21, 242n100; stereotypes, 34; in urbanism, 4–5, 13, 71–72; in zoo renewal, 4, 11–12, 15–16, 19, 25, 30, 72–73, 192–93, 225–28
Race Life of the Aryan Peoples (Widney), 182
racism, 16, 42, 225
Raffles, Stamford, 35

Ramona (Jackson), 183
Rancho California advertisement, 157–58, plate 6
ranchos, colonial, 180–81
ranch-style housing, 168–70
Reclining Odalisque (Matisse painting), 136
Reed, Elizabeth, 150–53
Reed, Theodore, 84, 125, 191–92; and FONZ, 90, 93; on genetic freakery, 145–46; on Great Flight Cage, 97, 101, 104–6; on Lion House accident, 81–83, 110; on Lion House demolition, 108; on Mohini, 125, 128–30, 143, 144; on zoo architecture, 113–14, 118–19, 121–22; on zoological slum, 76–78, 127
reform, zoological. *See* zoo renewal
Regent's Park Zoo. *See* London Zoo
reproduction and open space, 177–79
Rewati (Bengal tiger), 125–26
Rhinoceros (Dürer woodcut), 194–96
rhinoceroses: black, 195–97, 198; and race, 194–99, 219–21, 242n100; as violent, 210–13; white, as endangered, 24, 192, 193, 219–21; white, image of, 213–21; in Wild Animal Park, 191–92
"Rhino" radio advertisement, 212–13
Richards, Francis, 80–81
Riis, Jacob, 33–34
Ripley, Dillon, 97
River Park development (Washington, D.C.), 73
Roberts, Chalmers, 71, 75
Robert Taylor Homes, 51
Robinson, Mrs. L. Nobel, 90
Roediger, David, 16
Roger Williams Park Zoo (Rhode Island), 224
Rosaldo, Renato, 202
Rosler, Martha, 62
Ross, Nancy, 84
Rothfels, Nigel, 6
Rumford Fair Housing Act (California, 1962), 171–72
"Running Room" *(Zoonooz),* 186–88
Rydell, Robert, 142

Saarinen, Eero, 106

Sackler, Howard, 146

safari parks, 65, 199–200, 202, 205–6, 209–10, 211–12

Said, Edward, 127–28, 129

San Diego Glass & Paint advertisement, 188

San Diego Magazine, 157–58, 162, 181, 212, plate 6

San Diego race riot (1969), 163

San Diego Realty Board, 172

San Diego Union (newspaper), 179, 181, 200

San Diego Zoo, 22; Cascade Canyon, 119–20; Horn and Hoof Mesa, 165–77, 183; inter-species integration, 172–73; Ituri Forest, 224; North Country architecture, 166–71; Skyfari tram, 177; and urban development, 161–62. *See also* Wild Animal Park; Zoological Society of San Diego

San Jose Zoo, 65

Scharf, George, 35–36, 37

Schatz, Arthur, 49–50

Schmick, Paul, 132–33

Schmitt, Peter, 40–41

Schneider, R. Michael, 3

Schroeder, Charles, 159, 163–64, 182–85, 191, 199–200

Science News (magazine), 29

Scott, Ralph, 128–29, 138

Seattle Times (newspaper), 223

Sea World (San Diego), 159–60

Second Annual Autumn Safari (Zoological Society of San Diego), 205–6

segregation, 32, 93, 160, 171, 260n55

Sekula, Allan, 61

Senderowitz, Judith, 146

sexuality, 128, 135

shame: and animal displays, 64; and conceal-ment, 29; defined, 49; and urban design, 30, 31–46, 55, 70; of white middle class, 22, 29, 33, 70

Shame of the Cities, The (Steffens), 33

"Shame of the Naked Cage, The" (Morris), 27–28, 48–51, 72–73

Shaw Metz & Associates, 51

Shedd Aquarium (Chicago), 224

Sherborn, Florence, 143–44

Shukin, Nicole, 19–20

Shuster, Harry, 211–12

Singh, Martand, 128–29, 130, 132, 138

"Sketchbook of East Africa" (Faust), 205–6

slums: documentation of, 247n49; National Zoo as, 76–90; and "super-tribal" citizens, 54–55; and urban reform, 74–77, 108–11; use of term, 74; and zoo renewal, 29, 73–74, 84, 126

Smith, Barbara Herrnstein, 234n30

Smith, Bradley, 212

Smith, Henry Nash, 181

Smith, Robert, 193

Smithsonian Institution, 38, 43–44, 80, 84, 107, 114. *See also* National Zoo (Washington, D.C.)

Smokey Bear (Wendelin watercolor), 155–56

Snitow, Judith, 146

social hierarchy, 9

Society for the Prevention of Cruelty to Animals (SPCA), 64

sociobiology, 48, 55

Sociobiology (Wilson), 48

Some Laughed Long & Hard & Loud (Weems photograph), plate 2

Sontag, Susan, 204

Spacemaster I advertisement, 168

SPCA. *See* Society for the Prevention of Cruelty to Animals

spectatorship, 206, 216–17

Spots and Stripes (newsletter), 148–49, 150, 154

Stacey, Jackie, 148

Stange, Maren, 33

Starr, Kevin, 181–82

Steffens, Lincoln, 33

Steiner, Hadas, 47–48

stereotypes, racial, 34

Stern, Alexandra Minna, 143

suburbanism, 13, 71, 92, 170, 172–77, 193

Sugrue, Thomas, 71

Sullivan, Marguerite, 181, 202
"super-tribal" citizens, 54–55
Sveilis, Emil, 75, 77
Szarkowski, John, 56, 62

Tecton (architectural firm), 46–47
Third Church of Christ, Scientist (Washington, D.C.), 117
"Third Meaning, The" (Barthes), 20–21
Thomas, JoAnn, 186
Thompson, Marshall, 211
Tomkins, Sylvan, 48–49
Tompkins, Jane, 184
tract housing, 168
Trotter, Morris, 93–95
"True Life Adventure" (Disney series), 210
Tsavo National Park (Kenya), 205
TWA airport terminal (Idlewild, New York), 106

Umfolozi Game Reserve (South Africa), 192
underclass: and humanity, 34; use of term, 242n100
United Nations Organization for Education, Science and Culture (UNESCO), 3
urban decline, 4, 13–15, 32–33, 52–53, 71, 74–75, 83, 87–89, 180
urbanism: growth crisis in, 31–32; and middle class, 13–14, 71–72, 91–92; and poor African Americans, 30, 51, 54; and zoo renewal, 13–22
urban reform, 4–5, 51–55, 74–75; and blackness, 13–15, 71–72; public housing, 51, 54, 74, 109; and shame, 31–46, 51; and slums, 74–77, 108–11; and suburban flight, 32–33, 71; and whiteness, 12–14, 17–18; and zoo renewal, 22–23, 104, 161–62

Vaux, Calvert, 39
Virgin Land (Smith), 181
Vogt, Julie Ann: Lion House accident, 78–83, 110–11

Walter, Eugene J., Jr., 237n74
Washington, D.C.: 1968 riots, 75; urban decline, 71, 89; urban renewal, 115–16
Washington Post (newspaper), 65, 71, 82–83, 84, 86–87, 107–8, 116, 122, 138–39, 140
Washington Star (newspaper), 89, 90–91, 106, 109, 111, 112, 128, 132–33
Watts, Mary, 143–44
Wayne, John, 210–11
Wayside Shop advertisement, 188–89
Weaver, Robert C., 4
Weems, Carrie Mae, 63, plate 2
Wendelin, Rudy, 155–56
White, George, 137
white flight, 13–14, 71, 104–6, 108, 162
whiteness: aspirations of, 4; as choice species, 96; of middle class, 4, 16, 24, 33, 102, 142, 159; and open space aesthetic, 4, 188, 190; and rhinoceros corporeality, 194–99; and shame, 22, 29, 33, 70; and spectatorship, 216–17; and superiority, 141; and tourism, 193; and urbanism, 11–14, 17–18, 71–72, 91–92; in wilderness, 41–42; in zoo renewal, 4, 11, 15–16, 19, 25, 30, 31, 34–35, 51–52, 72–73, 90, 179, 192–93, 228
White Rhino Saga, The (Player), 197
"White Tiger in My House" (National Geographic), plate 5
white tigers. See Bengal tigers, white
"Why Look at Animals?" (Berger), 2
Whyte, William H., 158
"Why Zoos Disappoint" (Berger), 1–2
Wicker, Tom, 242n104
Widney, Joseph Pomeroy, 182
Wild Animal Park (San Diego), 6, 159, 177–90, 191, 200, 202, 213, plate 7, plate 8; monorail train, 208–9; Nairobi Village, 206–8; as safari park, 199–200, 202, 209–10; white rhinoceroses in, 191–92, 213–21. See also San Diego Zoo
Wild Animals in Captivity (Hediger), 67, 174, 176
wilderness: concept of, 41, 204

wildlife conservation, 7, 66–67, 126, 159, 191, 200

wildlife tourism, 199–210, 211

Williams, Raymond, 231n5

Wilson, Edward O., 48

Winant, Howard, 16, 267n13

Winogrand, Garry, 30–31, 55–64

Wirtz, Patrick, 19

WNEW-TV, 148

Wolch, Jennifer, 19

Wolfe, Cary, 9

Woodland Park Zoo (Seattle), 25; Maasai Journey, 223–24, 226–28

Woods, Phil, 83

WTTG-TV, 147

Youth Opportunity Corps, 113

Zeckendorf, William, 71

Zoo Atlanta, 10, 65

Zoological Society of Cincinnati, 35

Zoological Society of Philadelphia, 35

Zoological Society of San Diego, 11–12, 14, 22, 158–59, 160–61, 191, 199, 205, 212. *See also* San Diego Zoo

Zoonooz (magazine), 14, 15, 165, 166–67, 170, 171, 172–73, 175, 184, 186–88, 192, 205, 213–18, 220

zoo renewal: animal advocacy in, 64–70; antiurban, 55, 73, 91–95, 106, 126; and bad feelings, 2–3; blackness/whiteness in, 4, 11, 15–16, 19, 25, 30, 72–73, 90, 116–17, 179, 192–93, 223, 226, 228; criticism, 227–28; defined, 7–8; gender/sex in, 15–16; greening in, 23; middle-class values, 31, 34–35, 51–52; and modernist design, 46–55; naked cage discourse, 22, 27–31, 48–52, 54, 65; naturalistic environments, 38–41, 46, 66, 108, 114, 116–23; photography in, 31; post–World War II, 6–7, 28; race in, 4, 11–12, 15–16, 19, 25, 30, 72–73, 192–93, 225–28; relation to urban reform, 4–5, 22–23, 30, 34–35, 51–53, 108–10; and slums, 29, 73–74, 84, 126; and universal human being, 10–11; and urbanism, 13–22; and urban reform, 22–23, 104, 161–62; use of term, 4

zoos: as amusement, 64; breeding, 95–96; criticism, 2, 8–9, 227–28; and empire, 8; European practices, 35–37; exotic in, 9–10; flight distance concept, 174–76; funding structure, 239n33; as heterotopias, 18–19; history, 5–13, 21; humans in, 10–11, 223–27; and incarceration, 19; within public parks, 38–39; as retreats, 37–38. *See also specific zoos*

LISA UDDIN is assistant professor of art history and visual culture studies at Whitman College.